Praise for

Keeping Finance Personal

"As someone who has had to overcome serious financial shame and anxiety in her own life, Ellyce's book is a refreshing, emotionally thoughtful exploration of what it means to build a healthy relationship with money. She takes you on a journey toward a more sustainable and joyful life: one that doesn't require erasing your identity or history, and one which allows us to be full human beings—not just numbers on a spreadsheet."

—Chelsea Fagan, CEO of The Financial Diet

"*Keeping Finance Personal* breaks away from the traditionally individualistic approach to personal finance by addressing wealth inequities at the systemic level. It is a remarkably comprehensive yet accessible guide to personal finance told through a social justice lens that will benefit many readers."

—Michelle MiJung Kim, award-winning
author of *The Wake Up*

"An eye-opening journey into identity and finance! This is a must-read for anyone eager to discover a more inclusive and empowering approach to personal finance."

—Alyssa Davies, author of *The 100-Day Financial
Goal Journal and Financial First Aid*

Keeping Finance Personal

Ditch *the* **"Shoulds"** *and the* **Shame**
and **Rewrite Your Money Story**

Ellyce Fulmore

hachette
BOOKS

Hachette Go, an imprint of Hachette Books
Hachette Book Group
1290 Avenue of the Americas
New York, NY 10104
HachetteGo.com
Facebook.com/HachetteGo
Instagram.com/HachetteGo

First Edition: January 2024

Published by Hachette Go, an imprint of Hachette Book Group, Inc. The Hachette Go name and logo is a trademark of the Hachette Book Group.

The Hachette Speakers Bureau provides a wide range of authors for speaking events. To find out more, go to hachettespeakersbureau.com or email HachetteSpeakers@hbgusa.com.

Hachette Go books may be purchased in bulk for business, educational, or promotional use. For information, please contact your local bookseller or Hachette Book Group Special Markets Department at: special.markets@hbgusa.com.

The publisher is not responsible for websites (or their content) that are not owned by the publisher.

Print book interior design by Bart Dawson.

Library of Congress Cataloging-in-Publication Data

Names: Fulmore, Ellyce, author.
Title: Keeping finance personal: ditch the "shoulds" and the shame and
    rewrite your money story / Ellyce Fulmore.
Description: New York, NY: Hachette Go, 2024. | Includes bibliographical
    references and index.
Identifiers: LCCN 2023038173 | ISBN 9780306831317 (hardcover) |
    ISBN 9780306831331 (ebook)
Subjects: LCSH: Finance, Personal. | Money. | Finance—Management.
Classification: LCC HG179 .F79 2024 | DDC 332.024—dc23/eng/20231024
LC record available at https://lccn.loc.gov/2023038173

ISBNs: 978-0-306-83131-7 (hardcover); 978-0-306-83133-1 (ebook)

Printed in the United States of America

LSC-C

Printing 1, 2023

To everyone who has felt the crushing weight of financial shame, know that you are not alone. May this book be a guiding light, empowering you to rewrite your story and create a life where financial stability and joy coexist.

Contents

Start Here

*(and don't you dare
skip this section)*

This book is for the financially frustrated.

It's for everyone who feels stuck with their finances, those whose bank account seems to whisper, "You'll never be good with money." If you've picked up this book, there's a part of you that believes you should be doing better.

Shame has been your companion. "Shoulds" have stolen your attention. Comparison has made you feel inadequate. You are told to be more motivated, disciplined, and focused, to sacrifice all your time and energy in pursuit of being successful. Told that if your hard work hasn't resulted in a stacked bank account by now, that's somehow your fault. Maybe you've tried all the budgeting techniques, read the finance books, and followed the advice, only to find yourself back where you started. You are still drowning in debt, or struggling to save up for your goals, or not advocating for your worth when negotiating your salary. You're undercharging and underearning, hoping that one day things will just work out. You've done everything you thought you were supposed to do, implemented what you've been taught (or not taught) about finances, but it still feels like the system is working against you.

I believe that being good with money has nothing to do with numbers. Or at least, it's a lot less of a numbers game than most of us have been conditioned to believe. The narrative we've been given is that if you learn how to properly manipulate your money, create the perfect budget, work hard, and follow the formulaic system for success, you'll be wealthy and happy. **This narrative is a lie.**

You can learn all the different money strategies in the world, do all the "right" things according to the experts, and still struggle with your finances. There's no magic formula for being "good with money" or making the "best" financial decisions. In fact, I don't believe there's such a thing as the best or right choice when it comes to your money. There are only decisions that align with and make sense for your life and decisions that don't.

When I started my own journey with personal finance, I was drowning in $35,000 of debt, had $60 to my name, and could not bring myself to look at my bank account. As I navigated through my own struggles, I had an epiphany: my money problems had less to do with my lack of financial literacy than with my own unique identity and how I experienced the world around me. Personal finance is deeply personal.

The identities you hold, your lived experience, the way you navigate and perceive the world, your personal values and goals, your access to power and privilege, or subjection to barriers and systems of oppression all have an impact on your money. Getting diagnosed with ADHD allowed me to finally create a money system that worked for my neurodivergent brain. Coming out as queer allowed me to stop hiding behind certain clothes and makeup and gain more self-confidence. Dating a woman helped me understand the importance of safe spaces and the impact of discrimination. Changing my name taught me the power of being my authentic self. Living through political turmoil made me more aware of how I was voting with my dollars. All these experiences changed my perspective on how I manage, spend, and understand money. The problem with so much of the traditional finance education out there is that it doesn't consider who you are as a person. **That's why I decided to write this book.**

If you are looking for a step-by-step process on how to build wealth, this book will likely disappoint you (although don't panic—I've still included some practical tips!). But I think you picked up this book because the practical tips haven't solved the problem. You don't need another book telling you how to save more money, pay off debt faster, and become a millionaire. You need a book that's going to stop telling you the *how* without context and instead explore the *why*. Why do you struggle with saving money? Why does it never feel like you have enough? Why can't you stop spending your whole paycheck on (insert your shopping kryptonite of choice)?

In order to understand the why behind your money behaviors, we have to look beyond the numbers. The perfect budgeting spreadsheet or debt repayment plan will never address the root of your money issues. If you want to achieve a financial transformation, you'll need to dig a little deeper.

WHY YOU NEED THIS BOOK

I know that you need this book because I've been listening. I founded my financial literacy company, Queerd Co., as a safe and accessible digital community where people of all identities can visit, find support, and feel valued where money is concerned. Queerd Co.'s goal is financial equity that considers privilege, systems of oppression, race, gender, sexual orientation, mental health, disability, and other identities and lived experiences. There are *over half a million* of you in this community, and I've had the pleasure of working with hundreds of clients and hearing thousands of stories. This book is for all the people who don't fit into the mold that traditional finance advice is aimed at. I hear you, I see you, and I wrote this book for you.

Like many of you, I was not taught financial education by my parents or in the classroom; instead, I had to figure it all out as an adult. Despite this, I have a lot of privilege that made achieving financial stability possible. I am an able-bodied white woman who was raised in a middle-class, two-parent household. Opportunities were handed to me because of that privilege. Yes, I am also queer and neurodivergent, but my white and thin privilege outweighs those marginalized identities.

I am aware that my experience is narrow and does not encompass everyone's lived experience. Everything I learn, write, and teach is filtered through my own lens and bias. Which is why, throughout this book, you'll find expert opinion, advice, encouragement, and personal stories from folks with a variety of lived experiences. This book was an opportunity for me to pass the mic to folks who aren't always represented in the personal finance space. My hope is that you will relate to some of the people who have shared their voices and stories throughout these pages.

Finance advice is often rooted in restriction, guilt, shame, and generally making people feel like sh*t for not knowing things about money, which leaves them feeling discouraged. Trust me, I get it. That's why we are taking a shame-free approach that will fuel self-discovery, learning, and productive change, giving you permission to take control of your finances in a way that reflects and honors who you are.

HOW TO READ THIS BOOK

By now, you're probably itching to dive in because I've made it sound so exciting, right? You're almost at the juicy stuff, but first, you need to know how to approach this book.

I'm going to lead you down a path that will challenge you, make you feel uncomfortable at times, and perhaps even make you consider putting down this book. But I will be holding your hand along the way, guiding you through challenging subject matter, and providing encouragement and a way forward. Each chapter will explore a different aspect of identity and help you understand how it's impacting your relationship with money. Every part of who you are is woven into your finances, and in order to change your reality, you need to start embracing that fact.

Throughout our journey I will urge you to take what you need and leave the rest. I want to emphasize that point now. Some of the information or tips given may not resonate with you, and that's okay. Every reader needs a customized approach, but I trust that you are capable of discerning what is or isn't going to work for you.

I encourage you to go slow as you read and step away when it starts to feel like too much. Most importantly, I encourage you to not just consume the information but actually implement what you've learned. Each chapter ends with a Putting It into Practice section that includes homework and action steps. You can complete the homework in whatever way works best for you. If you're not a fan of journaling your thoughts, you might type them out, voice note yourself, write them on a whiteboard, talk about them out loud with someone else, reflect on them in your head, or use any other method that you please. I'm not picky about how you do it as long as you at least try. Do not skip over this homework; the action steps and reflection questions are where the magic happens.

Being neurodivergent myself, I've tried to make this book as approachable as I can, with the inclusion of illustrations and interviews, mental health, and personal finance boxes throughout. Here is a brief legend so you know what to expect:

The microphone illustration represents the Passing the Mic boxes, which include the interviews and stories of some incredible people.

The battery illustration represents the Mindful Moment boxes, which include mental health tips or considerations that tie into the specific topic discussed in that particular chapter.

The piggy bank illustration represents the Financial Sidebar boxes, which provide practical financial tips for you to implement.

The speech bubble illustration represents voices from the Queerd Co. community that occur outside the dedicated interview boxes.

In addition to these boxes, I've provided resources for topics that may require or inspire you to seek further explanation. The plant illustration is placed throughout the book, letting you know that there are more resources provided in the back. Keep an eye out for it as you read!

If you're ever unsure of what a particular term means, you can refer to the glossary linked in the resource section at the back of the book. However, I want to cover a couple important terms right now, so that we are all on the same page as you begin this journey.

- **Patriarchy**—an unequal social system in which men hold a disproportionate share of power and privilege
- **Capitalism**—an economic and political system in which the prices, production, and distribution of goods are controlled by private owners, with the primary goal being profit
- **American dream**—an American social ideal that believes all Americans have equal opportunity for success and prosperity
- **2SLGBTQIA+**—the acronym that will be used when referring to gender and sexually diverse communities; the 2S at the front honors and recognizes Two-Spirit and Indigenous people as the first to build communities on Turtle Island (North America)*

YOU ARE HERE

Let's do a little exercise together to gauge how you currently feel about money. I am going to present a couple of words to you, and I want you to pay attention to how each word makes you feel. Tune into what emotions come up for you, what thoughts pop into your head, and how your body reacts. Ready? Let's get into it.

---

* I myself am a part of the 2SLGBTQIA+ community and had lengthy discussions with the community about which acronym was the most inclusive and comprehensive. This is the most updated language at the time of writing, but there will inevitably be changes in the future as language evolves.

Word #1: MONEY

Word #2: DEBT

Word #3: SUCCESS

Word #4: WEALTH

Did you feel negative emotions come up, positive emotions, or a mix of both? Did you find yourself getting smaller, hunching your shoulders, feeling a tightening in your chest? Or perhaps you felt expansive and excited and held your head higher? Each of these words are simply letters on a page, but we attach meaning and emotion to them. How you think, feel, and speak about a word gives it a personality. Your history with money plays an important role in the way you feel about the words "money," "debt," "success," and "wealth." Whether you had a positive, negative, or mixed reaction, there is likely room for improvement because you picked up this book.

YOUR MONEY STORY

Your money story is a personal narrative around finances. It's your understanding and thought process around money, based on your unique set of beliefs, upbringing, and lived experience. It's sometimes also referred to as your money mindset, and we'll use the terms interchangeably throughout this book.

As someone with ADHD and self-diagnosed autism, I have a lot of "rules" for different areas of my life. For example, I always wash my face before I brush my teeth, use small forks for breakfast and big forks for lunch and dinner, and sleep with a heavy duvet all year round. I don't have to think twice when faced with a choice in these scenarios. Your money story operates in the same way. It is the ultimate "how-to" instruction guide for your finances. It dictates how you make every decision—such as how much you tip at a restaurant, what kind of car you drive, where you decide to live, the type of work you do, and the purchases you make. The biggest factors that influence your story are:

1. **Your childhood:** how you were raised; what you were taught by your caregivers; the environment, neighborhood, and socioeconomic status you grew up in; your family system and culture; and childhood experiences
2. **Your lived experience:** your knowledge and understanding of the world based on what you've personally experienced and lived through
3. **Your trauma:** the situations you've been exposed to that have left an unhealed wound, usually presenting as emotional or psychological distress

Imagine your money story as a bookshelf full of knickknacks. The idea here is that your money story is an accumulation of many things throughout your life, and everything on that shelf impacts your finances. Some of those knickknacks will sit on the shelf for most of your life, forgotten and collecting dust. Others you might look at almost daily and smile at as you pass by. Each item on the shelf represents a chapter in this book and is an important part of your money story to consider.

The beautiful thing about your money story is that you can edit and rewrite it as many times as you'd like. You know that feeling when you're reading a really good book but that one chapter or scene just infuriates you? Or (spoiler alert) when we found out Gossip Girl was Dan? What a disappointment. Your money story doesn't have to be like that! You can rewrite it however you wish.

Money is one of the most complex parts of our lives and rewriting your money story will involve a paradigm shift. Throughout the rest of this book you'll learn how that story is created, the various ways it impacts you, and how to rewrite and then embrace your new story. I will challenge you to abandon the narrative that there is a "right" way when it comes to managing your money and redefine what success and wealth mean to you. It's time to ditch the "shoulds" and shame and rewrite your money story. Ready?

MONEY STORY

Your money story is a collection of your lived experiences, much like items on a shelf. Each numbered item you see in this illustration corresponds to a chapter in the book.

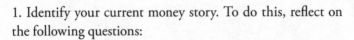

PUTTING IT INTO PRACTICE

Your first piece of homework, how exciting!! This one is really important, so whatever you do, don't just skip past this!!

1. Identify your current money story. To do this, reflect on the following questions:

- o What are your core beliefs around money?
- o What emotions do you associate with money?
- o What financial behaviors and habits do you think are holding you back right now? Where do you think those behaviors stem from?
- o What are some of your childhood memories around money? (We will dive into your childhood in detail in Chapter 7!)
- o What attitudes around money did you observe in your neighborhood or school growing up?
- o Do you feel like your financial goals are achievable? Why or why not?

Remember that you don't need to write these out if journaling isn't your thing, but please record your answers in some way so that you can refer back to them. We will be referencing and adding to your money story as we go along, and at the very end you'll have a chance to reflect on where you started.

CHAPTER 1

Safe and Sound (Ellyce's Version)

THE SECRET TO CULTIVATING SAFE MONEY SPACES

My least favorite class in university was STATS 101: Introduction to Statistics. It wasn't because I wasn't good at math, or because I found it boring. In fact, I always excelled in math, and I found the application of statistics to the real world interesting. No, the reason I dreaded this class so much was because I felt so uncomfortable in the classroom.

My professor was a nerdy white man in his midthirties named Carl, who attempted to bond with the class through (bad) pop culture references. During the first lecture, I felt optimistic that he was going to be a good teacher. He was friendly, organized, spoke clearly, and his cringeworthy sense of humor still made me laugh. But by the second lecture, I had gone from laughing at his jokes to staring blankly at his lecture slides. Carl was a brilliant man and knew what he was talking about, but unfortunately, he seemed to miss the major fact that we, the students, did not know what he was talking about. It was like trying to read a different language.

Now I know you're probably thinking, Ellyce, why didn't you just ask questions so you could understand? And that is a valid thought. I refused to raise my hand for two reasons. One, hardly anyone else in the class was asking questions so I felt stupid that I needed to, and two, I was so lost that I didn't even know what to ask. In reality, based on the vibe in the room, everyone else in the class probably felt equally terrified to raise their hands. Let's just say that Carl was not very welcoming to any questions that suggested you didn't understand a concept.

Plus, my undiagnosed ADHD brain could not watch the lecture slides, listen to the professor speak, and take notes all at the same time—can people's brains actually do that? But I am not a quitter, and I was determined to maintain my high GPA, so I did everything I could to succeed. I spent my Saturday nights poring over the textbook and struggling through equations, instead of slamming back $5 Jäger bomb shots at the bar like every other college student. Every free moment before, after, and even during other classes, I was studying stats. I even hired a tutor to help me prepare for the final so I could ace it.

Although I am literally shrinking in my chair as I type this, I want to be completely transparent in these pages: I received a D+ in STATS 101. I am not a D+ kind of gal. I am an A+, 3.9 GPA, Dean's List kind of gal, so this one hurt.

After having time to reflect on this class and experience, I have come to some conclusions as to why I did so badly.

1. The professor did not meet us where we were at. He was teaching our class as if we were all math majors taking advanced statistics and completely skipped over the basics.
2. The classroom was not a safe space to ask questions. The professor's response to many queries had an air of "if you were listening, you would know this," and asking for clarification only seemed to annoy him.
3. I felt alone in my struggles. Everyone else appeared to be frantically taking notes and intently listening, and I felt like I was incompetent for not following along.

That is the power of unsafe spaces:
they keep you silent in fear of shame.

YOU ARE NOT ALONE

I'm confident that many of you can relate to my awful statistics class experience. We've all been in settings where we didn't feel comfortable asking questions. It creates a barrier to understanding and learning that can leave you feeling isolated and inadequate. Raise your hand if you've ever felt this same feeling of inadequacy when trying to learn about finances. If I were to put all of you reading this book into one big lecture hall—or rather a football stadium because I'm dreaming big here—I know that the majority of you would have your hand up right now.

I can confidently say this because research shows only a quarter of millennials understand basic financial concepts and over half of Americans feel anxiety around money. If you're not a millennial, don't pat yourself on the back just yet, because according to the 2021 TIAA Institute-GFLEC Personal Finance Index, financial literacy is low across all generations of US adults, with Gen Zs actually struggling the most. Worldwide, over 60% of adults struggle with financial literacy. Like I said, most of us have our hand up right now.

I want you to close your eyes and imagine all those people around you in that football stadium with their hands raised: know that you're not alone. You are surrounded by people from all different ages, gender expressions, lived experiences, races, sexual orientations, and religions. All these beautiful humans have felt the same way you have, including me. I don't know about you, but I have a warm and fuzzy feeling picturing that because it makes me feel seen and understood. **This is why safe spaces are crucial.**

> *"A safe space is a place where anyone can relax and be able to fully express themselves, without feeling uncomfortable, unwelcome, or unsafe on account of gender, race/ethnicity, sexual orientation, cultural background, religious affiliation, age, and physical or mental ability."*

Imagine if the environment in STATS 101 had been more welcoming and the professor had encouraged questions, checked in to see where we were at, and provided extra resources to fill in any gaps. Maybe I wouldn't have struggled with the shame of that grade, or developed test anxiety, or pursued a different major because I was too intimidated to take another class like that. The impact of an unsafe space can linger long beyond the situation itself.

One of the most important first steps in your financial journey is finding safe spaces where you can learn and ask questions without judgment. The lack of representation in the financial industry for marginalized groups can create a barrier to financial advice and education. When you enter a financial institution that doesn't feel like a safe space, it immediately puts your brain into fight-or-flight mode. How are you supposed to talk about the house you want to buy with your same-gender partner when you're not even sure if the people you're speaking to are 2SLGBTQIA+ friendly? Money is already an uncomfortable topic that can bring up feelings of shame for many of us, and adding a layer of fear on top of it makes it next to impossible to feel confident asking questions.

THE IMPORTANCE OF SAFE SPACES

When I first decided that I was going to get my financial sh*t together, I went to the bank. It was of course the same bank that my parents used, the one I had been with since I was old enough to open a checking account. I sat down with an older, condescending white man who resembled my dad, probably named Doug, Jerry, or Steve. He proceeded to throw financial terms at me that I had never heard and make misogynistic comments like "when you have a husband he will take care of this for you." I blacked out during that appointment and ended up investing money into something called a Guaranteed Investment Certificate or GIC (if you're an American reading this, a GIC is comparable to a Certificate of Deposit or CD). A GIC is a very low risk investment, which can be useful for some savings goals, but the return often doesn't even keep up with inflation. Considering I was looking for help managing my money, not with investing, opening a GIC made no sense, but I just did what Steve said. He never took the time to explain anything to me, and I didn't dare ask any more questions for fear of feeling even more like a silly girl detached from the real world.

Reflecting on this interaction years later, I can identify what should have happened instead and hopefully save some of you from the Steves of the world. I came into that bank seeking to set up a solid financial foundation. Instead of giving dubious investing advice, this advisor could have spent time educating me about setting up a safety fund (aka emergency fund), how to properly use a credit card to build credit, and *then* maybe how to start investing for retirement. Instead, he skipped straight to investing, didn't explain anything, and just chose an investment option that would make the bank money.

Now I realize not every financial advisor out there is a Doug, Jerry, or Steve, but there are still many who may not have your best interest at heart. The term "financial advisor" is very broad and can encompass any sort of financial professional you pay to help you manage and plan your financial future. You don't necessarily need a financial advisor, depending on your situation and goals, but if you are going to work with one, you want to make sure they are a good fit. When going into a meeting with a financial advisor, I suggest bringing a list of the topics you want to cover. Figure out exactly what you want to walk away with from this appointment and be clear about that from the start. I've included more tips on choosing an advisor and some example topics to bring into a meeting in the resource section.

RESOURCE

Working with a Financial Advisor, page 311

If your advisor doesn't take the time to listen to you or won't explain why they are suggesting something, leave. Trust me, it's not worth the potential long-term damage. Don't worry, though, I got you covered on how to find safe financial spaces at the end of this chapter.

FINANCIAL SIDEBAR

Although this isn't your typical personal finance book, I couldn't resist slipping in some tangible financial tips in each chapter. I want to introduce you to the Financial Priorities Flowchart, a breakdown of what aspects of your finances to focus on first. This isn't the be-all and end-all formula, and throughout this book we will explore just how different everyone's approach to money will be, but it does provide you with a starting point.

1. Are your monthly bills covered?
The first place your money should be going each month is to your necessary expenses. If you're currently unable to pay your bills each month (or are putting them on a credit card), then **this** is your

financial priority. You need to create your own safe space by making sure all your basic needs are being met. Focus on trying to lower your monthly expenses and increasing your income wherever possible.

2. Do you have a 3-to-6-month safety fund saved up?
Once you don't have to worry about covering your monthly bills, your next priority should be saving up money to protect you from unexpected expenses. If you don't currently have a full safety fund, **this** is your financial priority. Yes, even before tackling your debt (although please don't stop making your minimum payments!).

Many of you will be starting here, and the Financial Sidebar in Chapter 3 will walk you through exactly how to do this!

3. Do you currently have any high interest debt?
High interest debt is any debt with an interest rate of approximately 8% or higher. (The differentiation between high and low interest debt is based on the average stock market return of 8%.) The most common type of high interest debt is credit card debt. After your safety fund is built up, you can now switch your focus to paying down your high interest debt. **This** is your financial priority.

4. Do you have any low interest debt?
Low interest debt is any debt with an interest rate of around 7% or lower. You can start tackling this debt after you've covered priorities 1 through 3. Once you reach this point, you can actually balance paying off your low interest debt while also saving and investing!

5. Is there anything you're saving for in the next 5–7 years?
This would include any money you're saving for upcoming financial goals like a big trip or down payment on a home. If those purchases are happening in the next 5–7 years, you can focus on saving **and** investing for retirement. If there's nothing on the horizon that you're saving for, then your financial priority can just be investing.

I've provided a visual of the Financial Flowchart on the following page.

FINANCIAL FLOWCHART

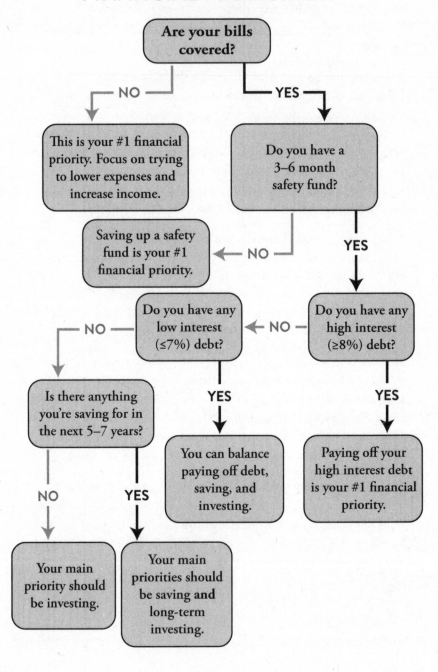

Not having the space available to ask questions without judgment and learn in a way that I understood held me back from getting ahead with my money sooner. In fact, it led me to rack up $15,000 of high interest debt because Doug, Jerry, what's his name, kept telling me that I needed a credit card and should accept this line of credit, etc. The experience of growing up in a household where money was a taboo subject reinforced the barrier to handling my own finances. As a result, I stopped getting advice from Steve and was too scared to seek out any other financial support.

In my story, the short-term impact of this encounter was embarrassment, shame, fear, discomfort, and impulsive financial action. The medium-term impact was my accumulation of high interest debt, increased anxiety and depression, and avoidance of financial planning. The potential long-term impact could be no retirement savings, decreased quality of life, and a negative impact on generational wealth should I decide to have kids.

THE COST OF UNSAFE SPACES

Research shows that I am not the only woman to encounter a Doug and that women face different systemic and societal barriers with their finances. It's not shocking that women make up only 23% of certified financial planners, 17% of senior leaders in investment banking, and 9% of senior executives in private equity. Those percentages are much lower for women of color, with only around 1% holding executive-level positions. Many women prefer to learn from other women who can relate to their experience and use language that speaks to them. With few women occupying positions in the finance industry, and even fewer Black women, Indigenous women, and Women of Color (BIPOC Women), the access to safe spaces decreases significantly.

So what happens when women feel unsafe or marginalized when seeking financial support? According to a study from Wealthsimple, women invest 40% less than men do. Although there are many factors at play here, over half of women say they don't invest due to fear. Again, we see this further amplified for marginalized groups. A 2021 survey from CNBC found that 59% of Black women and 48% of Hispanic women aren't investing at all, compared to 34% of white women. The barriers to changing those statistics are even greater for BIPOC folks, as they face more discrimination at financial institutions. Women, and especially marginalized women, are already at a disadvantage, and the lack of safe financial spaces out there leaves us all playing catch-up to men. It's a pretty good bet that having more safe spaces for women to learn about finances would help tackle this issue.

While there is more research to be done regarding nonbinary, genderfluid, and trans folks' experiences in navigating financial services, we do know that these populations are consistently marginalized as they try to access services that most gender-conforming individuals take for granted. As a result, many face yet another barrier that further widens the gap between them and financial security. If there were more safe spaces for those who do not identify as straight, cisgender men to learn in, we could begin to close some of those gaps. When I asked queer money coach Ada Vargas (they/them) how being nonbinary affects their finances, they told me,

> *"When learning about money, you're either learning from educators who are not marginalized, aka a bunch of white dudes, or you're learning from people who are marginalized. I learned from both but I still didn't feel heard or seen or represented because a lot of what I was consuming was finance for women and 'girl power,' things that were really triggering for my dysphoria. I was being misgendered constantly by an audiobook that's like, 'you can do this, girl!' so it was difficult to consume [financial resources] as a nonbinary person."*

Each human reading this book right now has a unique combination of identities. With every intersecting identity, especially marginalized ones, you add another layer of complexity to finding those inclusive spaces. In order for financial spaces to be safe, we need to reduce the barriers people may face due to their gender, race/ethnicity, sexual orientation, cultural background, religious affiliation, age, and physical or mental ability.

PASSING THE MIC

Charity's Story: Finding Safe Spaces as a Black Entrepreneur

My friend Charity (she/her) sat down with me to discuss finding safe spaces as a Black woman running her own business. Charity is a marketing manager and lifestyle content creator who is passionate about helping young adults recover from burnout and learn to love themselves. She is also a fellow late ADHD-er and just received her diagnosis at age 23. Here is her story:

As a Black business owner, I am embarrassed to ask investing questions and I think a lot of that comes back to ethnicity. A lot of Black people are just learning how to survive, and we are often a few steps behind, always playing catch-up to white families. I'm trying to learn how to understand finances, how to invest, how to build generational wealth, and I'm running my own business. In the entrepreneurial community, when I ask questions, I often get a response like "you're not doing xyz yet?" and it leaves me with the feeling that I "should know better." Even if it's unintentional, this type of response makes me feel unsafe, and I'm scared to open up about my finances in fear that people will place me into a Black stereotype. I want to walk into a room and feel respected by others, and as a Black woman, not understanding aspects of finance often takes away that respect.

My biggest example of the lack of respect I have received occurred when I went to open a bank account for my business. The bank teller wouldn't even look me in the eye and spent the whole time addressing my white-passing boyfriend. Even after my boyfriend repeatedly said, *"It's her company,"* the teller still refused to address me. I feel strongly that it was because I am a woman, and I am a Black woman. I ended up not opening my account with that bank because the situation felt so uncomfortable. When I did find another bank, I opened up the account online because I was too afraid to feel the same way I felt that day. I'll never get that situation out of my head, because it truly felt dehumanizing. It holds me back from wanting to speak to a financial advisor in the future in fear that it will not be a safe space for me.

HOW TO FIND SAFE SPACES

Whew, okay, so I don't know about you, but I could use a long hug or a glass of wine after that section. If you're feeling angry, take a second to put the book down and scream into a pillow as loud as you can. I'm serious, it's an effective coping strategy—even my therapist said so. Right now, you might be wondering how can you possibly get ahead with all these barriers working against you. The starting point is finding safe spaces.

In clinical settings, psychologists have found that if a patient feels safe enough, they are more likely to listen to criticism and alternative ideas and therefore more easily change their thought patterns. The physical space sets the initial tone, but the ability to facilitate inclusive conversation is the key. This is part of the reason why I personally love virtual therapy, because I can sit on my bed with my heating pad and hug my squishmellow while crying about the stress of running my own business. We can apply this same principle to learning financial information as well.

Charity shared with me that she is now a part of an online entrepreneurial group that is entirely Black, Indigenous, and other women of color, and that during their weekly Zoom meetings her screen is "Black girl magic." She says that finding this safe space has allowed her to feel comfortable and express herself more. When I asked how that has impacted her finances, she said, *"I know that I have a support system where I can ask questions about my finances without judgment, and overall, I feel better about where I am at in my life."*

Just like Charity was able to cultivate a safe space for herself online, you can also create this space for yourself. In order to get ahead with your money, you don't have to work with a financial advisor in a bank. The medium in which you find safety can come in many different forms, such as an online forum, Facebook group, blog, YouTube channel, friends or family, or a coach, mentor, or creator you trust. In order to find these spaces, I recommend that you come up with your own personal list of red and green flags. Red flags are the aspects that signal to you that this is not a safe space. These can be physical red flags, such as an intake form only offering "female or male" as gender options or the lack of diverse staff at your local bank. They can also be less tangible, such as an icky feeling you get or slight microaggressions you pick up on.

MY RED FLAGS

- No indication of being a 2SLGBTQIA+ affirming space
- Absence of options to select pronouns and alternative genders other than M/F
- Heteronormative language
- Lack of diversity
- Lack of inclusive practices
- Non-accessible information
- Unwilling to accommodate my ADHD
- Giving advice before hearing my goals
- Not listening to my questions/concerns
- Condescending language
- Anyone named Doug, Steve, Jerry, or Carl (kidding...mostly)

HELLO DOUG

There are many more, but you get the general idea. My own list of red flags makes it easy for me to identify unsafe spaces. Now that I have this clarity, I run away as fast as I can from those environments because I know firsthand the negative impact they have on me. On the flip side, your green flags are the aspects of a space that signal to you that it's safe. Many of these will simply be the opposite of your red flags, but treat this list like a wish list and add to it everything you would want in your ideal setting to learn about money.

MY GREEN FLAGS

- 2SLGBTQIA+ affirming space
- Inclusive language and practices
- Accessible information
- Implements diversity, equity, and inclusion (DEI) practices
- Mental health and trauma informed
- Good listener
- Passionate about their work

I can apply my green flags to anything I want, beyond just financial information. For example, when I am trying to make friends in a new city, or deciding on what gym I should join, or even when following someone new on social media. Set boundaries with yourself and decide today that you are done trying to shrink yourself to fit into an uncomfortable space. When you surround yourself with safe spaces, you open yourself up to more happiness, support, and confidence, a greater sense of security, and ultimately more power. In the resource section of this book, I've included a list of some supportive online financial communities you can explore.

RESOURCE

Finding Safe Spaces, page 312

WRAPPING IT UP

Remember the three reasons I didn't do well in my introduction to statistics class?

1. The professor did not meet us where we were at.
2. The classroom was not a safe space to ask questions.
3. I felt alone in my struggles.

Well, I am happy to inform you that this is not my STATS 101 class, and I am no Carl (although you may still get some cringeworthy humor). My promise to you is that I will do everything in my power to create a space where you feel welcome, understood, and seen. You will finish this book with a greater understanding of how your identity impacts your ability to build wealth as well as clear action steps for rewriting your money story and improving your finances. There are three reasons why I am confident you will feel that way:

1. I Will Meet You Where You're At

Whether you're just starting out on your financial literacy journey or have been struggling to budget for years, this book can help you. In fact, it doesn't matter if you're working a minimum wage job right now or are a seven-figure entrepreneur, the content in these chapters will make you view and understand your money in a new way.

2. This Classroom Is a Safe Space

There's a reason that the first chapter of this book focuses on safe spaces. I truly believe that you will struggle to take control of your finances if you do not have a safe space to learn in. The goal of this book is to make sure you feel heard, through sharing my experience and the experiences of many other incredible humans. Please know that there are no stupid questions and there is no place for judgment here.

3. You Are Not Alone in Your Struggles

You have a whole football stadium supporting you and cheering you on. Although right now it might feel like you're the only one who is struggling and everyone else around you is killing it, I promise you that is not the case. You are not alone.

Although it is impossible to learn everything about money in one book, I hope this one will give you the confidence to keep advancing your financial education and seeking out the supportive environments to do so. Remember that safe spaces take many different forms and that by finding those comfortable places to learn, you can begin to take back your power.

PUTTING IT INTO PRACTICE

1. Reflect on the following questions:

- o What are some signs of an unsafe space for you? Where do you feel unease in your body?
- o What have been some of the consequences of a lack of safe spaces in your life? (career, mindset, relationships, finances)
- o What are some signs of a safe space for you? Where do you feel at ease in your body?

2. Write out your list of red and green flags. Once you've done so, come up with a list of questions you could ask to screen for any red flags. For example, you might ask a financial advisor how they typically work with their clients and how involved they are in the process, or what their professional background and experience is.

Do your best to remove yourself from any unsafe spaces and seek out more comfortable ones. I've included a list of financial resources I know and trust in the resource section at the end of the book to help get you started. One easy step you can take right now is with your social media. Unfollow or mute accounts that don't make you feel great and start following accounts and creators that have your green flags.

CHAPTER 2

Little Miss Identity Crisis

HOW YOUR SENSE OF SELF SHAPES YOUR SPENDING

For as long as I can remember, I wanted to go by my middle name, Ellyce. There wasn't anything inherently wrong with my first name, it just didn't feel like me. I can't really explain it other than it never resonated or connected with me in any way. When I moved after college, I thought that would be the perfect time to make the switch because nobody would know me in my new city. But change is hard, and scary, and I didn't know how to alter this major piece of me that I'd had since I was born.

Then COVID-19 hit, threw the world into quarantine, and forced me to face everything I was hiding about myself. After breaking up with my boyfriend, coming out as queer, and starting to date a woman for the first time, suddenly, changing my name didn't feel as hard. In September 2020, I decided to start going by my middle name, and a couple of months later I made it official with a legal name change. Looking back now, I feel like I had more courage because I was sheltered from outside perceptions during that time. In fact, the only people observing were those on social media, who only saw the parts of me that I chose to show. I did a lot of reflecting during those first few months of lockdown, and I was ready to step into my true identity rather than the one I let others create for me. Despite this readiness, I still remember how simultaneously terrifying and freeing it felt when I texted my close friends to let them know I was going to make the switch.

Fortunately, I have great friends, who accepted me with open arms and immediately did their best to call me Ellyce. Unfortunately, my parents did not take it as well. Understandably so, as I was changing the first name they had picked for me (to a different name they also picked for me, but that's beside the point). I remember going home for Christmas that year, 4 months into being referred to as Ellyce by everyone around me, and my dad refused to call me by that name. I knew the transition for my parents would be more challenging, as they would have to change something that had been the same for 25 years, but I still hoped for the best. I broke down crying to my mom on my last day visiting and explained to her what it meant to me. My previous name always represented a version of myself that wasn't authentic. I was hiding from my queerness, masking in order to conceal my ADHD behaviors, and running from the person I was meant to be. I truly felt like I had shed this version of my identity and with it my old name. That raw conversation was the turning point for my mom, and soon after, my dad. As I write this, I am happy to report that they now wholeheartedly embrace calling me Ellyce.

Your first name is a part of your identity that you don't have any say in. In fact, many of us are told who we are before we can decide who we want to be. This often starts even before you're born, with gender reveal parties and comments like "They're going to be a heartbreaker." Our parents choose everything from the clothes we wear, food we eat, books we read, and movies we watch. Societal norms begin influencing us before we are old enough to walk or talk. We are told that girls should wear pink and boys should wear blue. We are told that women should be kind, caring, and gentle and that men should be strong, powerful, and fearless. This narrative continues throughout your life and can change based on what you look like and where you live. If you're really tall, you've probably been asked if you play basketball. If you are a person of color, you may have experienced stereotyping regarding what you're "good" or "bad" at based on the color of your skin. The identity being assigned to you is so intertwined in your life, you probably don't recognize many of the ways it has affected you. As a result, many of us grow up with a skewed sense of identity, because it becomes nearly impossible to separate out who we really are from how others perceive us. That's one reason changing my name proved so difficult—I was identifying a disconnect between the real me and the version of me that other people thought I was. Once I had identified this, I made the first step to connecting again through my name change.

UNDERSTANDING YOUR PERSONAL AND SOCIAL IDENTITY

Who am I, and how am I perceived by others? These questions form both the foundation of identity and the foundation of my approach to personal finance. Identity is a concept that is difficult to concisely articulate. That is because your identity is complicated—while some parts are solid and never changing, other aspects are fluid and ever-changing. Before you immerse yourself in the rest of this book, it's important to understand the connection between your identity, intersectionality, and your money. This connection is the reason why this book will be different from any other personal finance book you've read. I am going to challenge you to look at your money in a new way—through an intersectional lens. If you're unfamiliar with that term, don't worry, I'm going to walk you through everything you need to know.

For the purpose of this book, we are going to try to keep the definition of identity fairly simple, as there are many different ways people define and categorize this term. You can think of your identity as being made up of 2 parts:

1. **Personal identity**—the characteristics you have that determine the way you define and see yourself
2. **Social identity**—the characteristics you have that determine how others define and perceive you

Your **personal identity** is formed by characteristics that you feel attached or connected to. It is made up of the parts of yourself that denote who you are and create your sense of self, such as your values, career, personality traits, religious and political beliefs, hobbies, and goals. For example, you may identify as a dancer, a sibling, a teacher, an activist, and a scary movie fan. The combination of all these things and more creates your unique personal identity and the foundation of your self-concept.

But your **social identity** also contributes to your self-concept. Rather than being a personal choice, it's the aspects you have very little control over because you're born with them. Social identity derives from distinguishing characteristics, such as age, race, ethnicity, gender, socioeconomic status, and sexual orientation. Some characteristics, like race, are more easily noticeable and recognizable by others, whereas attributes like disability or socioeconomic status may be less noticeable. Interestingly, the term "race" is largely a social construct and even defined by the US census as *"a person's self-identification with one or more social groups."* Both visible and invisible identities are important and will inform the way you navigate the world, but visible identities speak louder to others. Social identity helps us understand our privilege and barriers as well as how the world perceives us.

Your social identity begins to form at an early age. It's the first thing people see about you, and they often base perceptions and expectations on it, as in the case of the gender and racial norms and stereotypes placed on you as a kid. As you grow older and discover more about yourself, you join other social groups. If you were to look at me, you would notice I am a young white woman. You probably wouldn't know, just by looking at me, that I am queer and neurodivergent, or that I struggle with depression. But all these social identities largely dictate the "groups" I identify strongly with. The same is likely the case for you. These groups will often have a big impact on your own sense of who you are. You'll base this sense on the expectations of people both inside the group and outside it.

Although I am explaining personal and social identity separately, it's important to note that they are completely woven together and sometimes hard to pull apart. They work together to form who you are, and as I mentioned earlier, this woven identity can change over time and circumstances. My sexual orientation has shifted from straight to bisexual, to pansexual, and now to queer. With each of those shifts came changes to the way I saw myself, the groups of people I connected with, who I supported with my money, and many other decisions. "Identity" is a fluid and complex term, and

for the purpose of this book, it's important to reflect on the aspects of your self-concept that impact the way you see and move through the world. Take a moment to look at the table below (adapted from the University of Michigan's table of social identities) and select the ones that you hold.

SOCIAL IDENTITY	EXAMPLE
Age	Child, teen, young adult, middle-aged adult, senior/elder
Ethnicity (heritage and ancestry)	Navajo, Puerto Rican, Latinx, African American, Irish, Punjabi
Religion or spiritual affiliation	Hindu, Buddhist, Taoist, atheist, Christian, Jewish, Two-Spirit
Sexual orientation	Gay, queer, lesbian, questioning, asexual, bisexual, heterosexual

Socioeconomic status	Working class, low income, middle class, upper class
National origin (the geographical location you identify as your home)	Japan, Mexico, Ukraine, United States
Gender	Transgender, man, gender fluid, woman, nonbinary
Sex	Intersex, male, female
(Dis) Ability	Disabled, nondisabled, chronically ill, deaf, visually impaired, temporarily disabled
Mental health/neurodivergence	ADHD, autism, neurotypical, allistic, facing mental health challenges
Race (physical characteristics that define a person as being a part of a specific group)	Biracial, Black, white, Asian, Indigenous

Based on what you identified above, let's take it one step further and reflect on how you feel about these identities:

- What part(s) of your identity do you think people notice first about you?
- What parts of your identity are you least and most comfortable sharing with other people?
- What part(s) of your identity are you most proud of?
- What part(s) of your identity did you struggle with the most growing up?
- What part(s) of your identity do you feel you receive privilege for most often? (if any)
- What part(s) of your identity do you feel you face barriers/oppression/discrimination for most often?

POWER, PRIVILEGE, AND
INTERSECTIONAL IDENTITY

Now that you've reflected on some of the identities you hold, let's discuss how those identities interact with one another, as well as with the world around you. I know I'm throwing a lot of definitions at you, but I promise to get back to funny and relatable stories once you make it through.

Kimberlé Crenshaw, a civil rights advocate, law professor at UCLA and Columbia, and scholar and writer on civil rights, critical race theory, and Black feminist legal theory, coined the term "intersectionality" as a way to further understand how our identities impact the way we move through society. Intersectionality is a framework that emphasizes the importance of viewing an individual's various overlapping identities collectively instead of independently. It gives us a clearer representation of how someone's unique kaleidoscope of social identities contributes to the barriers or opportunities they experience.

In one of her research papers, Crenshaw presented multiple court cases that emphasized the need for an intersectional approach. For example, in *DeGraffenreid v. General Motors*, five women introduced a suit against General Motors for discriminating against them because they were Black women. The women were told they could not bring a suit based on both race discrimination and sex discrimination, and that they would have to choose one. I know—the audacity, right? We can see intersectionality at play here, because these women were not discriminated against solely because they were women, or Black, but because they were women *and* Black.

The identities you hold will determine your proximity to power and privilege. Certain identities—such as being white, cisgendered, or male—give you access to more power and privilege. Other identities, such as disabled, Indigenous, or nonbinary, give you less access to power and privilege. You can have power and experience the impact of systems of oppression simultaneously. For example, I, as a white woman, experience privilege because of my race, but I also face disadvantages because of my gender and sexual orientation. Despite those disadvantages, in our current systemically racist society, I still hold more power and privilege than someone who is Black. Multiple things can be true at once. Keep this in mind as we move forward. Nuance, especially in financial spaces, is critical.

THE WHEEL OF POWER AND PRIVILEGE*

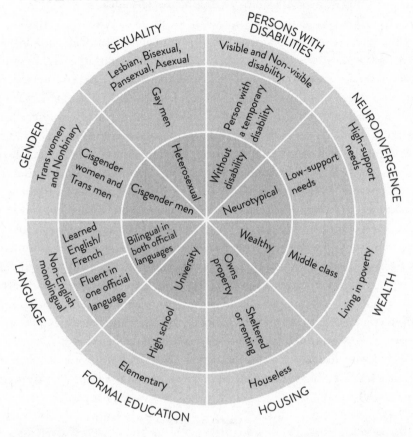

HOW YOUR IDENTITY IMPACTS YOUR MONEY

As we just discussed, intersectionality is important because it highlights that identities are not isolated. Instead, it provides a framework that shows us how every part of who we are is woven together. Traditional personal finance advice often attempts to put money in a vacuum, but once you understand that your financial situation is created from the intersection of your many identities, you can use that knowledge to make changes. You can stop

---

*   Adapted from the Government of Canada, https://www.canada.ca/content/dam/ircc /documents/pdf/english/corporate/anti-racism/wheel-privilege-power.pdf.

following the cookie-cutter advice from traditional financial experts and start creating a financial plan that supports the person you are.

Whether you realize it or not, your identity is already impacting a lot of the financial decisions you make. This is a connection that psychologists began to make in the 1950s and '60s and has been backed up since. In 2002 two American economists, George Akerlof and Rachel Kranton, introduced the concept of identity economics. According to traditional economic theory, people make buying decisions based on economic factors, meaning whatever choice makes the most sense financially. Sounds boring, doesn't it? That would mean that every time you went to buy a new piece of clothing, or electronic, or vehicle, or home, you would make a decision solely based on the "smartest" choice financially. Now I don't know about you, but I will continue to purchase Air Force 1s even though they are pricey for plain white shoes and don't provide good arch support for my flat feet. They're cute, okay?

Essentially, traditional economic theory ignores the fact that humans are human and have unique emotions, desires, fears, and identities that will influence their buying decisions. It keeps things black and white, but identity economics shines a light on all the gray areas. This approach recognizes that economics, psychology, and sociology are all connected and impact one another. Your sense of self affects your decision-making process.

If I were to tell you to go buy a pair of shoes that you would wear on a regular basis, with no budget, what shoes would you pick? According to

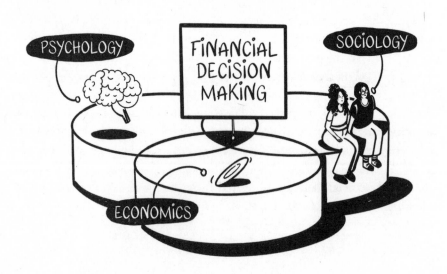

traditional economic theory, I would guess that most of you would come back with the shoes that cost as little as possible while providing comfort and durability. The main factor in your decision would be whether or not the shoes met your basic needs. But we all know that isn't what you would do, because let's be real, I did say no budget. According to identity economics, I would guess that you would all come back with different types of shoes, for different reasons. Some of you might pick out Air Force 1s, like I would, because they match with everything, are comfy, and look cool (at least in my opinion). Others would come back with a designer pair of heels, because you value high-quality, name-brand products. Or maybe you'd pick a pair of riding boots because you're an equestrian. Sounds more accurate, right? That's how humans work. We make decisions based on who we are.

The marketing industry quickly caught on to this idea and began using identity economics to its advantage. As a result, instead of advertising a product, many companies began to advertise a lifestyle. Lululemon doesn't spend time convincing you why their leggings are the best, they sell you on the aesthetic active lifestyle. Coca-Cola doesn't talk about how delicious their soda is, they sell you on the idea of happiness, togetherness, change, and impact.

Or consider the marketing done by Subaru that has branded the company's vehicles as the choice for sapphic women (women who love women). Subaru was struggling with sales in the '90s and decided to market their cars to five specific groups of people who they felt were their ideal customers. One of those groups was lesbians, and so Subaru launched a campaign to appeal to their active, laid-back lifestyle. These ads came out at a time when 2SLGBTQIA+ advertising was not mainstream, and the few companies that had done this in the past received backlash. Subaru created a safe space that appealed to the lifestyle of many queer folks. To this day, Subaru is chosen as the favorite car among lesbian consumers and seen as the most gay-friendly car brand.

Today we can see the power of identity economics in the use of social media, and in how influencers and content creators can create a sense of shared identity, connection, and belonging on their platforms. I spend way too much time on TikTok, and let me tell you, it has quickly become my biggest source of spending. You might have heard the phrase "TikTok made me buy it," because people are seamlessly promoting products within their regular content. They build an online community that you pride yourself on being a part of and, because of that, you would probably buy anything from them. The Kardashians secure multimillion-dollar brand deals in which they simply pose with a product, because they don't need to spend time convincing their audience to buy. People will buy because it brings them into the Kardashian lifestyle.

There are some flaws and critiques around identity economics, as it attempts to simplify the impact of identity and behavior and groups together personal sense of self and societal norms. There's no clear way to indicate which aspects of a person's identity have the largest impact on spending behavior. But it does provide enough evidence for us to know that both the norms forced upon you and identities you choose to hold will influence how you spend your money.

In the interviews I conducted for this book, I spoke to many people about how their self-concept impacted their finances. Let's hear from some of them so you can further understand the complex, nuanced, and deeply personal relationship between identity and money.

 ## QUEERD CO. COMMUNITY COMMENTS

"I grew up hearing from my grandparents over and over again, 'It's your duty to support your mom and to give back to your parents.' That pressure was so evident starting at such a young age, and it continued to play a role throughout my life in terms of how I viewed making money as the primary form of support for my family and my loved ones. So in terms of money and my identities, they're inextricably intertwined, and it's impacted every single aspect of how I had to navigate different systems as a person of color, as a queer person, as a woman, as an immigrant. And I think money can be such a source of both trauma and empowerment."

—Michelle MiJung

"I think that my disability and being in this world made me believe that I shouldn't have money. I was always undercharging and doing stuff for free. I look at my own financial journey over the last couple of years, and I sat in that place of struggle for a long time because that's what I felt like I deserved. That scarcity mindset is really hard to unlearn."

—Tiffany

"The biggest aspects of my identity that impact my finances are that I'm a trans man, and I have ADHD, anxiety, and depression. I'm a very frugal person and I don't typically spend money on things I don't need. But anything transition related, such as therapy, gender-affirming surgeries, and hormone therapy, I will spend the money on because it's a necessity."

—Stevie

"Getting my hair cut goes into making sure I'm feeling gender euphoria and feeling good and comfortable in my life. And so, I started going into men's barber shops, and that was a very scary thing to do because I was putting myself in a vulnerable position to ask for a 'men's' haircut. I have to really think about my safety in those environments and is this $15 haircut worth it instead of paying $80? It ended up being just fine, but the initial anxiety of starting to go there, and having it be my go-to place, was a big barrier to entry for me to just get my hair cut."

—Ada

"I feel trapped being on Social Security benefits. How do they expect me to live off this? We didn't choose to be disabled. We still like to look good. We still like to have fun. We want to go out, travel, spend time with family and friends, buy clothes, or things like that. I'm trying to manage my best, but it has definitely impacted me because I feel like I can't explore or do what I want."

—Keisha

"I spent my early twenties trying to make myself fit into a mold, whether it be with diet programs, diet food, diet pills. That's where most of my money went. And then on top of that, trying to dress myself in a certain way to be able to fit the beauty standard. Which involved buying certain products, footwear, clothing, doing my hair a certain way, etc."

—Zoe

As you can see from these stories, there are complex ways in which our sense of self may influence our spending behavior or financial decisions. I want you to think back to the aspects of your identity you explored at the beginning of this chapter. Choose three and reflect on these questions: **How have each of these aspects of your identity directly, or indirectly, impacted your financial decisions and behaviors? How has it shaped your money story?**

For most of us, there are probably aspects of our identity we are proud of and happy to shout from the rooftops, and some aspects we'd prefer to hide or run away from. Spending money can be a way to cope with a part of your identity you don't like—or that others don't like. How you feel about those aspects will influence how identity-based spending manifests for you personally. The basis of consumer culture is the assumption that we can find fulfillment and a sense of self through the products we buy. You might find yourself trying to hide parts of your identity, attempting to fit into a different identity, proudly embracing your identity, or most likely, doing a combination of all three.

FINANCIAL SIDEBAR

Since this chapter is all about getting to know yourself better, I figured it would be a good idea to get to know your finances better too. That being said . . . welcome to the Financial Audit walk-through! The Financial Audit is an opportunity to get every account, card, bill, debt, and savings down on paper. This work will also set the foundation for upcoming financial tips, so I highly recommend you don't skip past this one. You can record this information in the format you prefer, but I've also provided the link to my Financial Audit template in the resource section. Let's do this!!

Audit Your Income

If you have a **consistent** income, record:

1. Your payment schedule, aka what day(s) of the month you get paid (e.g., the 1st & the 15th, biweekly, every Friday)
2. The amount of each paycheck after taxes (aka what hits your bank account)
3. Your total monthly income (on average)

If you have an **inconsistent** income, record:

1. How much your income was for each of the past 6 months
2. Your average income—by adding up the past 6 months' income and dividing that sum by 6
3. Your highest monthly income
4. Your lowest monthly income

Audit Your Bank Accounts

For every bank account, record:

1. The account type (i.e., checking, regular savings, high yield savings)
2. The name of the bank or financial institution where the account is held
3. Any monthly fees you pay for the account
4. How you use the account (e.g., to pay bills, receive income, spending, all of the above, etc.)

Audit Your Expenses

For every bill/subscription/essential expense, record:

1. What the expense is (e.g., rent, car insurance, Netflix subscription)
2. The cost of the expense per month
3. The monthly due date of that expense
4. Whether or not that expense is automated

Audit Your Debt

For any debt you have, record:

1. The type of debt it is (e.g., student loans, credit card)
2. The amount owed
3. The interest rate (%)
4. Your minimum monthly payment/required monthly payment
5. When that payment is due
6. Whether or not that payment is automated

Audit Your Savings and Investments

If you do not have any savings or investments at this time, don't worry! Skip the stress, and skip this section.

For any savings/investments you have, record:

1. What you're saving for (e.g., vacation, retirement)
2. The type of account you're using (e.g., regular savings, high-yield savings, Roth IRA, TFSA)
3. The current amount you have saved/invested

4. The goal amount you want to save/invest
5. Your monthly contributions (if applicable)

There you have it! You have just completed your Financial Audit. Everything is out on the table, and you are ready to take those next steps. Congrats!

TRYING TO ESCAPE YOUR IDENTITY (AND WHY THAT'S EMPTYING YOUR WALLET)

A society built to reject anyone who doesn't fit into the white supremacist, capitalist, or patriarchal ideal leaves many people fighting every day to escape their own identity. Earlier in this chapter I asked you to reflect on the parts of your identity that you've struggled with in the past. Think about the ways your finances have been affected by these challenges (e.g., not getting hired at a job because of the color of your skin) and how that has shaped the way you make decisions about money and handle money, or the access you've had to money. If you have parts of your identity that you are not proud of or you wish you could run away from, you most likely have spending behavior rooted in trying to escape your identity.

For a long time, I struggled with internalized homophobia. I never even had a phase of "being in the closet," because I had simply shoved that part of my identity so far down that I didn't know it existed. Retrospectively, there were so many signs that I can't believe I ignored for years, but at the time I just thought everyone had the same experience. Like, it's completely normal behavior to get nervous when a cute girl tucks in your shirt tag or sits on your lap, right? When I did finally start

to suspect that I might like women as well as men, I told myself it was just a physical attraction and that I would never date a woman. Despite this realization, I still sought only male attention and validation. I spent a lot of money trying to look more desirable to men, in an attempt to escape from the part of me that knew I liked other genders. I feel most comfortable with minimal makeup, my natural hair color, and clothes that look like I stole them from my grandparent's closet. But I spent hundreds of dollars a year getting eyelash extensions, buying makeup from Sephora, bleaching my hair, and staying on top of the fashion trends.

I want to emphasize here that spending money on any of those things is not bad in any way. In fact, I encourage it, as long as it's because you *genuinely* like those things and not because you hate yourself so much you want to hide who you are. That's what I was doing, attempting to look as straight and feminine as possible so that I would get more attention from men. Another note here: you can be heterosexual and present more androgynous or masculine, and you can be queer and present more feminine. There are no rules, but there were rules in my head at the time. I knew that if I dated a lot of men and talked a lot about them, then people would be less likely to start asking other questions. For me, my spending was rooted in my desire to try to escape my identity.

In the story I just told you, I was suppressing my queerness while actively trying to fit in with some of my straight friends. My friend and wonderful DEI consultant, Jalali (she/her), shared her own powerful example of spending to escape her identity.

> *"While I loved my curly hair, I believed that there were limitations to showing up as myself naturally in many settings. I think about how I compromised myself in my younger years as a woman of color trying to fit in: every job interview, every formal event, every graduation picture, and every girls' trip, because I was trying to meet the societal expectations and pressure I was facing in an attempt to assimilate and bridge my own fear of not fitting into the mold of the group, or meeting the expectations of those in the space. I knew that there was hair discrimination in the workplace, and I wanted to get ahead of that, often losing my authenticity in the process. I continued to spend my money to get my hair blown out and straightened to the T, constantly.*

Not only damaging my hair and my self-esteem, but also weakening my confidence in showing up authentically in these spaces. I would strategically budget just for this."

Reflect on the aspects of your identity that you might be trying to escape from. The parts of yourself that you desperately wish you could change or hide from. The identities that you try to push down and cover up with something else.

- What are some purchases that you might be making that are helping you attempt to escape your identity?
- How do you feel about these purchases?

SPENDING TO BELONG

Most of my clothes growing up were either hand-me-downs or thrifted items. My mother is very frugal and has been a thrifter for as long as I can remember. I've always loved going thrifting with my mom, except for the period when I was in junior high and high school. Suddenly, thrifting became gross and I didn't want to do it—I know, I was a total brat. Instead, I wanted to be wearing a TNA sweater (that cost $80, by the way) to school so I could fit in with my friends. I got a job in seventh grade so I could buy myself expensive clothes and a cell phone. I wanted so desperately to fit in with the "cool kids" in my class, and I was willing to spend all my money to do so. But guess what happened? I bought myself the expensive clothes, and I still didn't feel like I fully fit in or was accepted. It's a feeling I've carried with me for most of my life. I thought if I could just buy the right stuff I would feel included, and when that didn't happen, I turned again to spending money to cope with my own feelings of inadequacy.

Spending to belong is another way identity and finances can intersect. In this case, the motivation behind spending is the deep desire to belong in some way. It's the need for validation from others. Spending money either to escape your identity (by buying things to camouflage who you really are) or to belong (by purchasing items that mark you as part of a particular group) often overlap, and you might experience a longing for both at the same time. Attempting to create a "new identity" for yourself by buying certain things can stem from the desire to break free of your real identity.

The beauty industry, in particular, is built on this desire to spend in order to belong. We've been convinced that we can simply buy "perfect." The industry tells us over and over again we aren't good enough and that we need to change something else about ourselves. Women are told to shave everywhere. Told to appeal more to the male gaze. Told to dress in sexy clothes—but don't show too much. Told to do our hair and wear makeup—but not too much. Women of color are told their natural hair is unprofessional and that they should change it. Men are told to hit the gym more, to be muscular and strong. Nonbinary folks wrestle with constantly being told they are "too feminine" or "too masculine," which is not surprising considering the binary nature of the beauty industry. I've heard similar stories from folks who self-identify as fat and don't feel "thin enough" to exist in many spaces. These unrealistic beauty standards make us think negatively about our body, weight, and appearance, and as a result we pay the price, literally.

According to Helga Dittmar, author of *Consumer Culture, Identity and Well-Being*, if you feel there is a gap between who you are and who you wish to be, you're more likely to be swayed by advertisements selling you the "solution." Companies know this and will specifically market toward "deficits" people commonly identify, effectively widening the gap and handing you the remedy on a silver platter. Purchase this product and you'll be one step closer to who you want to be.

Like my seventh-grade self, most of us have experienced this pressure to buy in order to fit in. Looking, acting, or behaving in a way that mirrors the identities you want to have can help you feel more connected to that group. Research shows that one of the root causes of materialism is the desire to be accepted. If you perceive that you aren't fitting in with a certain group or struggle with low self-esteem, you spend money to cope with those feelings. You will make financial decisions that further align or assimilate you into that social group. If you weren't born with the identity you wanted, you might convince yourself you can buy that identity, change the way people perceive you, and create yourself over again. Do we see the harmful cycle this puts you in? I specifically want you to think about the aspects of your identity you reflected on earlier that you struggled with growing up, or are least comfortable sharing now.

- What decisions do you have to make differently because of those identities?
- How are you using your money in order to fit in or belong?

EMBRACING YOUR IDENTITY

I want to be clear that just because these systems profit from our insecurities, this does not mean that everything we buy to make ourselves look a certain way is a negative thing. The reality is that it costs money to portray any aesthetic or vibe we want, even if it's embracing our identity. The material goods you own can communicate your personal and social identity both to yourself and to others. They can also help you hold onto your sense of self during periods of immense change or crisis. Think about how money can help you amplify your identity, specifically the aspects that you're really proud of and want to communicate to the world. Spending money to embrace your identity can also just be for you, an investment into your sense of self.

PASSING THE MIC

Stevie's Story: Learning to Embrace All Sides of Yourself

I had the pleasure of chatting with Stevie Gregg (he/him) about his gender transition and lifelong journey of becoming his true, authentic self. Stevie has a master's degree in business and currently works in the financial industry in addition to being a talented artist and writer. He is passionate about being a voice for future generations of trans youth and advocating for the 2SLGBTQIA+ community. Here is his story:

My gender transition is a big part of my identity. I was assigned female at birth but transitioned to a physical male body in order to reflect my inner male identity. I started my transition about 15 years ago, and I'm still learning new things about my identity.

I used to love doing my own nails as a teenager, but once I started transitioning, I had to fit this new, masculine mold. I needed to convince others around me that my identity was legitimate, and that required me to present more traditionally masculine. I got really into fitness and was spending a lot of money on the gym, supplements, and fitness classes. I wanted that hot guy persona of being buff and muscular.

It was all part of my journey, but now I'm past that and onto a new phase of my identity. I recently got my very first manicure and it feels like I've reached a place where I don't need to convince anyone else of my identity anymore. I'm free to express my gender in any way that feels good to me, regardless of what other people will perceive from it. I'm sure my consumption habits will change as I go through the process of really embracing all sides of me, like masculine, feminine, whatever.

It's hard to even verbalize how important it is to just be your true, authentic self. When you get the opportunity to be who you want to be, your confidence, happiness, excitement for life, and the future all just skyrockets. Before embracing my identity, I was scraping by mentally, and I didn't have any plans for the future. Now I get to live my life fully as a trans man and that's a privilege most people don't even realize they have been naturally given.

Stevie's story is a great example of how money can be a tool that helps you embrace your true identity. He wasn't wasting money when he was going to the gym, or when he paid completely out of pocket for one of his gender-affirming surgeries. These were necessary costs in order for him to feel like his true self. Even now, some people might view manicures as a luxury expense and consider them a waste of money, but don't underestimate the importance of these purchases for an individual. Spending money on products or expenses that uphold your identity can give you a return on investment that far outweighs the monetary cost. So let's collectively agree to stop commenting on how other people spend their money, okay? To you, a manicure may be frivolous, but for Stevie a manicure represents his freedom from the traditionally masculine mold.

WRAPPING IT UP

Embracing your identity means loving and acknowledging all parts of yourself. It requires you to understand the privilege you have and the barriers you face and to recognize your proximity to power. When you are able to embrace your identity, you're no longer shying away from the parts of yourself that you were bullied for, that you kept secret, or that made it difficult to navigate your daily life. Instead, you're empowered by who you are, welcoming in the good and the bad bits, so that you find a way forward that elevates your authentic self. Here are some questions to get you thinking about how to embrace your identity:

- What are some purchases you've made that helped you embrace your identity? How did they make you feel?
- How could money be used as a tool to embrace your identity?

Being able to embrace your full identity is going to take work, and it will be a journey. But allowing yourself to have that journey, and to really explore who you are, has the power to change your trajectory. You will have more confidence moving forward and creating a holistic financial plan that fully aligns with you.

PUTTING IT INTO PRACTICE

1. Look back at your past month of spending. Do this by pulling up your bank statements for every account or card that you use and recording all your purchases that month. This should be easier after completing your Financial Audit! The main focus here is discretionary spending (so not including essentials like food and shelter). You can use pen and paper for this, a simple Excel sheet, or the link I've provided to my free tracking template in the resource section. If that still sounds too overwhelming, start with just reviewing last week's spending. You want to get a better idea of where your money is going. This can be intimidating, but the goal here is to understand your spending, not judge it. Remember the importance of safe spaces? Give yourself the grace to create one now.

2. Now that you've tracked some of your past spending, I want you to reflect on the following questions for each individual purchase:

o Why specifically did you buy that thing? What was the purpose or intent?

o What does that purchase say in relation to your identity?

o What was your emotional response—did this give you a sense of joy, fun, or contentment when you purchased it, or did you feel embarrassed, guilty, or uneasy?

o Did you make this purchase in order to fit in or belong in some way?

o Did you make this purchase in an attempt to hide or suppress part of you?

o Did this purchase help you embrace your identity in any way?

Keep in mind that sometimes it's not that deep, and you might have bought yourself a coffee just because you wanted a freaking coffee and that's okay. Don't overthink it.

3. After completing the reflection questions, I want you to make two lists.

- o **List 1:** previous purchases you've made that feel good and help you embrace your identity. These spending habits give you a return on investment, usually in the form of happiness, fulfillment, or confidence.
- o **List 2:** purchases that you identified as rooted in trying to escape your identity or be accepted. These are oftentimes driven by consumer culture.

Your goal is to cut back or stop spending money on anything on the second list and redirect that money to purchases on the first list. Start by committing to how you want to spend moving forward. For example: "Next month I will spend less money trying to keep up with the trends I see on social media and instead invest in an item of clothing that feels 100% like me." Before you make a purchase, try taking a pause and asking yourself, **Does this purchase fall onto list 1 or 2?** to see if you can catch unaligned spending.

CHAPTER 3

Live, Laugh, Lexapro

HOW TO NAVIGATE THE CYCLE OF MENTAL HEALTH AND MONEY

I've held at least one job since I was 12 (because this was when my parents told me that if I wanted a cell phone, I had to pay for it myself) and I had never been more than 5–10 minutes late for a shift until my summer job in university. One morning I slept in and woke up at 9:30 a.m. when I was supposed to be at work at 8:30 a.m. Of course, this resulted in a panicked frenzy with me running around trying to grab everything while frantically texting my coworkers. I prided myself on being a reliable employee and being this late made me feel sick to my stomach. When I burst into my boss's office that morning to explain, I had barely opened my mouth before I started crying. I told him the truth of why I was late—I had started medication for anxiety, which made me groggy and drowsy and just out of it. Thankfully, I had an understanding boss who told me it was okay and that he wouldn't record me being late. He then proceeded to ask me genuine questions about how I was feeling and what type of work

I felt comfortable doing that day. I was responsible for operating the fork-lift and telehandler (a big machine with a retractable arm that we would use to crush garbage) and my boss agreed that I could take a break from operating the machinery until I had become used to the medication. I felt seen and understood in that moment, and the pit in my stomach started to ease.

In that instance, my boss made my mental health a priority, but that scenario might have played out very differently. I could have been written up for being late and forced to operate the machinery even though I was feeling out of it. I could have hurt myself or somebody else because I felt pressured to do my job. I could have been yelled at or fired. If I had been late frequently, would my boss have continued to meet me with the same amount of kindness and understanding?

Mental health is often not taken seriously in the workplace, and even if it is, there are not enough systems in place to support the people struggling the most. Without these support systems, individuals deal with the inability to take mental health days, the loss of wages, and the potential difficulty landing or keeping a job. If your job is at risk, so is your income. If your income is at risk, so are your finances. If your finances are at risk, so is your mental health, and the cycle continues.

The story I just told took place in 2018, but it wasn't until 2020 that I was diagnosed with ADHD, anxiety, and depression (more about my ADHD journey in the next chapter). Prior to that, I didn't understand the profound impact that my mental health had on my money. As much as we've progressed as a society, there is still a stigma around mental health and a taboo around money. Combine the two and you've got the perfect recipe for guilt, shame, and isolation.

THE IMPACT OF YOUR MENTAL HEALTH ON YOUR FINANCES

Mental health and money are interesting and complicated topics because they affect each other in many different ways. Struggling with your mental health can have a negative impact on your finances, and struggling with your finances can have a negative impact on your mental health.

If left unaddressed, this creates a continuous negative cycle involving mental health and money. Escaping this cycle is challenging because it's hard to know what to tackle first—your mental health or your money? My answer—tackle both, and that's what I'm here to help walk you through.

Let's start by talking about the impact that mental health challenges may have on your money. I'm sure that almost all of us have struggled with our mental health at some point in life. Whether it's something you struggle with daily, periodically, or just once in a while, you know what it's like to just not feel okay. The way that your mental health impacts you will vary from person to person. It might feel like a dark cloud that won't go away, which keeps you stuck in bed, and sucks all the energy and motivation right out of you. Maybe it feels more like a quiet voice that whispers negative and intrusive thoughts as you go about your day. Or perhaps it comes and goes, disappearing for months at a time only to appear again when you least expect it. However mental health struggles show up for you, it's probably had an effect on your finances. You're not alone in feeling that way; many folks in the Queerd

Co. community have expressed how much their mental health impacts their money.

QUEERD CO. COMMUNITY COMMENTS

"I feel so much guilt over my debt, and a lot of it was due to undiagnosed/untreated mental illness, but I haven't gotten past the stigma."

"One of the worst things I've ever done was coping with bipolar disorder by recklessly spending. I'm almost 24, still living with my parents, in a mountain of debt."

"I'm drowning. I can't collect my own thoughts; so how the hell do I support a family when I can't even support myself?"

"I just quit a good-paying job because I COULDN'T handle the mental stress it had on me."

The comment section on many of my videos feature thousands more comments like these. You're truly not alone in what you're struggling with. The research backs up the observation that folks who experience mental health challenges are more likely to struggle with their financial situation.

Let's dive into some examples of mental health challenges that might affect your money.

IF YOU STRUGGLE WITH ... LACK OF MOTIVATION OR INTEREST

When you feel down, or anxious, or just not quite yourself, you often lack the motivation to manage your finances. Your brain is focusing on other things like getting through the day without crying or pulling yourself out of bed to brush your teeth, and it doesn't have the capacity to work on anything else. The last thing you probably feel like doing during times like these is looking at your bank account, especially if you're not feeling great about your money. Additionally, if you're feeling hopeless about life, or about the future, you may not even see the point in caring about your finances. Like . . . is the planet even going to be around that long, or will we all be living in a barren wasteland?

Okay, I'm about to give you some really profound advice here, so pay attention.

What if during the times you don't have the motivation to manage your money— you just didn't manage your money?

Now before you gasp in shock, I want to be clear—I'm not suggesting it's a good idea to ignore all your bills and debt payments for weeks on end. What I am suggesting is that there might be a better way. Hands down, one of the best things I've learned on my personal finance journey is the power of automation. The solution to a lack of motivation is to automate your financial systems so they run on autopilot without you. Don't worry, we will cover how to automate your finances later in Chapter 9, but first let's start with creating some financial security.

One of the greatest gifts when you're struggling with your mental health is having financial peace of mind. This is the difference between not being able to afford missing a day of work and being able to take two weeks off to focus on your mental health. We need to get you out of survival mode before we worry about all the systems. You can create the space needed to take care of yourself by saving up a safety fund!

FiNANCiAL SiDEBAR

What is a safety fund?

A safety fund (also called an emergency fund) is money you've saved to protect yourself from unpredictable expenses. Those birthday presents you forgot to save up for don't count as unpredictable since birthdays happen every year without fail. I'm talking about events like losing your job, unexpected vet bills, a car accident, a medical emergency, etc.

You learned in Chapter 1 that saving up a safety net should ideally be one of your first financial priorities, even before paying off debt! The reason for this is that it can protect you from going into *more* debt when unexpected expenses arise. I know saving for potential emergencies doesn't feel so fun, but it can be your key to finally breaking the cycle of debt and just having peace of mind when it comes to your money. Just imagine not having to stress when you have to pay $500 for dental work, or when your cat needs a procedure done. You deserve to prioritize your own well-being and financial security before worrying about quickly paying back your debt to these huge corporations. Now I'm not suggesting you default on your debt payments (please keep making your minimum payments!); rather, I believe you should focus on saving up your safety fund before you aggressively start paying down debt.

How much money should you aim to save in a safety fund?

A good starting point is saving up 3–6 months' worth of your living expenses in your safety fund. You'll want to add up everything essential you pay for in a month (rent, utilities, minimum debt payments, bills, groceries, gas, etc.), plus anything else you need to pay for to function properly as a human (therapy, medication, gym membership, etc.). You should already have an idea of this number from your Financial Audit. Now multiply that number by 3, 6, 9, 12—whatever number makes you feel comfortable—to come up with your goal safety fund amount. If you own property or have dependents, you're going to want to increase that number, because both of those examples come with many more unexpected expenses.

Where should you keep this money?
Your safety fund should be easily accessible in a high yield savings account (HYSA), also referred to as a high interest savings account (HISA), and not invested. In case of an emergency, you'll want to be able to access your money immediately if needed. A HYSA is simply a regular savings account on steroids, and all you need to know is that it earns you more interest (yay!). It's super easy to open one online for free, just do your research and make sure you go with a HYSA that is either FDIC or CDIC insured (this means your money is protected up to a certain amount). Or, if you go through a credit union, you want to make sure your money is NCUA insured. Check out the resource section at the back of the book for more guidance on this. There are tons of HYSAs out there that have no fees, no hard credit checks, and take less than five minutes to activate.

IF YOU STRUGGLE WITH . . .
IMPAIRED DECISION MAKING

Often when our mental health isn't doing so hot, we're operating in survival mode. Have you ever made a decision when you were struggling and later been like—"Oof, why did I do that?" Like the time I decided to cut my own bangs when I was feeling depressed (yikes). When we are in crisis, it's next to impossible to make decisions from an objective point of view. Many options or choices become closed off to us the deeper we get into a mental health crisis. It's almost like we have blinders on, and we can only see one option right in front of us and can't see all the other options to choose from. This is why we are more likely to make poor financial decisions when we are struggling. When you're in survival mode, you'll make decisions that might make sense in the short term but often don't take into account the long-term impact.

Some people struggle with impulsivity or manic episodes that can impair their decision-making ability. In this case, you make decisions from a place of panic and urgency. Instead of being able to sit down and review all your options, you feel the need to make a decision immediately and move on. You make a choice in the moment without considering future consequences or repercussions.

One of the best tools I have for dealing with poor decision making is the 24-hour rule. Here, the idea is that whenever you are faced with a big financial decision, you should wait at least 24 hours before making the final call. I started implementing this rule when I was trying to cut back on impulse spending, and I've carried it with me ever since. Here are some examples of times when I've applied the 24-hour rule:

- When I get an idea for a new hobby and want to buy $100 worth of supplies for it
- When the stock market drops and I have a moment of panic
- When I see literally any influencer talking about a skincare product and I'm convinced I need it
- Oh . . . and *definitely* if I get the urge to cut my own bangs again

Another tip is to write down a list of responsibilities and tasks that you know you should only attempt to tackle when you're feeling good mentally. When the darkness lifts and you have more clarity to make thoughtful decisions, start working your way through that list. Take advantage of the days your brain feels good and give yourself permission to release those responsibilities when things are hard. I know society has told you that you should be balancing work, homelife, finances, health, and social life all the time, but the truth is that doesn't work for many of us. I live a very "unbalanced" life, but I'm honest about my energy and I am less likely to make poor decisions.

Now as much as I wish I could tell you that those two tips will prevent any impaired decision making in the future, that's not realistic. The truth is that you inevitably *will* make decisions in the future that you later regret. The sooner you can make peace with that fact, the better off you'll be. In the grand scheme of your life, a couple of financial missteps won't sabotage anything.

> *Managing your money is not about being perfect and never making a mistake, it's about figuring out how to create sustainable habits and behaviors.*

IF YOU STRUGGLE WITH . . . ANXIETY/WORRY

If you battle with anxiety, you may avoid checking your credit card statements or opening up that letter about your taxes because it'll trigger panic or worry. That was me. I would delete emails and throw out letters about my student loans without reading them. FYI—I do not recommend this approach. But I was already anxious; I didn't need Lisa from the federal student loan office to make it worse. Money can be very anxiety inducing because it's this Big Important part of being an adult that we often feel unprepared to handle. Anxiety thrives off doubt and what-ifs, and it makes you constantly question everything. How am I going to pay off that debt? Where did all my money go this month? Will I ever be able to own a home? Having anxiety makes it hard to ground yourself in the present, and many of your thoughts revolve around fear of the future. We're so busy worrying about all the "what-ifs" that it keeps us paralyzed and unable to take control.

PASSING THE MIC

Alyssa's Story: Learning How to Sit in Discomfort

My friend and fellow finance creator Alyssa Davies (she/her) shared with me her experience navigating the impact of mental health on her finances while juggling full-time work, entrepreneurship, and family life. Alyssa is the founder of Mixed Up Money, an award-winning personal finance blog, and a two-time published author. She is passionate about providing judgment-free financial education to her community and does so through her creative illustrations and weekly money polls. Here is her story:

Prior to becoming really financially aware and realizing I had to worry about my future, I was carefree and didn't have very much anxiety. But then I hit a wall with my debt, and the anxiety came. I was barely making ends meet, and I was going into overdraft every single month trying to pay my bills. The anxiety took over and, to be honest, I have not been able to control it since.

Most of my anxiety and stress comes from work because it's always been about making as much money as possible so that I never get back to the place that I was in. There's not a lot of breathing room for me, so any chance I can opt for convenience in my life, I will take it. I don't question it, because if I do, that's just one more thing to worry about. For me this shows up as paying for the closest parking spot because it's too anxiety inducing to look for one down the street and then try to find my way back. Or constantly going over budget on takeout when my partner and I are overloaded and exhausted.

I think that most of the time we are spending irrationally or really out of sorts financially it's because we are trying to deflect from the fact that something else is going on, and it ends up putting us in a cycle. When I'm really anxious, I'm immediately like, I need to dissociate, or I need to buy something that's going to fix the problem. I'm working on learning to accept and sit in that discomfort rather than running away from it and using money as my outlet, because that's when I get stuck in that cycle.

Personally, I couldn't deal with my mental health until my money was organized because I couldn't afford to deal with it. That sounds awful, but I didn't feel like I had an option. When it comes to which one you should tackle first, I think it's more a matter of what is the immediate danger in your mind. But ultimately, you'll end up tackling them together because they are so intertwined.

If you struggle with anxiety like Alyssa and me, it can be easy to dissociate or try to ignore the discomfort rather than facing those anxious fears head-on. One of the only helpful things that came out of my years of horrible experiences with doctors when I was seeking a mental health diagnosis was being introduced to an exercise by a sleep psychiatrist to help quiet down those anxious, racing thoughts.

This is called the constructive worry exercise. Oftentimes our worries and anxiety can stem from situations outside our control, and thinking about them won't actually bring us any closer to relief. This exercise was designed to be used when you're being kept up at night with these thoughts, but it also works well anytime.

For this exercise you're going to need a piece of paper with a line drawn vertically down the center of the page. On the left side write *"worries"* and on the right side write *"solutions."* As you follow the instructions, give yourself some grace, be honest with yourself, and do your best at each step. Take breaks as needed.

1. Write down all the anxieties, worries, concerns, and thoughts that are swirling around your head under the "worries" column.
2. Next, go through the list of everything you wrote down and brainstorm all possible solutions in the "solutions" column. Jot down 2–3 practical ideas that would make the problem at least

a little bit better or water down the intensity of the anxiety you feel around it.

If the solution is simple—go tackle that worry right now. Unless of course you're about to go to sleep or it's the middle of the night: in that case, maybe wait till morning.

If you realize after writing a worry down that it's actually not that important, then delete it from your list (and your brain). I like to imagine that those worries are a file folder that I remove from the depths of my brain and throw into a paper shredder.

If you can't solve the worry right now and it has to wait till a later time, write down when you will tackle the solution. Tomorrow? Next week? After you talk to your partner?

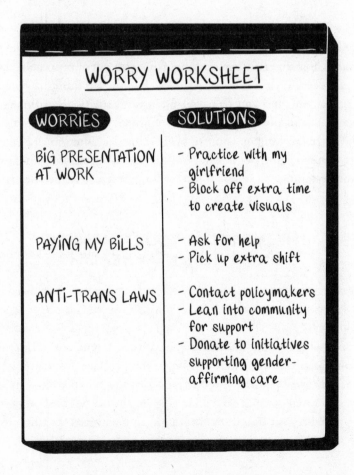

If you're not sure what the solution is, ask your support system if they have any ideas.

And most importantly, if you realize that the worry doesn't have a solution because it's outside your control, write that down (and maybe highlight and star it too, so you don't forget!).

3. Come back to this sheet periodically. Add in any other worries that have come up, cross things off, and work through your solutions one by one until those worries have been addressed.
4. If you find yourself feeling anxious about something, go to your worry worksheet and see what solutions you can try. Remind yourself that you've done everything you can and handled it as best you could.

Now, I know completing this worksheet will not magically heal your anxiety, but it is one tool that can help you view your worries from a different perspective. Sometimes just getting those thoughts out of your brain and onto paper can offer some relief. Especially when you are thinking about your finances, this method can help you brainstorm solutions to things you're anxious about and allow you to understand what's simply out of your control.

The key is working on consistently making decisions that feel good and support your goals and not beating yourself up when you make one bad decision. The best thing you can do is just readjust for next time and keep moving forward.

THE IMPACT OF YOUR FINANCES ON YOUR MENTAL HEALTH

Now let's explore how your finances affect your mental health. According to a 2019 US survey on stress, financial worry was the number one stressor across all ages, with 52% of people saying money regularly stressed them out. This isn't surprising because money affects so much of our day-to-day lives. Your financial stress shows up when you go to work and ask for a promotion. It shows up when you buy groceries and provide for your family. It shows up when you pay your bills or go to the doctor. It shows up when you go out with your friends or book a vacation with your partner. If you're worried about money, this will impact many of your daily activities. Some common ways your finances could impact your mental health include:

- Triggering feelings of anxiety or panic
- Constant worry leading to difficulty sleeping
- Strain on relationships and social life
- Feelings of shame and isolation
- Inability to afford to manage mental health

When I was struggling with my debt, the weight of my guilt, shame, and stress around debt was constantly with me. It affected my confidence, my job, my mental health, and my quality of life. If you've ever joked with your friend about how your student loans are making you depressed—turns out that may be true. Your financial situation can act as a catalyst for temporary or ongoing mental health struggles. Folks who are low income or experiencing poverty will likely have to navigate financial hardship in a variety of ways and are more prone to unemployment. Barriers such as difficulty accessing affordable housing and paying bills lead to increased mental health challenges. And research shows that debt depression—experiencing depressive symptoms as a result of the emotional stress of debt—is a real thing.

I believe that a lot of the negative emotions we feel around debt are a result of the messaging we've received as a society that debt is bad. We're told that debt is a result of poor financial management and impulsive spending and that we need to strive to be debt-free as quickly as possible. In reality, debt is often a result of systems outside of your control and being debt-free isn't a necessary requirement to achieve financial security. In fact, it's almost impossible to live debt-free if you choose to go to college or buy a home. For many of you, the debt you took on was actually a helpful tool. Maybe that debt helped you get a college degree, or purchase a safe vehicle for your family, or travel and have life-changing experiences, or simply just *survive*. I want you to take a moment and think about how you can reframe your debt as a tool.

It's easy to look at your money and feel like something is wrong with you. We've been conditioned to associate our self-worth with our net worth. When you're struggling to pay your bills or your account dips into the red, you might feel worthless. You might convince yourself that these negative emotions will go away once you pay off your debt or make more money, but achieving financial stability can take time. Here are some suggestions to get you started:

1. Break Down Your Goals

Start small when it comes to making financial changes. Identify what specific aspect of your finances is causing you the most stress right now. Think about the end goal that would remove that stress for you. **How can you break down that end goal into smaller, bite-size pieces?**

For example, if you're struggling with debt depression, paying off your debt might be the end goal. Instead of focusing on the fact that you're $80,000 in debt and have no idea how you'll pay that off, start with thinking about how you'll pay off $100 of debt. As you start tackling these smaller milestones, you'll begin to feel more confident about achieving your end goal.

2. Start Talking About Money

I've found that sometimes the most reassuring thing when it comes to coping with financial stress is simply knowing that you're not the only one struggling. Having a safe space to open up and share your struggles can help you feel less shame about your situation. In 2019, 53% of people reported that they feel better after talking to someone who experienced a similar situation to theirs. Ease into the conversation by talking about simple and broad money topics first and begin to share your personal situation when you feel comfortable. Always approach money conversations with an open mind and without judgment. If you don't have anyone in your life to talk to about money, consider finding an online community (*hint hint* like Queerd Co.) where you feel seen, heard, and understood.

3. Seek Out Professional Support

Regardless of the personal experience I have and research I've done, I'm not a mental health professional. The information I provide will never replace the work of a professional, and many of you may require that additional support to manage your mental health. Being supported in your mental health means that you have more capacity to tackle your finances. Speak to a healthcare professional about your options to see if you could benefit from medication or therapy.

THE COST OF SUPPORT

When it comes to trying to work through the mental health challenges we just covered, many people will suffer alone or in silence because of the barriers that stop them from seeking out help or being able to access support. The obvious barrier is cost, but another barrier is the lack of diversity that exists in the mental health professional industry. Most of the research finds that Indigenous, Alaskan, and white adults, as well as those who report two or more races, experience the highest rates of mental health issues and are more likely to access mental health services. However, it is noted in some research that the cultural stigma around mental health for many Latinx, Black, and Asian communities may explain the seemingly "lower rates." An important part of therapy is being able to feel heard and understood by your therapist, which becomes a challenge when your therapist has no way of relating to your experience. Folks in the 2SLGBTQIA+ community are 3x more likely to suffer from mental illness and 2–4x more likely to access mental health services than heterosexual people, so it's imperative that those services are safe spaces and that we look for therapists who can meet our needs.

What should you do when you can't afford therapy or don't feel like therapy is a safe space for you? An article from *PsychCentral* outlines some suggestions on how to find more affordable options and alternatives to therapy. Specifically:

Check your insurance. If you have insurance, check to see what your coverage is like and what benefits you're eligible for. See if your employer offers an Employee Assistance Program (EAP) that will provide you with some free counseling sessions. Make sure that any professional you're seeing will accept your insurance.

Inquire about sliding scale options. Some therapists will offer sliding scale payment options based on your income or make adjustments to the session (e.g., shorter time frame, virtual appointment) that allow for a lower rate.

Go to a psychologist training clinic. Often found on college campuses, these clinics will have therapists who are in training but are always overseen by a fully licensed professional. These clinics often offer lower-cost services.

Take advantage of community mental health services. Check out local mental health centers to see what kind of programs or services they offer. You might be able to find free group sessions or get assistance finding a therapist.

Join local or online support groups. If you are living with addiction, substance abuse disorder, domestic violence, disability, or mental health challenges, there are support groups out there that can help you. For example, the National Alliance of Mental Illness (NAMI) offers free peer-led support groups for folks struggling with their mental health.

Take advantage of free/low-cost resources such as books, podcasts, and apps. If all the above suggestions are still out of your budget or not accessible for you, try utilizing all the self-led resources available to you. Read books that will help you navigate your mental health struggles. Listen to podcasts discussing mental health and recovery and interviews with people sharing their personal experiences. Download apps for meditation, breathwork, and overall support. Check out the resource section for specific recommendations!

RESOURCE

Free Mental Health Resources, page 313

I'm not going to sugarcoat it—managing your mental health is expensive. The tangible costs include medication, therapy, and other treatment. I pay over $150 per month (works out to be around $5 per day) for my medication, and I know I am extremely privileged to be able to afford that. I spoke with one of our Queerd Co. community members, Hannah (she/her), about her experience living with diabetes and the potential detrimental effects of not being able to afford insulin. Here's what she had to say.

"I didn't really understand the financial burden of my diabetes until I moved out and discovered how beneficial benefits actually are, how much they cover, and how expensive it was to basically just live. I'm very fortunate now that I pay maybe about $150 to $200 a month out of pocket for expenses related to my diabetes, but there was a time when I was struggling. I was making minimum wage, working two jobs while in college, and money was going out faster than it was coming in. I would ration my insulin just so I could afford to pay my rent and eat and all those kinds of things. Rationing insulin is a huge cause of death for diabetics, especially young people, and I did that for a really long time. I'm not proud of it, but I had to live somehow. I could have lost my eyesight, I could have had my limbs amputated, I could have had a heart attack, but I was fortunate that I could afford enough to keep me alive."

The reality of the costs of mental (and physical) health can be sobering, and ultimately, we just have to do the best we can with what we have and continue to fight for better systems. Later on in this chapter we will explore some ways to advocate for yourself and invest in your well-being.

MENTAL WELLNESS IN THE WORKPLACE

Another way that your mental health impacts your finances is through the effect it has on your career. This impact starts when you are young and continues all the way up until adulthood. If you struggled with your mental health as a child, this might cause you to be distracted in class and unable to complete your work when you go home for the day. If you have ADHD, you might have a hard time taking tests or staying on task during childhood and/or young adulthood.

These struggles can carry into your career as well. You might face "employment issues" such as arriving late, poor performance, and missed days due to your mental health. This creates a domino effect leading to struggles getting raises or promotions, often being passed up due to poor performance or too many sick days, and having to frequently "start over" at new jobs. Each transition leaves you with a period where you lack benefits and access to support, only further exacerbating your mental health challenges.

Perhaps this is why only half of Americans feel comfortable discussing their mental health at work. The research on disclosure makes sense: Why would you put your own career and potential access to healthcare at risk? You may have been told in the past, either directly or indirectly, that you are a burden to the company or not a good employee because of your mental health. The real issue here is that employers are not setting up proper systems to support their staff.

What Can Employers and Employees Do to Address Mental Health at Work?

If you are an *employer* (even a small business with one employee!), here are some suggestions:

- Offer employee assistance programs
- Create company policies around health and wellness (and actually walk the walk)
- Work job accommodations into your budget (time off, mental health days, remote work, time to reach productivity milestones, etc.)
- Put money into training managers/supervisors on interventions and how to work with performance difficulties in a mental health and trauma–informed way
- Create a return-to-work protocol after extended leave
- Implement job-employee matching (finding a role/environment that fits that person)

As someone who manages a team of three people currently, here are some of the things I do to support my employees' mental health:

- Flexible timelines and schedules that accommodate days or weeks off on short notice
- Team days off after triggering or upsetting political or social justice issues/events
- Ongoing team diversity, equity, and inclusion training that helps us navigate difficult topics and use appropriate and inclusive language

Right now, my employees are individual contractors who work very part-time, but as Queerd Co. grows, it's a goal of mine to make sure I offer an amazing benefit plan with lots of mental health support to my team.

If you are an *employee*, here are some suggestions:

- Identify, diagnose, and manage your mental health to the best of your abilities (you may not have access to a medical diagnosis but self-diagnosis is still valid when properly researched and understood)
- Know your legal rights as an employee where you live, as well as company policies (when requesting accommodations, bring these to your HR department)
- Learn and practice coping skills that you can use at work
- Engage in self-awareness training (asking for accommodations involves knowing what you need first)
- Find your community (oh look, the importance of safe spaces again!)
- Join a union if that's an option for your role
- Apply for any subsidies available

INVEST IN YOUR WELL-BEING

Those of us who struggle on a consistent basis with our mental health often rely on adaptations to complete necessary daily tasks. I used to resent the fact that I had to pay more money just to get through life the same way as those without mental health challenges, but I've since realized that spending the money to enhance my life is worth it, every time. I've embraced the fact that certain tasks are going to be harder for me; I can either be constantly angry about that, or I can learn and accept the adaptations that can help me.

For example, grocery shopping and cooking are the bane of my existence. I struggle with all of it, from planning out weekly meals and navigating a grocery store to actually wanting to eat that meal once it's cooked. Instead of dealing with all that, I would often end up ordering takeout. If I was tight on money or trying to save more, I would end up skipping meals because I couldn't decide what to eat or didn't have the energy to make anything. Obviously, this practice made my mental health even worse—*and the cycle continues.*

I'm sure many of you grew up being told "why pay for something if you can do it yourself?" and held onto that belief as adults. I remember how shocked I was when my sister told me that she hired a cleaner for her little 300-square-foot studio apartment. I mean, it was so tiny—why would she waste money on that when she could clean it herself? But my sister is an accountant, balancing working sixty to ninety hours a week at a Big 4 firm, trying to have a social life, and managing her own mental health. I didn't understand that the money it cost to hire a cleaner was less than the impact of trying to do it herself.

I used to think that paying for something like cleaning services or grocery delivery (a) cost too much and (b) wasn't worth the money, but I know now that isn't true. I've learned that it's worth paying for tools or services that take away or reduce barriers for you, if you're financially able to do so. I started getting my groceries delivered, which allowed me to skip the grocery store and save time. I even hired a cleaner, and let me tell you, I'm never going back. The cost of me cleaning my entire house by myself? *An entire Saturday and my sanity.* The cost of hiring an amazing cleaner (and supporting a small business) to clean my house way better than I could? *PRICELESS.*

Choosing to pay for these services meant that I had to adjust my budget and shuffle around my spending so that I could afford to do so. It meant less money for me to spend on fun things like going out for dinner or buying new clothes. This trade-off initially felt restrictive and took some time to adjust to, but having this support meant that I had more time and energy to spend taking care of myself, building my business, and spending time with loved ones. It meant that I was a better version of myself for everyone around me, and I actually had more motivation to go out and enjoy my life. I've since reframed the question from "*Why* pay for something if you can do it yourself?" to "*Why not* pay for something that will enhance your life?"

Think about the tasks in your daily life that are a constant sore spot for you, but that you know are important for your well-being. How could you make these tasks easier? Basically, if there's a task that feels overwhelming and it's financially feasible, you can probably pay someone to handle it for you. Here are some ideas:

If you struggle with cooking:

- Order grocery delivery
- Sign up for a prepared meal service
- Try a meal kit service (e.g., HelloFresh)
- Pay for a meal plan from a dietitian
- Take cooking classes

If you struggle with moving your body:

- Invest in home equipment
- Sign up for a class
- Hire a personal trainer
- Buy a workout plan

If you struggle with adulting ('cause let's be honest, adult responsibilities suck):

- Hire an accountant at tax time
- Pay for done-for-you laundry services
- Hire a cleaner for your home (highly recommend!)
- Pay your neighbor to mow your lawn or shovel your walkway
- See a travel agent for your next trip

There are lots of free ways to manage or adapt tasks in your life too, but I want to demonstrate that investing money into your well-being can have a huge return on investment. Remember that money is a resource—just like time and energy—and sometimes your time might be worth more than the price. When you're trying to decide whether or not paying for something is "worth it," think about what other resources you would gain in return. Minimizing your daily challenges can help improve your overall mental health, making it more doable to manage your money.

If you're working with a tight budget, here are some ways you can build more ease into your daily life that are free or are more low-cost:

- Buy items in bulk that you use often (e.g., toilet paper) to save on costs and reduce your trips to the store
- Double recipes when cooking meals and freeze the leftovers so you have meals ready to go on low-energy or tough mental health days
- Declutter your home—especially your main living areas—so there is less stuff to clean and put away (you could also sell some of this stuff for a little extra cash injection)

MINDFUL MOMENT

This chapter has been hard to write because there is just so much ground to cover. It's impossible to reduce the connection between mental health and money into a few pages when it has such a big impact on your life. In the following chapters of the book, you'll see Mindful Moment boxes just like this one so that I can keep reminding you to check-in on your mental health and consider it in relation to whatever topic we are discussing.

WRAPPING IT UP

We've seen in this chapter how much your mental health can impact your finances, and, unfortunately, how little support exists out there. It's important that you either advocate for yourself or find someone who can advocate for you. Take advantage of as many resources and services as are available to you. Apply for any government assistance you qualify for. Join support groups that make you feel seen and understood. Advocate for yourself and others on a government level. GO VOTE. Look into employment lawyers. Join a grassroots movement.

I've had hundreds of conversations with folks who struggle with their mental health, and the overarching theme I've noticed is the extreme shame they carry. For many, this is the biggest burden resulting from their experience of trying to manage their money. Despite the barriers working against you, I promise you can still have a solid financial future.

I know the feeling of guilt after making an impulsive purchase.

I know the embarrassment of admitting how much debt you have to a family member.

I know the pit in the stomach when you compare your life to that of people on your social media.

I know the pain that comes with the lack of understanding from those around you.

Please hear me when I say, *it's not your fault*. Your financial situation is not your fault, because you were not given the proper tools to succeed. Society did not teach you, the education system did not teach you, and your parents probably did not have the tools themselves to teach you. Many people face systems that have been set up to prevent them from gaining the tools to build financial health. The financial information out there rarely addresses the effect of mental health on your money.

Imagine you're trying to put together a piece of IKEA furniture and they forgot to include any Allen keys or screwdrivers. You have all the right screws and all the furniture pieces in front of you, but no way to put them together. That's where you are right now. You are missing some of the tools you need to build your financial future, but once you collect those, you're more than capable of putting everything together. By the end of this book, you'll be well equipped with tools and confidently building.

PUTTING IT INTO PRACTICE

1. Reflect on these questions:

   o What aspect(s) of your mental health make managing your finances challenging?
   o What patterns or behaviors are sabotaging your financial success?
   o In what ways does your financial situation change as your mental health worsens or improves?

2. Start working on building up your safety fund. Refer back to the financial sidebar in this chapter if you have no clue what I'm talking about right now. Set up an automatic transfer into this account every paycheck or once a month. The dollar amount doesn't matter, start with what you can, even $5 a month, and increase it as you're able to.

3. Build mental health expenses into your budget. You already learned about opening up a high yield savings account for your safety fund and now I suggest you open two more high yield savings accounts specifically for mental health. The first one can be used to save up for mental health expenses such as therapy or medication. The second one I like to call the "oh sh*t fund," designed to protect you during times of mental health distress. So if you did in fact cut your own bangs in a state of mania or depression and you need to get a haircut to fix it, you can use money in your "oh sh*t fund" to cover it instead of throwing off your monthly budget. Set up monthly automatic transfers to each of these accounts and slowly build them up.

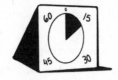

CHAPTER 4

Keep It (Neuro) Spicy

TIPS AND TRICKS TO GAMIFY YOUR FINANCES

Before diving in, I want to note that even if you don't have ADHD, you will still likely find this chapter helpful. You've probably also experienced many of the challenges or behaviors that I cover—like struggles with motivation, impulse spending, and difficulty sticking to a budget—to some degree. Although this will show up and affect you differently than someone with ADHD, the tips I provide will still be helpful and applicable. So please stick around!

When I first was confronted with the thought that I might have ADHD, the idea was quickly brushed off because I did so well in school. I was a smart, hardworking child—the kind of child nobody really worries about, because it was clear I was going places. I got all As in school, a record only tainted by one B in my Grade 3 gym class. Not only was I doing well in school, I had a solid group of friends and was training 20 hours a week as a competitive gymnast. I was every parent's dream child. Staying out of trouble, getting good grades, hanging around good people, being active, and working hard. Adults didn't have to worry about me, and that soon became the problem.

Going into university, I was confident that I would excel, but my first semester was a wake-up call. At one point, I doubted my ability to keep going, but the fear of failure kept me trying. I started out in the science department, and after a rough first year (remember my stats class?), I switched into kinesiology. Looking back now, I can attribute my success in college to the group of friends I made after that switch. We would meet daily to study for hours on end, quiz one another, share class notes, and cheer one another on. Even though I had a rough start to university, I ended up finding my footing and graduating with distinction.

All this to say, I was viewed as a successful person. From the outside looking in, I was doing well in all facets of my life. It wasn't until I graduated and started my own business that my success started to fall apart. Without the structure of a class schedule, accountability from professors, and support from my friends—who had also moved on to their careers—I began to struggle. I left college without a clear idea of what I was going to do with my life and who I wanted to be. As my friends drifted apart, I had trouble making new ones.

Oh, and I also graduated with $35,000 worth of debt.

At this point in my life, I had curated the image of myself that others saw. I was smart, successful, self-sufficient, and the helper to everyone else. I was the friend people would always come to for advice. I was the girlfriend who would put all my energy into enhancing my partner's life while neglecting my own. I did such a good job of upholding this image that nobody noticed I was struggling. The worse things got, the more ashamed I felt. I was embarrassed that I had student loan debt for a degree I wasn't even using. I was terrified to ask for help because that would expose me as a fraud, an imposter who appeared to be living her best life when in reality she was having panic attacks, fighting to keep up with work, and drowning in debt. I tried to stick to a schedule and set goals for myself, but I could never seem to follow through with my intentions. My daily inner monologue sounded a little something like this:

Just go finish that thing, why can't you just go do it?
Stop being so lazy.
How did you get yourself into this situation?
You can't afford to buy that, you're in debt.
You don't deserve it either.
What is wrong with you?
You're such a failure.

So what went wrong? How did the smart, hardworking child become the lost, helpless adult? For me, the answer was undiagnosed ADHD. It wasn't that anything went wrong, it was that school had been my safety net and once I graduated, I was free-falling. I know many people with ADHD struggle to get through school, but for me, it provided the structure, external accountability, and support that my brain required. After that went away, I was stuck navigating a world that wasn't designed for me. As I grappled with my shame and self-loathing, I pushed people away as a form of protection. It felt like the problem was me and that I needed to change to find that success again. I was alone in this struggle. The responsible ones, the smart ones, the helpers, and the high achievers too often get left behind because no one thought to worry about us.

THE SCOOP ON ADHD

ADHD stands for attention deficit hyperactivity disorder. The American Psychiatric Association defines ADHD as a "developmental disorder characterized by symptoms of inattention, hyperactivity, and impulsivity." The name is misleading because people with ADHD don't necessarily have a deficit of attention, but rather, the inability to focus their attention. ADHD coach Brett Thornhill says, *"It's like your brain keeps switching between 30 different channels and somebody else has the remote."*

The stereotypical view of someone with ADHD is a hyperactive boy who can't pay attention in class, has seemingly endless energy, and is constantly moving, fidgeting, and talking. But ADHD is also the person with their head in the clouds, the daydreamer. They are easily distracted and have problems sustaining their attention. With ADHD you can present more hyperactive symptoms, more inattentive symptoms, or have a balance of both. In addition to these types, ADHD exists on a spectrum and can impact people in different ways, to varying degrees. All three types interfere with the individual's functioning in multiple settings. ADHD is very real, very challenging, and can often be debilitating.

I have the combined type of ADHD, so I experience both hyperactive and inattentive symptoms without one of those being far more prevalent. While I did well in school, almost every report card mentioned that I was a chatterbox. When I wasn't busy talking, I was staring out the window, doodling, or working on homework for another class. None of these behaviors was flagged as a problem because of my grades. This is often what happens to women and girls with inattentive ADHD.

Since my moment of free-falling, I have found solid ground. I've built a successful business, transformed my financial situation, and found myself in the happiest, healthiest relationship I've ever had. It turns out the problem was never me, or my undiagnosed ADHD, but the fact that society is not designed to accommodate anyone who diverges from the norm. Of course, I would be remiss if I didn't point out that my privilege greatly contributed to this outcome as well.

In this chapter we are going to touch on some of the common challenging aspects of managing money with ADHD, and how you can work with your brain instead of against it. I want to acknowledge that there is a lot of research currently being done on ADHD, especially in women, so some of this information might change as new discoveries are made. It's important to note that everyone experiences their ADHD differently, and some of the money struggles I talk about won't be applicable to you. Whether you're reading this chapter for yourself, or to support someone else in your life with ADHD, give yourself the space and grace to experiment and find what works.

HOW ADHD IMPACTS YOUR MONEY

I opened up a $10,000 line of credit when I was in college to help cover some of my expenses as a student. I remember thinking to myself I'll only use like $1,000 and pay it off once I'm back at my full-time summer job. But it only took me two months to max out that $10,000 line of credit because I couldn't stop impulse spending. Yes, I know, I'm wondering how that was possible too. Prior to my diagnosis, my brain was feeling so out of it most of the time that I would spend money just to feel *something*. This line of credit was the gateway to even more spending, and before I knew it I had a maxed-out credit card, two lines of credit, and my student loans.

This is how I ended up in $35,000 of debt, $15,000 of which was high interest. I would look at my credit card statement and not even remember half the purchases I made. It seemed like everyone around me had it all figured out, and here I was, free-falling. The shame I felt followed me everywhere: when I went out for dinner with my friends, paid for my groceries, treated myself to a Starbucks, or bought another shirt that I definitely did not need. I felt so out of control, but at the same time I didn't know how to change my money habits and behaviors.

Turns out, my struggle with impulse spending and debt was not a unique one. 65% of folks with ADHD say that having ADHD makes managing their money more difficult. But that's not all. If you have ADHD you are . . .

2x more likely to suffer from anxiety linked to finances
3x more likely to struggle with debt
3x more likely to miss bill payments either occasionally or often
3x more likely to struggle with sticking to a budget
4x more likely to impulse spend

. . . than those who don't have ADHD.

ADHD isn't confined to one area of your brain or one major impact on your life. It affects how you take in sensory information, how you think and process, and how you respond and behave. When it comes to your finances, it's going to impact how you understand, spend, and manage money. It will influence your emotions and mood, which we know both play a big role in financial decisions. Our challenges can lead to earning less and paying more than folks without ADHD. Just like every other chapter in this book, understanding how this piece of your identity impacts your money story, behaviors, and patterns is crucial for changing your situation.

When I was first diagnosed and started to learn more about how certain traits affected my money, I looked online to learn more. I was met with tumbleweeds, a couple YouTube videos and vague articles, but nothing that I could relate to. In fact, many of the articles giving advice on ADHD and money were filled with tips like "just make a budget" or "stop impulse spending." Thank you, Janet, I never thought of that!! Much of the advice available completely misses the mark because it suggests using systems and tools designed for and by neurotypical folks instead of actually catering to neurodivergent brains. For those of you unfamiliar with those terms, "neurodivergent" refers to those whose brain and cognition differs from what is considered "typical" by society. This can include folks who have ADHD, autism, dyscalculia, dyslexia, dyspraxia, BPD, and more. The term "neurotypical" describes those who display "typical" cognitive function. Please be aware that this language is always evolving, and new terms might be in use by the time you read this book.

To fill the gap I had identified, I started creating content around how my ADHD impacts my finances. If you follow me on social media, you know I talk about ADHD and mental health on an almost daily basis. I've had multiple videos on ADHD and money go viral, and here are some of the comments I have received:

 **QUEERD CO. COMMUNITY COMMENTS**

"I'm diagnosed with ADHD and I overthink all my spending to the point that I won't buy necessities."

"*tears* I always felt like such an idiot for the way I handled money. I'm trying to heal now that I know I have ADHD. Thank you."

"Every time I try to bring up that I think I need to be tested for ADHD my family tells me that I just lack discipline."

"23 years of untreated ADHD has left me with a lack of independence and no vision of a future."

I hope after reading these comments, you know that you're not alone. I hope you feel validated, that it's not just you struggling with your money. I hope you know that your financial challenges are clearly not your fault. I've said that a lot throughout this book, but I will say it a million more times in an attempt to override society's overarching message that your struggles are solely your problem.

Despite me saying all that, I know there will still be some of you who don't believe me. You still feel like you're lazy, not motivated enough, and a failure. A lot of that stems from the misconceptions and lack of understanding that still exists around ADHD. To combat that, I'm going to share some of the common beliefs people with ADHD hold and the reality behind what's actually happening. I want you to understand that there are real, tangible reasons that your finances are suffering and that there are actionable steps you can take to change that.

3 LIES AND MANY TRUTHS ABOUT ADHD AND MONEY

Lie #1: "I'm Just Lazy."

Writing this book brought up a lot of shame for me. When I signed my book deal, I had a long time frame to complete the manuscript, almost a full month to write each chapter. I planned out a schedule for exactly how I was going to spend my time. I decided I would write a little bit throughout the week and then Fridays would be my dedicated writing day. The plan was perfect, but I couldn't stick to it. I know that my brain thrives off urgency, and I do my best work under pressure. Having almost a year to write this book with no real sense of priority didn't set me up for success. I'm writing most of this book in the last 2 months before my manuscript due date. Some might label me as lazy for putting it off, but I couldn't create that false sense of urgency for myself. I had to wait until the tension of the deadline closed in around me. I felt deeply shameful about this. I was embarrassed when people asked me how writing was going. There were low moments of beating myself up, calling myself lazy. But I'm not lazy, *I just have ADHD.*

ADHD impairs your executive function, the set of cognitive processes involved in planning, time management, prioritization, organization, and self-control. Executive function is what enables us to effectively accomplish what we want to do and reach our long-term goals. It's basically the manager of your life. When your executive function is impaired, this will directly impact your ability to organize your money and stay on track with financial goals. The general detriment to planning and time management will have other indirect effects on your finances as well.

If you have ADHD, I'm sure you have experienced couch paralysis. This is when you're stuck on the couch, scrolling on your phone or watching TV and just cannot seem to get up and do the thing. You want to go work, or study, or clean your house because it's important to you, but you feel glued to those cushions. Growing up maybe you were called lazy for this. Maybe your partner gets frustrated when they ask you to do something and come home to find you watching TV on the couch. You're not lazy, *you just have ADHD.*

Executive function has effectively left the building. The task you are faced with might have too many moving parts that involve your executive function, which can hold you hostage. I want you to think about when you may have experienced this situation around your finances.

Let's look at the earlier example from Janet, telling folks with ADHD to "just make a budget." Making a budget is seen as one of those tasks you "should" be doing. It's what all the financial experts tell you to do and seems pretty straightforward, right? For someone with ADHD, this "straightforward" task can end up being very overwhelming. Here's an example of what this might look like:

- Muster up the motivation to start (if it's not interesting, *I don't want to do it*)
- Get overwhelmed trying to organize expenses and subscriptions
- Have a hard time finding the time to sit down and do the work (maybe plan to do it but end up not having enough time)
- Feel frustrated or bored and abandon the project for a couple weeks
- Attempt to track spending but have a difficult time remembering to do it
- Struggle trying to pick out a budget system (none of them seem quite right)
- Spend hours setting up a system only to hate it in 3 days

Some of you may not struggle with budgeting and actually find this an enjoyable task, but you can likely relate to this example when it comes to one or more areas of your finances. Tasks that other people can just sit down and complete may feel like climbing a mountain for you. Creating a budget involves your executive function, which is partially out of commission. So sometimes it's easier to just avoid the task completely.

Repeat after me: I'm not lazy, I just have ADHD.

Lie #2: "I Lack Willpower."

One of the big reasons folks with ADHD struggle with their finances is because they lack the right motivation. You know you "should" be saving money, paying off debt, and planning for the future, but you can't seem to execute on those goals. You might find yourself constantly comparing your financial progress with that of others and being frustrated that you haven't reached certain milestones. Other people are doing all the things, so why can't you? This often leads to the belief that you just need to be more motivated, or have more willpower. But motivation is not the problem, it's that you're seeking the *wrong* kind of motivation.

Neurotypical folks respond differently to "shoulds." They can tell themselves that they should save up a safety fund, or that it's important for them to be investing for retirement and just go and do those things. *Wild, right?* As someone with ADHD, even if I know something is important, and I want to do it, it can still be a challenge to find the motivation to start and keep going. Dr. Russell Barkley accurately refers to ADHD as "a motivation deficit disorder." We are lacking the same motivation that neurotypical folks have and often don't like tasks that are boring, repetitive, or take a long time. Don't worry, this doesn't mean that you'll never be able to do these tasks, it just means that you need to tap into different types of motivation. Let's cover four common types of motivation for folks with ADHD, and later on I'll touch on how you can apply them to your finances.

1. Pressure/Urgency—motivation as a result of the sense of pressure or urgency you feel around that task

The reason why the long writing deadline didn't work for me was because I had no sense of urgency. This is why many folks with ADHD will procrastinate on tasks. Waiting longer will create pressure and drive for them. You can either manufacture the urgency or tension yourself, or in some cases, rely on that from others.

Pressure from yourself often shows up in the form of shame, anxiety, and negative self-talk. Raise your hand if you've ever shame-spiraled so hard that it motivated you to complete the task you were avoiding. *Whoops—me too.* Pressure from others can stem from your fear of failure, disappointment, or potential consequences. It can also be rooted in your desire to impress or please others. When my university friends all met every day to study, they expected me to be ready to be quizzed, and that created pressure that motivated me to show up prepared. This type of tension is way more up my alley because, while I will ignore my own deadlines, I hate letting other people down (recovering people pleaser over here!).

We can also experience financial pressure, when the fear of your money being at risk creates a sense of urgency. That's the whole premise behind late or cancellation fees. Businesses hope that the financial repercussions of not showing up will be enough to deter that from happening. It's a good thought, but I've noticed the financial pressure will vary based on the individual's perception of that "cost." For example, a cancellation fee of $5 is unlikely to stop me from canceling if I need to. I'll take the hit because $5 isn't a lot of money for me. For other people, that $5 means more and they might respond differently.

Now, pressure or urgency may not do it for you, and that's okay because we have 3 more types of motivation coming up.

2. Interest/Passion—motivation as a result of being excited and engaged in the task

Have you ever put off cleaning your house or cooking yourself a meal because you were too busy reading a good book? Or researching how to transport coral from a saltwater fish tank (my most recent google search)? Or spending hours perfecting your latest crafting project? You have no problem spending the whole day doing these things, while simple daily tasks feel impossible.

This is why it's more accurate to say that folks with ADHD have an inability to focus their attention rather than a deficit of attention. You can easily engage and zero in on the tasks that interest you but struggle to even initiate the tasks that don't. We know that people with ADHD can fixate for hours on end when it comes to tasks they find engaging. Often the repetitive and necessary tasks required to take care of ourselves, our living space, and our finances get pushed to the wayside. The challenge here is to find a way to make those less riveting tasks more personally interesting.

For example, I don't love doing the dishes. But I make this task more enjoyable by using a Scrub Daddy sponge (which I love) and listening to music or watching a show while I do them. You may not be able to make a task like filing your taxes more enjoyable, but perhaps you can do it in a way that's more interesting.

3. Competition/Challenge—motivation as a result of the thrill of winning something or beating someone when it comes to the task

With this type of motivation, we are aiming to turn those tasks you're avoiding into a competition or challenge, essentially gamifying the process. I notice this motivation the most when I'm doing a Peloton bike ride. During the class, there is a leaderboard on the side of the screen that shows everyone else on the ride. I usually keep this hidden, because if I glance at the leaderboard I suddenly feel the need to beat everyone. I suppose that's not a bad thing, but I'm not looking to pass out on every bike ride I do. Keep in mind that even competing against yourself and the idea of beating your personal best can be motivating. Competition and challenge tends to be hit or miss with ADHD folks. Either you love it or you hate it.

4. Novelty/Play—motivation as a result of the tasks feeling shiny, new, and fun

You know that feeling when you buy a cute new gym outfit and suddenly you have more initiative to exercise? That's novelty motivation at work. Your brain is stimulated by fresh and novel things, and you'll get a hit of dopamine from starting exciting tasks. The challenge is that once that novelty wears off, you will lose that source of motivation. This is why many folks with ADHD get excited about new hobbies or ideas and end up abandoning them before they finish. *RIP to all my 70%-finished projects.* The key here is to find different ways to keep the task fun and fresh until completion.

Trying to accomplish tasks that we see others doing easily, or that we've completed before in the past, can be very frustrating. It's no wonder we internalize the belief that we are lazy, or that we just don't care enough. But it's not about trying harder, or caring more, or being more disciplined. It's not about contorting yourself to fit into society's neat little boxes. It's about accepting that your brain has different needs. Your brain has less dopamine and requires more stimulation. You don't need to change—your approach to the task does. That's when you'll find the motivation that's right for you.

> **Repeat after me:** *I don't lack willpower,*
> *I just have ADHD.*

Lie #3: "I'm Bad with Money."

The day I took stimulant medication for the first time was like the day I put on glasses for the first time. I felt like superwoman. I remember going to the gym and realizing I could actually keep track of reps. Usually I'm like 1, 2—*what am I going to eat after this?*—5, 6, 7—*why is this person standing so close to me?*—8, 9—*oof this burns*—9, 10—*wait did I count right?* But on medication I could count without losing track, and actually focus on my muscle activation. I always say that without medication I have "bees in my brain." If you also have ADHD, you probably know exactly what I'm talking about.

Okay, now imagine unmedicated me—the person who has bees swarming around her brain, who can't count to ten reps without losing track—trying to sit down and manage her finances. I hope you're imagining an absolute disaster because that's what it was. I never understood just how hard it was for me until I started taking medication and experienced what it was like to have a quiet brain for once. And it wasn't until this realization that I also began to understand the profound influence that the right tools could have.

If we look at the research around ADHD and money, the conclusion might be that people with ADHD are bad with money. You've probably thought that about yourself at one point in your life because you've likely struggled with finances. According to research, adults with ADHD:

- Struggle with financial decision making, which leads to earning less, amassing more debt, and having less savings.
- Are more prone to impulsively spend and use avoidant or spontaneous decision-making styles when shopping.
- Scored lower on a Financial Competence Assessment Inventory (FCAI), which shows they struggle to understand relevant information of a financial situation or transaction.
- Are more likely to have low savings, high debt, excess credit card use, rely on payday lending, and make late credit card payments.
- Can tend to get stuck in a scarcity mindset and reject a more rigid structure surrounding money. Some folks might use impulse spending to balance that rigidity out, which could also explain the difficulty sticking to strict budgets.

I'm not contesting that having ADHD contributes to financial challenges. But these challenges are not because people with ADHD are less smart, or incapable of making good financial decisions. Symptoms such as disorganization, forgetfulness, unreliability, trouble planning, challenges with task completion, and poor time management contribute to difficulty paying bills on time, creating and sticking to a budget, managing cash flow, and maintaining good money habits.

"ADHD symptoms essentially increase the cost of self-control needed to perform various tasks that are necessary to maintain good financial health."

It's not that you're bad with money, but rather that you don't have the right tools to support you. If I put a bowl of soup in front of you and handed you a fork, you'd be like—what the heck, Ellyce, I *clearly* need a spoon. You recognize that trying to eat soup with a fork is ineffective and silly. That doesn't make the soup inedible or the fork a useless utensil, they just aren't the right fit for each other. The reason you haven't had success with traditional finance advice and tools as someone with ADHD is because they were all designed for the neurotypical brain. You were handed a fork and told to eat your soup, only to realize that everyone else is eating a salad.

The key to managing money as a neurodivergent person is to find the method and techniques that work for your brain. Medication was one tool for me but so was creating an engaging budgeting system, learning how to inject dopamine into my money goals, and understanding what type of motivation works for me. Accept that it may take time to find what works and that doing things differently is not a bad thing.

Repeat after me: *I'm not bad with money,*
I just have ADHD.

PASSING THE MIC

Lexa's story: Moving Past Money Mistakes

My online friend and ADHD finance creator Lexa VanDamme (she/her) shares her journey from struggling with undiagnosed ADHD to finding financial tools and systems that work. Lexa is the founder of the Avocado Toast Budget, a shame-free personal finance company. She believes everyone deserves to feel confident with money and that there's no room for shame in your budget. Here's her story:

When I was struggling with undiagnosed and unmedicated ADHD I very quickly got into $20,000 of credit card debt and didn't process what was happening. I just kept telling myself that it'll be okay, I'll pay it off, I'll figure it out. I've gotten this far, so it should be fine. And then I just kind of hit my financial rock bottom.

Looking back now, it makes sense that I was struggling. I was in an abusive relationship, I had undiagnosed ADHD, I was dealing with anxiety and depression, and going to school full-time. I remember the first time I evaluated my spending from the previous month and was horrified because I spent $900 on DoorDash and food delivery. But of course, I spent a lot of money on eating out, I could barely get up and function and complete everything I needed to do.

I thought that not being able to stick to traditional personal finance advice was a reflection of me and my worth. I didn't understand that it was never going to work for my ADHD, the kind of life that I live, and how I want my relationship with money to be. I'm in a good place where I recognize that sometimes I'm going to be really excited about money and finances and my financial goals, and sometimes I'm just not. I used to think that it was a bad thing and that I just needed to suck it up, but that never worked. Now I've set my financial systems up for success so even when I'm struggling with my ADHD or my depression, they can ebb and flow with me.

No matter how much debt you're in, how much you've been struggling with money, how much it feels like it's all your fault and you just suck at it, know that you are deserving of feeling confident with money and changing that relationship. You're so much more than your past money mistakes.

THE NEURO$PICY MONEY METHOD

I hope I've helped you kick-start the process of letting go of these unhelpful narratives and beliefs. In order to move forward with your finances, you'll need a new way of thinking and new strategies to implement. I created a program called the Neuro$picy Money Method in order to offer financial education and tools specifically for neurodivergent brains. I want to give you the sparknotes version in this chapter by introducing 6 steps you can take to start making changes.

Neuro$picy Method Step 1: Release Neurotypical Expectations

Part of this journey requires you to let go of the expectation that managing your money will look the same as it would for neurotypical folks. One of my favorite ways to release these expectations is through daily affirmations. I've provided some example affirmations (some of which I've adapted slightly to apply to money) from Sonny Jane Wise's book *The Neurodivergent Friendly Workbook of DBT Skills*, but feel free to also add your own. I know not everyone loves affirmations or finds them helpful, so just take what you need!

- It's okay if the financial strategies and tools that were designed for and by neurotypical people don't work for me.
- My brain works exactly the way it was designed to, and I deserve to find ways to support my brain.
- I can forget to pay bills, put money into savings, or call back my bank and still be worthy.
- The differences in the way my brain understands money are real and valid, and they deserve to be accommodated.
- People disagreeing with how I spend or manage my money does not mean my choices or opinions are invalid.

You can write these out on sticky notes for your mirror, add them as reminders on your phone, say them out loud to yourself, or print them out and put them up where you'll see them. The more senses (e.g., sight, smell, touch) you can involve, the more powerful this practice will be. Keep them visible and notice what happens as you start to repeat these affirmations daily.

Neuro$picy Method Step 2: Find Your Motivation

Earlier I went over four types of motivation that tend to work well for folks with ADHD. It's important that you understand which of these types work well for you and how you can implement them into your finances. If you're not sure which of these types of motivation is best for you, experiment until you do.

How to Leverage Pressure/Urgency in Your Finances

Make the financial tasks you're avoiding more urgent. One way you can implement this into your finances is by setting savings goals and debt repayment deadlines for yourself. Let's say you want to save $500 in the next 6 months. Come up with a deadline for every $50 of that $500. Mark them on a visual calendar or put reminders into your phone. Now if you're like me and you're just going to ignore these deadlines, keep reading.

Share your financial goal deadlines with a partner or friend and ask them to hold you accountable. Give them an exact date and time and specify what you're going to accomplish. Request that they check on your progress, and don't let them sugarcoat things. When I started writing this book, my editor made the grave mistake of telling me, "It's okay if you miss a deadline, I trust you to get the work to me." While I recognize my editor was just being kind and understanding, it took the pressure off, which removed my sense of urgency. Alison, I appreciate you and don't worry, we got it done in the end. If you're recruiting outside assistance to create urgency, make sure you're clear on what they need to do.

Another way to create a sense of urgency on a smaller scale is by setting timers. Let's say you're working on creating a budget for yourself, and one of the tasks you need to do is figure out all your monthly expenses. This involves the tedious work of searching through your account statements to find all the recurring bills and subscriptions. Try setting a timer for 20 minutes and see how much you can get done in that time. Timer goes off, you can move on. Committing to a night of searching your bank statements? *Not so fun.* In my case it's likely to lead to couch paralysis. Committing to 20 minutes of it? *That's more doable.*

If time isn't doing it for you, consider creating some financial pressure. One way to do this is to invest in a course or a program so you have some "skin in the game" and feel the need to show up and get your money's worth. Even the act of buying this book will be enough pressure for some of y'all. You spent your hard-earned money on this book (thank you, by the way, I am eternally grateful for your support), and that will motivate you to finish it and implement what you've learned.

How to Leverage Interest/Passion in Your Finances

When it comes to your money, think about what you could add to your tasks, or ways you could become more personally invested in it. Here are some ideas:

- **Add good company.** Body double with someone while working on your finances. This just requires having someone else around you, even if they are doing something completely different. Platforms like Focusmate offer virtual, worldwide body doubling.
- **Spice it up.** Take yourself on a money date. Order some good food, light a candle, put on music, and turn looking at your finances into a full experience by pairing it with things you love and enjoy.
- **Trick your brain.** One of my favorite ways to hype myself up for tasks I'm not interested in is to watch videos on YouTube of someone who is excited about said task. For example, I dread doing my taxes every year. But if I watch videos of creators passionately telling me about the system they have created to make filing taxes easier or how they celebrate after filing, I can borrow their interest.

Adding interest can literally be as simple as just listening to music you love or putting on your comfort show while you work on other things. If you're struggling to find your finances interesting, start with the aspects you're passionate about. Perhaps you're excited to save up for a big trip to Europe, or the idea of color coding your expenses lights up your brain. Sometimes just getting the ball rolling can build enough momentum to keep going.

How to Leverage Competition/Challenge in Your Finances

Your goal is to turn money into a game. An easy way to do this is by competing against somebody else. Start a savings challenge with a friend or partner. For example, see who can save up more money in the next 90 days, or who can save up $1,000 first. Sweeten the pot by adding a reward for the winner.

If you want to create a little solo competition, share your financial goals online. This way you've created some external pressure to compete against yourself to reach your goals.

How to Leverage Novelty/Play in Your Finances

This is all about adding the fun into money management. You can achieve this by changing things up often and approaching tasks in a new way. Don't be afraid to get weird and put your personal *neurospicy* spin on those tasks.

- **Change up your location.** If you always sit down and look at your money at your desk, do it from your couch instead. Tackle your budget while you're taking a bath. Plan out your financial goals while hanging upside down off your bed. Write out your monthly expenses while enjoying a latte at your favorite coffee shop.
- **Change the information.** Consume financial education in a different way. If you typically learn from listening to podcasts, try switching to watching YouTube or TikTok videos, joining a Facebook group, reading blogs, enrolling in a course, or reading finance books. Find new creators to follow and learn from.
- **Change the format.** Tired of that Excel sheet? Switch to budgeting in a bullet journal. Hate keeping tax documents in that sad brown folder? Set up a colorful virtual folder.

It's very likely that many of the tools or systems that work for you might stop working at some point when they lose their novelty. Lean into this and don't be afraid to switch up your money management methods every couple of months.

Neuro$picy Method Step 3: Stop the Impulse

Impulse spending is when you buy things on a whim, without any pre-planning. It often feels out of your control. Impulsivity is one of the hallmark symptoms of ADHD, and impulse spending is perhaps the most common challenge my online community struggles with when it comes to money. If you struggle with impulse spending, it can be hard to save money and pay off debt.

There are various mechanisms that contribute to impulse spending, and the key to curbing the impulse is understanding why it's happening. For folks with ADHD, impulsivity can be caused by a lack of communication between two areas of your brain, the thalamus and the frontal lobe, which is the higher-level thinking part of your brain. The thalamus is supposed to act as a sort of "gate" that stops us from doing things that might cause harm by sending a signal to your frontal lobe to inhibit an impulse. In an ADHD brain, this signaling doesn't work quite like it's supposed to, and more impulses get by unchecked.

Someone with ADHD is more likely to engage in impulsive behaviors without considering future potential consequences. This is largely due to the differences in the way your brain processes financial incentives, which includes your ability to choose between long-term or short-term rewards. As a result, people with ADHD have more of a tendency to undervalue delayed rewards and overvalue immediate rewards—a concept called delay discounting. Delay discounting can lead to poor decision making and adverse financial outcomes.

Another factor that contributes to impulse spending is the lower dopamine levels that folks with ADHD tend to have. Having low levels of dopamine can encourage impulsivity because your brain is actively trying to seek out a "dopamine rush." Impulse shopping becomes the ultimate temptation because it delivers an immediate reward. **Translation: we want dopamine and we want it now.**

Something I personally struggle with is how intangible and fake money feels to me. I mean, money doesn't seem real if you think about it. Its value is socially constructed, and I can't physically hold the numbers in my bank account. This disconnect makes it hard to understand the reality of my spending behaviors. Additionally, it can be difficult for me to imagine what the future will look like. I don't have a great sense of how long goals will actually take to achieve, or what my capacity will even be like at that time. This can contribute to the issue of delay discounting and essentially to a greater desire to spend in the short term. Living with ADHD means I have to work harder to help my brain understand the value of long-term goals.

I am proud to have mostly overcome my impulsive spending habits, but I still have my moments. Because guess what? You don't need to be responsible all the time. In fact, it's unrealistic to expect yourself to never impulse spend. It's going to happen, and that's okay. Set yourself up for success with helpful tools and systems and forgive yourself when everything doesn't go according to plan.

So how do you actually curb impulse spending? The Putting It into Practice section of this chapter will include some reflection questions about your impulse spending, and the financial sidebar will also give you a starting point, but ultimately I'm going to leave you on a cliff-hanger. In Chapter 6 we will be diving more into dopamine and impulse spending, and we'll discuss some solutions in detail.

FiNANCiAL SiDEBAR

Okay, okay, I'll give you something to work with! If you struggle sticking to your spending limits or want to curb your impulse spending, here are ways to set your money systems up for success.

1. Start Giving Yourself an Allowance
This tip quite literally changed my life when it came to my spending habits. Set aside a certain amount every month or each paycheck to specifically buy whatever you want! Your allowance is your fun money, which you get to spend without guilt.

Keep your allowance separate from your other daily banking so that it's harder to transfer more money to it. You can also do a cash allowance if that feels better for you. I personally load my allowance onto a separate card each month (I've put some suggestions in the resource section!), and then once I spend that money, that's it. In Chapter 6 you'll learn about my account organization system that stops me from being able to just reload this card.

2. Set Up Banking Alerts

You can choose what alerts you want to set up, but my favorite is a notification that tells you exactly how much money you have left in your account every time you spend. I set this up for my allowance card so I know how much I still have to spend, which helps me pace myself better throughout the month. You could also set up alerts to notify you when your account drops below a certain threshold, or when bills come out of your account. This is typically set up through your online banking, though every institution is a little different!

Neuro$picy Method Step 4: Reduce the ADHD Tax

Having ADHD is expensive. The additional money or resources that people with ADHD end up paying because of their ADHD is referred to as the ADHD tax. This doesn't just apply to money; having ADHD can incur other costs, such as time, energy, well-being, and self-esteem. Some specific examples of the ADHD tax are:

- Forgetting to pay bills, resulting in late fees and/or a hit to your credit score
- Always running late and having to eat out more because of it
- Failing to think about food in the fridge until it goes bad
- The cost of materials for new hobbies that often go unused after a couple months
- Putting off or getting overwhelmed with filing taxes
- Buying multiples of items because you forgot you already have some
- Having to pay more for apps or services that help you with daily tasks
- Losing items and having to replace them

- Neglecting necessary medical/health appointments due to the work involved

Add to that all the costs involved in managing your ADHD, such as therapy, medication, or other treatment. Another important example of the ADHD tax is how it affects your career. You might struggle to find accommodating jobs and ace interviews, navigate the workplace, meet expectations and deadlines at work, and overall find an environment that supports you. Let me introduce you to three different ways you can start reducing the burden of the ADHD tax.

1. Acknowledge that this isn't your fault.

The ADHD tax is often hard to recognize or pinpoint, and it can feel like we don't have control over it. A starting point is to reflect on the ways that it's affected your life, and where it's costing you the most. Reflection will also help highlight what you do and don't have control over so you can implement changes.

- In what ways has the ADHD tax personally affected you?
- In what areas of your life do you feel the cost of the ADHD tax the most?
- How do you feel when you realize that you've paid the ADHD tax? What emotions come up for you? What stories do you tell yourself?

2. Put the management of your ADHD and mental health first.

Your own mental well-being is the top priority, so I want you to put your energy into that first. If you're struggling mentally or don't have ways to manage your ADHD symptoms, that can exacerbate the ADHD tax. I recommend speaking to your doctor or mental health professional about the options available to you. If you're currently on medication, assess if the dosage is working well for you. Refer back to the examples in Chapter 3 about free or low-cost alternatives to therapy and support.

I also highly recommend exploring the possibility of other comorbid conditions. ADHD is often accompanied by autism, sleep disorders, anxiety, depression, and autoimmune disorders. These may be contributing to the challenges you're facing day-to-day.

3. Create systems that will limit the ADHD tax.

Find ways that you can "prepay" the ADHD tax to cut down on how much it costs you, such as buying prechopped veggies or multiples of items you often lose or run out of. Stock up on on-the-go snacks and meals available at home and at work. Cancel trial subscriptions as soon as you sign up. Add a 20% time buffer to tasks and mark travel or traffic time onto your appointments in your calendar. The biggest piece of advice I have for you is to adapt the daily tasks or areas that "tax" you, so that you're less likely to incur that cost. I also previously introduced the idea of having an "oh sh*t" mental health fund, and you could create a similar account to cover the cost of your current hyperfocus hobbies or impulsive purchases.

Neuro$picy Method Step 5: Set Yourself Up for Success

Forget about what society says you "should" be doing and start thinking about what actually makes sense for you and your life. Here are some of my favorite ADHD money tips that have worked well for me and my clients. Take what you need and get creative with it.

Automation is your best friend. I talk about automation multiple times throughout this book and that's because I'm its #1 fan. Set up auto-pay on your bills, subscriptions, and minimum credit card payments so you don't have to stress about remembering them. Pay yourself first by setting up automatic recurring transfers to your savings account whenever you get paid. **Bonus tip:** store your savings in an institution separate from your daily banking so it's out of sight, out of mind. You can find more details on automation in Chapter 9.

Keep things visual. Display a vision board with your financial goals, a sticker chart for rewards, visual savings and debt trackers, a spending breakdown, or a calendar view of all your bills or paycheck dates. Turn on notifications to remind you of important deadlines, and set up banking alerts to stay up-to-date with your accounts.

Focus on one goal at a time. Many financial experts will tell you to balance your savings, debt repayment, and investing goals. Sometimes, that can be too much. I find it helpful to focus on one financial goal at a time. That doesn't mean I'm neglecting everything else, because I have automations set up, but rather that I'm putting my energy toward one specific goal. If you struggle with conceptualizing money, make your future goals more visible and tangible. Focus on the daily and weekly steps instead of the goal as a whole.

Be realistic with yourself. When you're trying to figure out a money management system, I suggest starting with just one small area of your finances that isn't working very well for you and playing around with different tools. Think about what aspect of your money is causing you the most stress right now. You don't need to transform your entire system all in one go, although I'm sure your brain is currently trying to convince you to do that.

Remember that tools can expire. A financial system that you've set up might stop working for you after a while and that's okay. Financial tools will expire, just like milk. This is your permission slip to let go of the expectation that one system will work forever and instead get comfortable with experimenting and trying out different options. If this stresses you out, I suggest finding a couple of backup tools or systems that you like and consistently cycling through them as needed.

Neuro$picy Method Step 6: Make Money Fun and Rewarding

If you're completely bored with the idea of learning how to manage your money better or creating a savings plan, let's make it more fun. We already covered how different types of motivation can make these financial tasks more interesting, and now I want to take it a step further.

After you've applied the motivation tips, take a moment to think about how you could make money management more fun for yourself. This will require some self-awareness around what actually constitutes fun in your book. It's time to start getting creative with your finances. Any daily adaptations you've adopted to make your life easier? Roll them over to your bank account. I'm going to hit you with some ideas, but remember that my idea of fun may not be your idea of fun, so take what works and leave the rest:

- Name all your accounts and make them funny
- Use visual progress trackers that you color or paint in, kind of like a paint by numbers but for your savings goals
- Create a vision board for all your financial goals
- Start a Pinterest wish list of all the things you hope to buy one day
- Use Monopoly cash to visually represent your own money
- Celebrate every single win, big or small

Now for my favorite suggestion, the sticker chart. Sticker charts have been a game changer both for myself and dozens of my clients. You might think of sticker charts as "childish," but honestly that's why they are so fun. My brain lights up around bright colors and beautiful stickers, so these work well for me. I use bright neon posterboard from the dollar store and usually order some really fun stickers online (although you can snag these from the dollar store too!).

You can then set guidelines for yourself—for example, for every $50 saved, a sticker goes up. If you're saving a large sum of money, I suggest breaking this down into smaller chunks. For example, if you're trying to save $20,000, maybe create a new sticker chart for every $5,000 and add a sticker for every $100. To up the ante even more, pick some sort of reward at the end for reaching your goal. So once you reach the first $5,000 and your sticker chart is full, reward yourself before moving onto the next $5,000!

If you don't have a reward system built into your finances, now is the time to add one. There are multiple ways to do this. The most common reward system is the completion reward. You complete the thing; you get the reward. Another approach is the token reward system. You do the thing, and you earn a small reward that you can save for a bigger reward later (a sticker chart is a perfect example). The problem is that it can be easy to just give yourself the reward before accomplishing the task or convince yourself you don't deserve it at all. One way to make these more ADHD-friendly is to put the control of the reward into the hands of someone else.

Both of these systems involve getting some sort of reward *after* completing a task, which doesn't always work the best for me. I'm a big fan of momentum surfing, which involves rewarding myself first and riding the wave of dopamine to complete the task. If I'm struggling to start work, I'll often put on one of my comfort TV shows (nothing too stimulating) and once the episode ends, I'm usually feeling good enough to just keep working. You can also reward yourself during the task itself, say by eating your favorite candy while you work on your budget.

Regardless of which of these approaches you decide to try out, make sure that the reward itself feels special. The reward does not need to be monetary and could be as simple as cooking your favorite meal, or giving yourself a Saturday of self-care.

Managing your money with ADHD is freaking hard, and you deserve a damn reward for doing it.

WRAPPING IT UP

Reaching the financial milestones I wanted to would not have been possible without understanding the impact of my mental health. Learning how and why my ADHD was affecting my money allowed me to pinpoint what had to change. It wasn't enough to be financially literate, I had to understand my money story within the context of my mental health. By finding and connecting with other folks with ADHD, I began to forgive myself. I realized that it wasn't my fault, I just was never given the tools to succeed. This all brought me to where I am today, a place where I've accepted I need to do things differently, I'm equipped with the right tools, and I have systems set up that support how my brain works. Now it's your turn.

PUTTING IT INTO PRACTICE

1. Experiment with motivation and reward systems to find which ones work best for you. If you're struggling to get started on this, think about what's already working well in the other areas of your life listed below, and tools that you've implemented to help. Here are some examples:

- **Meal planning, grocery shopping, and cooking** (e.g., using Instacart, doing it together with a partner, earplugs while shopping, listening to music while cooking, looking up fun recipes on TikTok)
- **Physical activity, fitness, movement** (e.g., signing up for a new workout class, reminders on Apple watch, working out with a friend, buying a new outfit)
- **Skincare, personal hygiene** (e.g., using products that smell good, keeping them somewhere in sight, lighting a candle while showering, listening to a podcast)
- **Cleaning your home** (e.g., playing your comfort TV show in the background, having the pressure of someone coming over, hiring a cleaner, enjoying a clean space, simplifying the process)
- **Getting work done at your job, school, home** (e.g., deadlines, sticky notes, phone reminders, notion board, highlighting notes, flashcards)

Get inspired by the current systems or tools that help in other areas and think about how you could apply them to your finances.

2. If you struggle with impulsive spending, reflect on these questions:

- o When do you feel an urge to impulse spend? What type of mental or emotional state are you in?
- o Are there specific types of impulse purchases you tend to turn to? If so, list them out.
- o What do you think your brain is actually needing or craving in those moments?

3. Pick one of the systems you learned in this chapter to set up. This could mean setting up an allowance card or making a wish list on Pinterest, whatever feels doable and exciting right now. Yes, I said **one**. It can be tempting to try to make all these changes at once, but that will likely lead to burnout. Pace yourself.

CHAPTER 5

Let's Unpack That

THE EFFECT OF TRAUMA ON YOUR BRAIN, BODY, AND BANK ACCOUNT

This might surprise you, but my educational background is actually in kinesiology. Yup, I have a degree in exercise science, not finance. My focus in my kinesiology degree was adapted physical activity. I mostly studied access to recreation for disabled folks and spent a lot of time helping children and adults with physical and cognitive disabilities reach their movement goals.

Now you're probably wondering, Ellyce, why are you admitting to not having a formal education in finance? First, because financial literacy is for everyone, not just the people destined for Wall Street. Second, because my experience working with disabled folks, in financial aid, and with low-income families taught me way more about the way our financial systems really work than any Accounting 101 class could.

After graduating, I worked in the adapted physical activity department at a recreation center providing financial aid to disabled and low-income customers. Here my two worlds collided. I spent my days talking with countless families and individuals about their financial situation. Many of them told me this was the first time they'd ever shared these details. I've interacted with immigrant families, folks who were previously incarcerated, unhoused people, and disabled folks. I heard a lot of stories about the different systems they had to navigate in order to meet their needs.

Let me paint you a picture using an example of someone who is unhoused, living on the streets, and actively trying to change that. Their first step is getting a job, which involves being able to look for one. Most people use online job boards, but that requires access to either a smartphone or computer and the internet. Maybe this person lives in an area that has a public library nearby so they can start looking. They find a couple positions to apply for, but now they need a résumé. This means they for sure need use of a computer, and likely a printer. They also would need to either know how to write a résumé or spend time learning online. Let's assume they have access to all that, so they find a posting, they create a résumé, apply for the job, and land an interview. I want to note that many of the careers that are available to folks with no formal educational background, limited transportation options, and lack of computer access are often unsafe or unregulated. Now they need to have appropriate clothing for the interview and would likely want to shower and freshen up beforehand. They need to get to the interview, which is hopefully reachable by walking or the bus route. Let's just jump past all these barriers and pretend they land the job. Yay! Things are looking up, right? That depends. Many employers will pay via check or direct deposit, which requires access to a bank. In order to open up a bank account, you need a valid ID and an address. I could keep going but I think you get the picture. The systems needed to get folks off the street, help them fight addiction, get out of poverty, receive proper medical care, or generally improve their quality of life are often set up in a way that those who really need them have to work incredibly hard to access them.

The people who came into my office faced barriers like this every day and had to cross yet another in order to be able to use the recreation center. I tried to make the system I was working within as simple as possible for them. I would highlight the areas on the form they needed to fill out, like their signature, and do the rest of the work myself. I would rarely turn anyone away. If they came into my office, I did everything I could for them. The stories I heard illuminated the harsh reality of trying to get ahead in a system working against you. If these systems aren't helping the people who truly need it, what are they even doing?

Before we explore how these different systems impact your finances, let's take a step back and start with you as an individual. In this chapter, you'll explore how any trauma you've experienced can affect your finances. Once you have a greater understanding of the trauma of money, you will find it easier to connect the dots when it comes to how social systems might be working against you. You'll come to realize your financial situation is a lot less your fault than you initially thought when you picked up this book.

THE TRAUMA OF MONEY

We typically think of trauma as being related to horrible, life-altering experiences, but it can also be the result of repeated or sustained stressors. You may have heard people use the terms "big T" and "little t" trauma before. Big T Trauma is defined by the American Psychological Association as *"an emotional response to a terrible event."* Little t trauma, on the other hand, is differentiated by the fact that the cause of trauma doesn't involve a violent or terrible event. However, I believe that all trauma is trauma, which is why I prefer this definition from Dr. Gabor Maté: *"Trauma is not what happens to a person, but what happens within them. In line with its Greek origins, trauma means a wound—an unhealed one, and one the person is compelled to defend against by means of constricting [their] own ability to feel, to be present, to respond flexibly to situations."*

One specific type of trauma you can experience is financial trauma, which can mimic symptoms of post-traumatic stress disorder (PTSD). Here are some examples of financial trauma:

- Losing your job
- Living in poverty or financial distress for more than 3 months
- Growing up in poverty
- Experiencing chronic financial stress

- Inability to retire
- Economic abuse
- Domestic financial abuse

It seems pretty obvious that financial trauma will have a direct impact on finances, but what I want to spend time talking about is how *any* kind of trauma can actually affect your money. Have you ever felt that regardless of how much effort you've put in or how closely you've followed the "right" steps when it comes to your finances, you're still struggling? That's because many of our financial challenges stem from trauma that cannot be erased through financial literacy.

In 2023 I was certified through a course called the Trauma of Money, which opened my eyes to the complexity and importance of trauma and its connection to your finances. To explain exactly what the trauma of money is, I'm going to pass the mic to one of the Trauma of Money cofounders, Chantel Chapman (she/her).

"Trauma of money is the idea and belief that anything that can cause trauma can impact your relationship with money. The reason why is because trauma impacts your feelings of safety, security, and worthiness. What does money represent in our society? Safety, security, and worth. Even if the trauma has nothing to do with money, it will show up in your relationship with money."

Trauma can be individual, intergenerational, relational, societal, or systemic. Anything that we view as a threat to our life or sense of self can result in trauma. Folks with one or more marginalized identities likely experience trauma from facing systemic oppression in their day-to-day life. Just living in a capitalist society is traumatizing. Trauma is as palpable as the air you breathe. It exists around you at all times. It infiltrates every single area of your life, including, of course, your finances.

We've all experienced some kind of trauma, and this is not the time to gaslight yourself. You don't need to power through your trauma in the name of toxic positivity. Instead, you need to acknowledge it and begin to explore the effect it's having on you and your money story. Here are some financial behaviors that may stem from trauma:

1. **Avoiding money:** essentially ghosting your finances. This means you'll likely avoid things like opening mail from your credit card company, talking about money with your partner, filing taxes, or checking your bank account.
2. **Overspending:** spending more money than you have. Overspending is often a self-soothing response to a stressor.
3. **Underspending:** avoiding spending, even if you have the money. You are basically trying to prevent exposing yourself to the risk that comes with managing your finances.
4. **Lack of boundaries:** struggling with perceived worth and people-pleasing tendencies. As a result, you'll avoid things like negotiating raises and applying for a promotion. If you're self-employed, you might be undercharging for your services and not being clear with your payment terms or contracts.

TRAUMA MIND MAP

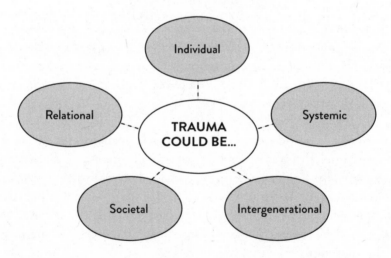

If any of those signs sounded familiar, don't panic. After reading that list, you might have thought *but most people do that!*, especially when it comes to avoiding money and overspending. And you're right! Because we all have experienced trauma. Later on in this chapter, I'll suggest some ways to start working through this financial trauma, but first you need to understand the effect it has on you. Keep in mind that *any* kind of trauma can have an impact on your finances.

> ### *In order to change your relationship with money, you need to address your trauma.*

Trauma and Your Brain

The experience of trauma can lead to unhelpful money behaviors and habits. To further understand why, let's look at what happens in our brains when we experience a trauma trigger. A trigger is anything that sends you into a trauma-activated state and could include sights, sounds, smells, experiences, memories, or certain people. When your brain is in a trauma-activated state, it will mobilize your amygdala, which will then sound an alarm to the rest of your brain to shut down your prefrontal cortex. Your prefrontal cortex is the part of your brain responsible for higher-level critical thinking. So when it says, "Peace out!" you're unable to make logical decisions around money. You've lost access to your executive function, impulse control, and rational thinking; instead, your emotional survival brain takes over.

Our prefrontal cortex is like our brain's Google Maps, scouting out all the possible directions we could take and suggesting the best option. But when it goes offline, it's like trying to navigate a new city without directions. Our survival brain is lost, confused, and frustrated, driving around with no navigation. As a result, we don't see all the options or the roadblocks and instead take the closest exit we can. When making financial decisions through an instinctive response, you are not critically thinking. Which is why the next day, week, or month you look back and question your past choices.

Trauma and Your Nervous System

Experiencing a trigger will also activate your nervous system. Daniel Siegal, a clinical professor of psychiatry, developed the term Window of Tolerance (WOT), which refers to the optimal state of your nervous system where you can function effectively. When you're inside this window, you're able to deal with daily stressors without throwing your nervous system off balance. You feel calm and relaxed and can successfully implement coping strategies when challenges arise. If your nervous system becomes overactivated or shuts down, you fall outside that happy medium. Overactivation is often referred to as your "fight or flight" response and is characterized by anxiety, panic, anger, inability to relax, sleep problems, and self-destructive behavior. A nervous system collapse or underactivation is your "freeze or fawn" response, characterized by depression, dissociation, numbness, exhaustion, disorientation, and chronic fatigue. Every person's window is different and can become wider or narrower. Experiencing trauma can narrow your window and make it hard to regulate your nervous system while a wider WOT will allow you to stay within that optimal range more easily.

To help you understand the WOT a little bit better, let's compare it to my coffee habit. (Fear not, my coffee habit does not actually cause me to move outside the WOT, but it's a fun metaphor!) If I have one cup of coffee,

I'm feeling good and in my optimal state. I'm in that happy medium zone where I haven't had too much or too little. But if I drink two cups, or even worse, zero cups of coffee, I'm pushed outside that window. Drinking two cups of coffee will overactivate my nervous system. I'm buzzing off the walls. Having no coffee (lord help me) will shut down my nervous system. In this case I'm lying on the couch, not wanting to do anything.

A balanced nervous system will be able to handle the ups and downs of daily life. It will be like having just one cup of coffee every day. You will experience daily highs and lows, but they won't feel extreme, and your prefrontal cortex (your higher-level thinking brain) stays engaged. You've found the sweet spot, the Window of Tolerance, that allows you to live mindfully and make wise money decisions.

In a trauma-activated state, you will likely either experience a shutdown or an activation of your nervous system. If you're living through chronic stress or trauma, it could feel like a roller coaster, with extreme highs and lows. If you're experiencing a chronic collapse, you might seek out substances to help you perk up. Chronic overactivation might push you to self-harm and numb the feelings. Engaging in these types of behaviors creates what trauma therapist Dr. Janina Fisher calls a "false window of tolerance." What we are really doing is distracting ourselves from the intense emotional or physical pain.

Different triggers that we experience will elicit different responses. Sometimes trauma may cause you to curl up in bed and cry, or it may push you to impulsively spend. There is a part of you that learned to freeze and a part of you that learned to fight back, and both will show up differently, depending on the context of the situation. Behaviors like spending or restricting money can create a false window of tolerance. We are tricked into believing that our impulse spending brought us back to our optimal state when in fact it's only temporary. As a result, many of us get stuck in unhealthy money behaviors because we believe they are solving the problem.

Making financial decisions when we are outside our WOT or operating within a false window of tolerance can have detrimental effects. It's difficult to make sound choices when your nervous system is dysregulated. So how do we make sure we are using our prefrontal cortex and stay inside our Window of Tolerance? The answer is mindfulness. This is one of the best ways to bring yourself back to the present moment and turn off those alarms in your brain, so you can feel grounded dealing with your finances.

I suggest creating a trauma evacuation plan for yourself. Similar to the fire evacuation protocols you learned in school, this plan will provide you with step-by-step instructions on how to evacuate trauma and return to your WOT.

Your Trauma Evacuation Plan

Disclaimer: I am not a clinical practitioner and these suggestions are short-term solutions that should not replace long-term plans for healing trauma.

1. Assess Your Brain and Nervous System

Begin by running a little diagnostic test on yourself to determine whether or not your prefrontal cortex is turned on and you're in your optimal window. This could be as simple as asking yourself, "Is my critical thinking brain on right now?" or taking your heart rate. It depends on what overactivation and underactivation of your nervous system looks like for you. Take a moment to assess how you feel in your body (comfortable, tense, relaxed, jittery), what emotions you're experiencing (anxiety, confusion, excitement, boredom), and the nature of your thoughts (sluggish, rapid, confused). The more you practice assessing yourself, the easier it will become to identify when you're in a trauma-activated state and your nervous system is dysregulated.

2. Remove the Trigger

If there is something that is still actively triggering you in that moment, remove either yourself or the trigger from the situation. Sometimes it won't be possible to remove the trigger, and in this case you may not be able to return back to your WOT, but do your best to continue on with the rest of the steps as they'll still be beneficial.

3. Find a Safe Space

Connect back with your body and the present moment. Ground yourself by using some mindfulness tools listed below, or other practices that you find helpful. If you've never done this work before, it will take some time to figure out the tools that are most effective for you. The list below will help get you started, but it isn't exhaustive. Experiment until you have a solid toolbox at your disposal.

Different tools to access your WOT:

- Take a couple deep breaths
- Get some fresh air
- Practice light stretching
- Hum, sing, or chant
- Take a hot or cold shower

I've provided some additional tools to access your WOT in the resource section, but let's walk through an easy one right now. This is a breathing technique called 4-7-8, based on ancient prānāyāma practices that can help promote relaxation. It's free, effective, and easy to do anywhere! All you do is inhale through your nose for 4 seconds, hold that breath for 7 seconds, and then exhale through your mouth for 8 seconds. Repeat this cycle 2–4 times, stopping if you feel lightheaded. Allow yourself to relax, get grounded, and focus solely on your breath.

4. Evaluate the Process and Improve for Next Time

When you're in a trauma-activated state, the most important thing is to ease yourself out of activation, which isn't always possible. For example, if you're unhoused, it will be difficult to get out of that state until you have shelter. In the long term, the goal is to move away from the situation that is triggering you and widen your Window of Tolerance to increase your resiliency. You can do this by evaluating the foundational system you have in place and how it's supporting you. Think about your sleep, nutrition, physical activity, stress, and social connections to see if there are areas of improvement. Become a little trauma detective and really get curious about what triggers your trauma and how it shows up for you. Later in this chapter you'll hear some tips from a trauma therapist on how to begin healing from trauma and widening your WOT.

THE SHAME WE CARRY

The trauma we experience will shape our beliefs and money story, ultimately impacting our sense of safety, security, and worthiness. The financial habits and behaviors that stem from this trauma can lead to harmful personal narratives. As a result, we can struggle with feelings of guilt and shame. Guilt shows up as an uncomfortable physical feeling of remorse for some offense, action, or behavior, either imagined or real. Experiencing money guilt means you will feel uncomfortable or remorseful for actions or choices you made with your finances. Those negative feelings are directed more toward the action/choice than your sense of self. Shame, on the other hand, is an intense physical feeling of being fundamentally flawed as a person. Money shame is a direct attack on your feelings of worthiness.

Guilt = I did something bad (e.g., I made a bad decision buying that new iPhone because now I can't cover my electricity bill).

Shame = I am bad (e.g., I made a bad money decision because I'm bad with money).

The guilt and shame around credit card debt is a perfect example of how impactful these harmful narratives can be. I run a series on my Instagram stories called Finance Confessions, where I ask my community to submit their money confessions, and here's how they feel about credit card debt:

 **QUEERD CO. COMMUNITY COMMENTS**

"Dreadful, it's a huge burden, and feels like I'm sinking."

"Incapable. Helpless. Hopeless. Undeserving of literally everything."

"Embarrassed, irresponsible, less than, not a 'real' adult like everyone else."

"AWFUL. Tied down. I can't move as freely through the world as I'd like."

But when I asked my community what factors contributed to them ending up in credit card debt, I heard things like the cost of living, medical bills, the pandemic, and mental health challenges. In my opinion, most of these reasons speak to the gaps in our social safety net and the inequity in our systems rather than us as individuals. I'm not saying we should just wipe our hands and say "f*ck it" when it comes to our credit card debt. I am saying that this shouldn't be solely your shame to carry. Your credit card debt is largely not your fault and it's clearly not an individual problem. It's a collective issue that so many people are struggling with, and that's what we need to look at.

The question of "whose shame is this?" was posed to those of us who participated in the Trauma of Money program, and I haven't stopped thinking about it. Whose shame are we really carrying around, and is it our shame to carry? Why are we taking on the burden of these f*cked-up systems? Recognizing that a lot of this shame is not our responsibility or fault can be freeing.

WHOSE SHAME IS THIS?

Take a moment to reflect on the following questions:

- What narratives do you hold around yourself and money? (You answered a similar question at the start of the book but note whether it's changed at all.)
- If any of those beliefs bring up feelings of shame for you, ask yourself: Whose shame is this?

WORKING THROUGH MONEY TRAUMA

Now that I've hit you with all this information, what are we going to do about it? How can you start working through and healing from the effects of trauma? This section will explore some solutions, and the Putting It into Practice section will give you some action steps to get started.

Since I'm not a mental health professional, I sat down with trauma therapist and educator Simone Saunders (she/her) to get her perspective on where to start when it comes to working through your trauma. Simone founded her practice, the Cognitive Corner, with the intention of creating a safe space that provides culturally responsive mental health support. Here are her suggestions:

1. Focus on What You Can Control

If you can't remove yourself from an environment that is triggering you, focus on the areas you are in control of. Trauma often strips your agency, so working to build choice and safety within that unsafe space is a good place to start. For example, if your workplace is triggering, maybe you go and eat lunch in a familiar space like your car, or you eat with a coworker who is your comfort person. Safety looks different for everyone and it's important to give ourselves and other people compassion around that fact.

2. Implement Somatic Practices

Trauma can disconnect us from our bodies, so connecting back to our bodies through what's called somatic practices can be helpful for working through trauma. This could be as simple as lying in bed for an extra 30 seconds in the morning and feeling the sheets on your body and the pillow under your head. It could be noticing what it feels or tastes like when you eat or drink something. Overall, just practice being more in tune with what your body is doing and feeling. Are you thirsty? Do you feel cold? Are you nervous? Connecting back to your body will also help you be able to notice when you're slipping outside of your window of tolerance.

3. Work on Widening Your Window of Tolerance

The key to widening your WOT is to step into discomfort without it being dysregulating. There are warning signs that you're about to leave your WOT, but we often don't know them or haven't paid attention to them. Maybe your palms get sweaty, your heart rate increases, you get tingly hands or feet, you start to dissociate, or you clench your jaw. Once you can recognize those signs, you can regulate yourself before you're outside your window. When you're processing a specific type of trauma with a therapist, they can help challenge you to push to the edge of your window without moving outside it. Over time this will help widen your WOT.

4. Seek Professional Help

If you've been struggling with trauma, seeking out professional mental health support is going to be the most helpful for long-term change. When looking for a therapist, if they offer an introductory or complimentary consultation, 100% take it. A consultation can give you a really good glimpse into whether the therapist might be a good fit for you or not.

If a particular type of therapy has not worked for you, try another method. Not all modalities of therapy are beneficial for working through trauma. Some approaches that are proven to work better for trauma are EMDR, accelerated resolution therapy, somatic-based therapies, and internal family systems. I'd even suggest looking into specific support groups for the type of trauma you're dealing with. Professional support won't be financially accessible to everyone right now, but you can explore low-cost or free resources that are available to you. Part of the work is the knowledge, but the other part is the actual application. Make sure you really implement some of the tools and strategies you're learning.

TRAUMATIC MONEY SYSTEMS

Experiencing trauma that has a negative impact on your finances makes you feel like it's your fault without considering the larger financial systems involved. Some of these systems inflict constant damage on individuals, preventing them from being able to access their Window of Tolerance. Black people, Indigenous people, People of Color, the 2SLGBTQIA+ community, disabled people, and those living in poverty suffer the most under these systems. There is not enough room in this book to address all the traumatic money systems; nor do I think you would enjoy reading hundreds of pages of depressing information, but I'm going to mention a few now. In order to heal from our trauma, we need to recognize the role that these systems play and how they shape our money stories.

White Supremacy, Banks, and Financial Institutions

White supremacy is perhaps the most prevalent source of trauma within society's systems. This racist ideology is the dominant paradigm that dictates our societal norms and laws. According to the author of *Me and White Supremacy*, Layla F. Saad, *"White supremacy is an ideology, a paradigm, an institutional system and a worldview that you have been born into by virtue of your white privilege."* It is like a poison, coursing through the veins of our social systems. Almost every (if not all) North American system and institution was designed to uphold white supremacist ideals. Now that's traumatizing.

The financial system itself has deep, racist roots. What started as an overtly racist and classist system became almost a natural part of the American capitalist structure, which ultimately required a discreet and subtle perpetuation of government-sanctioned discriminatory policies. This racism has never been addressed or corrected. It is still embedded in the practices of these financial institutions. There is so much to say about the wealth disparity affecting Black communities, but for now, I'll just give you a brief introduction.

After slavery was abolished, Black folks were still largely restricted from using banks, accessing credit, starting businesses, and owning property. Sherman's Field Order 15 was an order to give 400 thousand acres of land to those freed from slavery, which would have created a way for Black communities to start building generational wealth for themselves. After hundreds of years of enslavement and treatment as less than human, this allotment would have barely scratched the surface of reparations. Even so, it was protested violently, chaos ensued, and after Lincoln's assassination, it was quickly revoked. Any land that had already been purchased by Black folks was confiscated and returned to the previous owners.

The traumatic, racist impact of financial institutions continues today. A prime example of how banking systems are traumatizing is the sheer lack of accessibility for anyone living on the margins. A study conducted in 2022 found that a quarter of US households are either unbanked or underbanked. Not having a bank account means it's more difficult to pay bills and takes longer to wait for a paper check; moreover, the fees for cashing checks and writing money orders can add up to over $150/year. Only 12% of white Americans are under- or unbanked, compared to 40% of Black Americans, which greatly reduces their access to credit or savings. This percentage is not surprising considering the Black community suffered immense collective trauma when Freedman's Savings Bank, a bank specifically created for Black communities post-enslavement, lost millions of their assets.

These financial systems are carrying on the legacy of maintaining white wealth. The role of white supremacy in financial systems will be explored further when we discuss the racial wealth gap (and other notable wealth gaps) in Chapter 11.

MiNDFUL MOMENT

Whew, okay, this is a lot of heavy information, so let's take a break for a second. Take 3 deep breaths with me. Ready? *One* . . . . . *two* . . . . . . *three.* Now I want you to look around your space and point out *three* of each of the following:

- Sounds you can hear
- Things you can feel on your skin
- Objects that bring you joy

If you're feeling triggered, it might be a good idea to put the book down for a bit and come back to it later. I'm ready when you are.

Capitalism

The capitalist system in America flourished due to slavery. This was because of the value of cotton and the value of those enslaved for its production. The 3.2 million enslaved people in the United States were valued at $1.5 billion; their lives became a form of capital and pathway to wealth for white America. This led to the creation of new financial tools that allowed white men to build wealth by using enslaved people as leverage. Black folks were prevented from engaging in the economy for 246 years while white people got richer. It wasn't until the plantations were no longer profitable that slavery was ultimately abolished. Let me repeat that. It wasn't until America was no longer making money off enslaved Black folks that they decided it was okay to stop. Although by abolished, we really mean slavery was just rebranded into new forms of oppression.

Capitalism, North America's crown jewel, the foundation of the American dream. In reality it's a system that benefits the rich and continues to harm the poor. It's designed to keep our inequitable systems operating and lure you in under the guise of wealth for all. Capitalism consistently closes the door on marginalized folks and is set up to actively work against them.

The bootstrap mentality (this phrase was originally sarcasm because pulling yourself up by your bootstraps is literally impossible) transfers the responsibility of success to the individual at the same time that capitalism guards the tools required to get there. You can't pull yourself up by your bootstraps if you don't have any boots. Trying to earn a living and survive within this vicious system means subjecting yourself to relentless trauma, the worst part being our inability to escape or avoid triggers because it's literally our way of life. I think this quote from the *New York Times* nicely sums up the damaging nature of capitalism:

> *"If today America promotes a particular kind of low-road capitalism—a union-busting capitalism of poverty wages, gig jobs and normalized insecurity; a winner-take-all capitalism of stunning disparities not only permitting but awarding financial rule-bending; a racist capitalism that ignores the fact that slavery didn't just deny Black freedom but built white fortunes, originating the Black-white wealth gap that annually grows wider—one reason is that American capitalism was founded on the lowest road there is."*

The irony of me writing about the trauma that is capitalism while simultaneously benefiting from that system through this book (and my business in general) is not lost on me. How can I advocate for anticapitalism while profiting off the system? My answer is not perfect, but it's honest. Changing this system requires huge collective upheaval, and it's not going away anytime soon. So yes, I'm benefiting from capitalism while continuing to advocate against it. In writing this book, it is my hope that in some small way, I am contributing to greater access to financial education for those who would not otherwise have it.

There are so many more systems I haven't touched on. The "pink tax" (products marketed toward women cost more), the debilitating financial impact of the American healthcare system, the lack of access and safe care for trans, nonbinary, gender fluid, and disabled folks, the exorbitant cost of living with its corresponding unlivable minimum wage, the barriers to mental health support . . . and the list goes on. These systems are all detrimental to your finances because they either directly impact and negatively affect your money or they cause lasting trauma, which we now know hinders our ability to make sound decisions.

When we take a step back and look at the trauma these systems cause, it's mind-boggling to me that people still think individuals are solely to blame for their financial struggles. We carry around this financial shame, but the real question is—whose shame is this?

PASSING THE MIC

Edgar's Story: The Path to Healing Traumatic Financial Systems

Award-winning author and activist Edgar Villanueva (he/him) shares his experience working in philanthropy and witnessing the barriers that prevent communities of color from building wealth. Inspired to shift resources back to impacted communities and address the racial wealth gap, Edgar founded the Decolonizing Wealth Project and its corresponding fund, Liberated Capital. He is passionate about using money as medicine in order to decolonize wealth and commit to a path of collective healing. Here is his story:

> Being Indigenous and working in and around money and in philanthropy for 20 years, I had a lot of personal experiences that were really traumatic for me personally but also just stressful and frustrating in terms of trying to move resources to communities of color. I reached a point in my career where I realized that something wasn't right. What drove me to that point was the decline of my own health

due to stress and a particular day I had in a board meeting while working in the philanthropy space. In this meeting I was advocating to move money to a certain community and I received pushback and was basically told that I needed to know my place and keep my head down. That situation signaled to me that I was in an institution that wasn't serious about change.

I started journaling about my experiences and having conversations with others as a way to find healing and support and realized my experiences were really shared with a lot of folks. So I decided to write my book, *Decolonizing Wealth*, which was a path to healing and also a contribution that allowed me to bring these critiques that were really taboo to discuss to light. My world changed dramatically when my story started really resonating with people and there was the opportunity to do more, so we responded to that demand and launched the Decolonizing Wealth Project and the Liberated Capital Fund.

Less than 10% of grants from philanthropic capital actually reach organizations led by people of color who work explicitly with a racial equity lens. It's often about using any means necessary to continue to harm and extract, in order to build wealth. The creation of Decolonizing Wealth Project's fund, Liberated Capital, was an opportunity to create a model for the redistribution of wealth that centers the spirit of reparations by shifting resources directly to impacted communities who make all the decisions about how they use those resources. We're liberating the community but also liberating donors from the need to control and to dominate, and instead [helping them] join a community where they are able to engage in discussions and opportunities for healing, knowing that their resources are being deployed in the form of medicine.

THE POWER OF COLLECTIVE HEALING

Part of the process of healing from trauma involves tackling the impact of traumatic financial systems. If you are someone who benefits from these systems, you need to examine the role that you've played, so you can address any harm and commit to paying reparations. If you've been harmed by these systems, it's important to decolonize your mindset by unlearning internalized oppressive narratives. In order to heal as individuals, we need to participate in collective healing.

When it comes to collective healing, we should defer to those who have been harmed the most by these systems. I had the honor of speaking to Indigenous thought leaders Edgar Villanueva (who you just heard from) and Candace Linklater about their suggestions on how to begin healing from these traumatic systems. Candace Linklater (she/her) is a passionate public speaker, educator, PhD candidate, and founder of Relentless Indigenous Women Consulting Inc. She built a thriving online community called Relentless Indigenous Woman, where she discusses issues around the patriarchy, white supremacy, capitalism, colonization, and how these systems impact Indigenous people. Here are Edgar and Candace's calls to action:

1. Decolonize Your Heart

Candace shared with me that decolonization doesn't just involve being outwardly critical of these systems: it requires actually taking a look inward. She suggests getting honest about what internal dialogue and narratives you hold about the world that stem from colonization. Educate yourself on what colonialism is so you fully understand the impact it has had. Then, you need to really embody the process of decolonizing. It needs to be part of who you are, which involves a lot of internal responsibility, accountability, and humility. Ask yourself the hard questions and have meaningful conversations in safe spaces. Decolonizing your heart cannot happen in a checkbox kind of way, it has to be an ongoing process and an everyday commitment.

2. Embrace an Indigenous Worldview

Edgar believes that the process of decolonizing starts when we embrace an Indigenous worldview. Three Indigenous beliefs that you can start to adopt are (1) all our suffering and thriving are mutual; (2) the value of reciprocity; and (3) all your relations are important (including those to nature and the planet).

1. Understanding that all our suffering and thriving are mutual entails a shift in ownership from thinking this is *my* money to this is *our* money. Edgar shares how adopting this mindset can

decrease feelings of scarcity, because you start to view money and resources in a communal way.

2. Even when he was experiencing financial hardship, Edgar knew he could rely on the support of his community. This is the value of reciprocity. When you know that wealth you share will come back to you in times of need, that knowledge decreases the need to irresponsibly hoard resources (like the wealthiest 1% tend to do).

3. If you believe that all your relationships are important, you make decisions about resources and power in a different way. The individualistic Western mindset means that good people unintentionally make decisions that will harm others because they are out of sight, out of mind. Edgar shares the principle of seven generations, which states that every decision you make today will impact seven generations to come. Holding this value means you'll be more mindful of how your choices impact other people and the planet.

COLLECTIVE HEALING

THE PSYCHOLOGY OF SCARCITY

By this point you have a greater understanding of how trauma disrupts your nervous system, which ties into the psychology of scarcity. Scarcity is the belief that there isn't enough to go around; everything is finite. Many people do not realize they are struggling with a scarcity mindset and that this is influencing their financial decision making. This mindset might be present in folks who grew up in poverty, are currently experiencing financial hardship, or simply believe they don't have enough money.

The experience of having a scarcity mindset is similar to trauma in its effect on our bodies and minds. It will impede your cognitive capacity and executive function. Your brain will be focused on your current need (the resource that feels scarce) and will do anything to obtain it despite the necessary sacrifices. Keep in mind that your brain cannot differentiate between quite literally not having enough of a resource and the *belief* that you don't have enough. Wealthy people can still experience the feeling of financial scarcity, for this reason. Operating with a scarcity mindset will lead to a whole slew of other barriers and responses that make it challenging to escape the situation.

One benefit of scarcity is that it can produce a focus dividend, which means it allows us to concentrate on fulfilling the most important need at that current moment. Living in scarcity will also give you a greater appreciation of the value of that resource. This is why folks in poverty are incredibly skilled at finding the best deals in the grocery store, or why I'm so much more efficient at writing this book the closer my manuscript deadline gets. However, the perks of a focus dividend are far outweighed by the debilitating downsides of scarcity.

One of those downsides is the tunneling of your brain caused by scarcity. Tunneling is when your brain narrows in on the scarce resource so intensely that it prevents you from thinking about anything else. While the focus dividend can help you meet your needs, tunneling will push all other needs completely out of sight. In a situation of scarcity, you lack the energy and mental bandwidth to dedicate to other important responsibilities. You may develop trade-off thinking—if I buy this, then I can't afford to save for that. Your brain is focused on your scarcity, so it'll prioritize urgency over importance.

Having more money means that you don't need to engage in this trade-off thinking as frequently. Your decisions have less impact and result in fewer consequences. In contrast, poverty will lead to more trade-offs because each decision holds more weight. It's not uncommon to hear middle-class folks judge those in poverty for their "poor financial decisions" without understanding the weight of scarcity. For example, taking out a payday loan may be a solution to the person experiencing scarcity. They don't have the capacity to consider long-term repercussions because it's outside their tunnel. Researchers Shah, Mullainathan, and Shafir found that *"scarcity, of any kind, will create a tendency to borrow, with insufficient attention to whether the benefits outweigh the costs."*

It's not that people experiencing scarcity make less intelligent financial decisions, but rather that their cognitive capacity is more heavily taxed. This is called bandwidth tax and refers to our capacity to make sound decisions, follow through with goals, and resist any temptations that would derail our plan. When you're experiencing financial scarcity, you have less room for error, and your brain is running like an internet browser with 50+ tabs open. The bandwidth tax leaves you exhausted and more likely to act on impulse.

One way to offset bandwidth tax is through the creation of slack. Having slack means you have access to spaciousness. It's a mental luxury. Think of when you're packing for a weeklong vacation. If you have a large suitcase, you can throw in a lot of extra clothes and not worry too much about what you're bringing. I will literally pack 20 pairs of underwear and 15 different tops for a weeklong trip "just in case." On the other hand, if you can only bring a carry-on bag, you will be much more selective and thoughtful about the items you're packing. I might think twice about the underwear. No slack means there's more pressure to make the "right" decisions. You can't afford to make any mistakes. This is the cruel math of financial scarcity: the less you have, the more challenges you face.

FINANCIAL SIDEBAR

If you're struggling with a scarcity mindset, it can be helpful to implement the concept of "unbudgeting" in your finances. Unbudgeting is the process of removing limits for very specific expenses. I learned the term "unbudgeting" from fellow finance creator Bridget Casey (she/her), who says it can help relieve stress, remove a false sense of scarcity if you have one, and allow you to enjoy your money more. Bridget has shared how this practice has helped ease some of the scarcity she felt around expenses like groceries after growing up in poverty.

Pick one or two areas of your budget to completely unbudget and remove all restrictions. Before you panic, the idea is that you pick categories that won't derail your finances if you happen to go over budget. So think of expenses that you could technically overspend on and that still wouldn't add up to an unmanageable dollar amount. For example, I've removed any limits around coffee spending, because I know that even if I buy a coffee every single day, my finances will be okay. You can also choose to remove restrictions from a microportion of your budget if that makes more sense for you. So you might still budget the bulk of your groceries but choose to unbudget cheese or fancy tea. Or you continue to set a budget for entertainment but give yourself a free pass on movie tickets.

Unbudgeting might be a good option for you to create some slack if you're struggling with a scarcity mindset but aren't actually living in poverty. This might not be a good option for you if you typically struggle a lot with impulse spending and don't trust yourself to unbudget with care.

WORKING THROUGH
A SCARCITY MINDSET

A scarcity mindset is a whole other beast that you may or may not be experiencing alongside trauma. In order to make changes, you need to have the slack and bandwidth to do so, which is very challenging while operating in scarcity. There's no perfect or magic solution, but hopefully some of these suggestions can be a starting point.

1. Put Out Immediate Fires

The ultimate goal is to get outside the tunnel you've found yourself in, but first you need to work *within* the tunnel. Focus on putting out your immediate fires first. Lean on your support system and look into the resources available to you. Immediate financial fires would include catching up on the necessities and things that ensure your safety and security. For example, if you're behind on payments that will impact your heat, water, or electricity or that put your access to shelter at risk, those would be high-priority fires to extinguish.

2. Reduce Your Bandwidth

A great way to reduce your bandwidth is through automation. (I told you I'm the #1 fan.) By this I mean automation not just of your finances but of other aspects of your life too. The more responsibilities that you can put on autopilot, the less energy you have to dedicate to them. This allows you to work toward goals that got tossed aside due to tunneling. Refer back to the Invest in Your Well-being section in Chapter 3, the Reduce the ADHD Tax discussion in Chapter 4, and the Financial Sidebar in Chapter 9 for some suggestions on where to start.

3. Create Slack

This is the definition of easier said than done, but try to create some slack within your finances to ease the pressure of decisions. The best way to do this is by saving up a safety fund like we talked about in Chapter 3. Start with putting $5 per week or even $5 per month into a high yield savings account. As you slowly save up a little nest egg, this will give you more slack.

4. Practice Gratitude

You're probably tired of hearing the suggestion to practice gratitude, trust me, I've been there. But listen, this sh*t actually works. Research has consistently proved that gratitude practice makes you happier and more positive. When you're experiencing scarcity, practicing gratitude can help shift your mindset into more abundance. Right when you get into bed, spend 5 minutes writing down everything you're grateful for that day. Focus on what you *do* have, especially when it comes to money.

WRAPPING IT UP

We've covered a lot of concepts in this chapter, and you may still be processing how they all interact. Trauma can come in many forms and stem from our own backyard or larger financial and economic systems. Trauma and scarcity have a powerful impact on your nervous system and your money. The decisions you make, patterns you engage in, and financial behaviors and actions you take are a result of all these moving parts. Naming and understanding the trauma that you've experienced is a key first step in unraveling how it may be influencing your money. Trauma and scarcity won't just disappear overnight, but they also don't have to define your financial future. Tune in to your nervous system, work on widening your Window of Tolerance, commit to decolonization, and use money as medicine. In doing so, you open up room for healing.

PUTTING IT INTO PRACTICE

1. Let's add the impact of trauma to your money story. I want you to take a piece of paper and draw a line vertically down the middle (just like the Worry Worksheet you did earlier). On the left side you are going to list out your trauma (individual, intergenerational, relational, societal, or systemic), and on the right side you're going to write down all the ways that trauma has affected you. I specifically want you to focus on how it has impacted your financial

decisions, behaviors, and mindset around money. This is heavy work, so take as many breaks as you need!

2. Reframe the shame. Earlier you reflected on some of your core beliefs around money and the areas in which you're holding onto shame. I want you to take those unhelpful beliefs and reframe them in a way that's more encouraging. For instance, one of your core beliefs might be "I will never have enough money." With the lens of compassion, you can acknowledge the fear and scarcity mindset in that statement and reframe it as "I am capable and deserving of having enough money to live comfortably."

3. **Call to action:** Start using money as medicine. As Edgar taught us earlier, it's important to center the communities that have been extracted from and redistribute the wealth back to them. Prioritize Black, Indigenous, and other communities of color in your charitable giving and make sure that those organizations are actually led by folks who are a part of that community. I've included a list of organizations to donate to in the resource section at the back of the book.

RESOURCE

Using Money as Medicine, page 314

CHAPTER 6

Dopamine Dollars

HOW TO FIND AND FIX YOUR UNHELPFUL MONEY HABITS

$60.47. That was the number staring back at me from the dirty ATM screen. A wave of panic and shame washed over me. There I was, standing at a random ATM in Toronto, visiting my sister for New Year's, with strep throat and $60 to my name. I had been sent to this ATM by a walk-in clinic up the street, after being told their card reader was down and I would have to pay $80 in cash for the antibiotics they had just prescribed me. Usually, these would be covered by my extended healthcare plan (which I recognize is an immense privilege), but I had forgotten my benefits card at home so I would have to pay out of pocket.

The days before this had been full of shopping sprees, cocktails, dinners, and even a Raptors game. I was having so much fun that I didn't notice the money I was spending. Yet here I was, with $60.47 in my bank account. I had arrived in Toronto with $1,000, so how had I ended up with only $60 in my account within a few days? It was a glaring reminder that I needed to get my spending under control.

HIGHS, LOWS, AND WALLET WOES

I've always loved spending money. I enjoy shopping and picking out what I want, and I love the feeling of buying that item and being able to take it home. I live for the anticipation that comes after placing an online order and the thrill of finally opening up the package. Swiping my credit card gives me the same kind of feeling as swan diving off a cliff with a bungee attached to my ankles. It lights me up and delivers that sweet, sweet dopamine. If you also love spending money, you know that the good feeling goes away pretty quickly, and suddenly you're in this cycle of spending more in order to feel good again.

Dopamine is a neurotransmitter (these are chemical messengers that help different parts of your brain and the rest of your body communicate) that is heavily involved in your brain's reward and motivation systems. Whenever you engage in something you find enjoyable, like buying something you've been wanting for a while or sipping your favorite beverage, dopamine is released. It's often called the "feel good" hormone because, well, it makes us feel really good. This release of dopamine is like a pat on the back that encourages you to keep seeking out those pleasurable activities. Hence my infatuation with shopping.

Your desire for dopamine hinges heavily on the current levels you have in your body. This is known as your dopamine baseline. Because I have ADHD, my dopamine baseline is below average, which means I'm hard-wired to seek out more. If you have adequate levels of dopamine in your body, you won't feel the same need to chase dopamine. According to the Cleveland Clinic, here's how you might feel with low, adequate, and high levels of dopamine:

LOW LEVELS OF DOPAMINE	ADEQUATE LEVELS OF DOPAMINE	HIGH LEVELS OF DOPAMINE
Tired	Happy	Euphoric and energized
Unmotivated	Motivated	Poor impulse control
Unhappy	Alert and focused	High sex drive

Any increase in your dopamine baseline feels good, even if your baseline was adequate to start with. That's why chocolate, exercise, caffeine, sex, and drugs feel so good and can be sources of addiction. Now, because I have a lower dopamine baseline, these examples wouldn't have the same impact on me. If I'm unmedicated, drinking coffee doesn't give me energy, it just quiets my brain. Things that would spike the levels of someone with adequate dopamine will often just bring folks with ADHD up to baseline.

As humans, we are hardwired to constantly seek out pleasure and avoid pain (physical, mental, and/or emotional). That requires engaging in activities that release dopamine and make us feel good while avoiding the things that bring discomfort.

Researchers will often describe this pleasure and pain battle as a scale. A balanced scale is your baseline dopamine level, aka homeostasis. Although, factors such as mental health challenges or chronic pain can result in an unbalanced scale to begin with. When we engage in something pleasurable, we get an increase in dopamine and tip the scale toward pleasure. Because our brain is always trying to bring us back to homeostasis, our dopamine levels will drop following the surge, tipping the scale back toward pain. This is your comedown from that pleasurable feeling. We are all aware of what happens next—the craving for more pleasure. This is why it's hard to stop watching your favorite show after just one episode, limit yourself to one scoop of ice cream, or exit out of TikTok after five minutes. It's easier to keep going than it is to stop.

When our dopamine levels are low, we turn to pleasurable activities to cope with the negative feelings that arise. You can't get out of bed during an episode of depression so you order takeout every day. You come home from work feeling stressed so you plop on the couch and binge-watch TV to turn off your brain. It's not the behavior itself that you're attracted to—it's the addictive dopamine release that comes with it. You need something to cope with the sadness, emptiness, or stress and to tip the dopamine scale back toward pleasure.

THE WAYS WE COPE

Within stress research, coping refers to the behaviors you use to manage stressors. This set of behaviors can be conscious or unconscious, helpful or harmful, but the goal is to limit, stop, avoid, or tolerate stressors. Put simply, coping mechanisms are the ways in which you attempt to decrease discomfort. This response is normal and healthy. It's important that we have ways to work through difficult times. I want you to have coping mechanisms that you can turn to, but ideally, I don't want them to hurt you—or your wallet—in the process.

Before we dive into the different ways we cope, I want to reframe the language we are using to describe our coping mechanisms. I am not a fan of the descriptors "helpful/harmful" or "healthy/unhealthy," because that binary language often makes people feel ashamed of the behavior they are engaging in to cope and doesn't allow for nuance. What may be healthy for one person could be entirely destructive to another. Or you might have a tool or behavior you use to cope that you don't love using, but that serves an important purpose. I love the terms "survival resource" and "creative resource" that I learned from researchers Ogden and Fisher, and we will use that language to differentiate coping mechanisms moving forward. By reframing how we define "harmful" coping behaviors, we remove some of the shame around them and acknowledge the complexities involved.

Survival Resources

Survival resources are the behaviors, tools, and substances we instinctively turn to in order to make it through and cope with whatever we are facing. You feel tired, so you have some coffee. You're bored waiting for the bus, so you start scrolling on your phone. Your toddler drew on the walls with permanent ink, so you unwind with a glass of wine. When it comes to your finances, maybe you find yourself checking your bank account every day, or multiple times per day, because you're afraid of going into overdraft or having a bill bounce. We start implementing these survival resources without even realizing it. Remember that survival resources aren't inherently a bad thing and may serve an important purpose (e.g., keeping you safe, helping you relax). For now, I just want you to approach any resources you have with curiosity. In a safe and grounded environment, consider the following questions:

- What are the sources of pain or discomfort in your life right now? (aka your stressors)

- What survival resources do you use to reduce or avoid the effect of stressors?
- Are any of these survival resources having negative consequences on you, your finances, or your life overall?

Creative Resources

Creative resources go beyond survival and are the skills or competencies you develop that help you learn and grow from your experiences. These resources help soothe you emotionally, physically, mentally, or spiritually. These resources could be relational, artistic, somatic, emotional, intellectual, material, spiritual, natural, or psychological. While survival resources are all about surviving, creative resources are about thriving. A creative resource around money could look like having a dance party instead of checking your bank account, or enrolling in a financial literacy course when you find yourself stressed about money. We will explore more creative resources throughout this chapter, but let's check in to see where you're at with them:

- What creative resources do you use to reduce and overcome the effect of stressors?
- What current survival resources would you ultimately like to replace with creative resources?

When faced with pain, you will access either survival or creative resources to soothe it. Both resources have their roles and will help you in some way. Survival resources are often easier to access and require less work on our part, but they only provide quick, short-term relief. Creative resources, on the other hand, require more of your capacity and energy to access but will provide you with more tools and long-term support. I want to challenge you to be honest with yourself about what forms of coping you're using that may not be ideal and that you would ultimately like to change.

WHEN COPING HAS CONSEQUENCES

Engaging in a specific survival resource over and over again can turn into a habit. This is when the behavior becomes automatic and much harder to change, because you don't even consciously realize what you're doing. Interestingly, the survival resources that are more likely to develop into habits are those that give your brain a nice dopamine boost. The more dopamine released, the more addictive that thing is.

Shopping started out as a survival resource, a tool I could easily access when I felt bored, sad, stressed, or anxious. But I was unknowingly forming a pattern of behavior around these negative emotions. If I felt bad, I would go shopping. Problem solved—or so I thought. In reality, I was spending money I didn't have (remember the $10,000 line of credit I told you about earlier), racking up thousands in high interest debt, and living beyond my means. By the time I admitted that something needed to change, my shopping behavior was ingrained and habitual and my bank account was in the red.

Moving forward, the survival resources that you begin to use continuously and habitually, despite the consequences, will be referred to as vices. Although I want to avoid placing any value judgment on the behaviors you use to cope, I think it's important to acknowledge the formation of habits that aren't in our best interest. We'll use the term "vices" to differentiate between the one-off, or less impactful, survival resources from habitual coping strategies that have a negative impact and that you can't seem to stop turning to.

Previously, shopping became a vice for me. Currently, my phone is my biggest vice. I need constant stimulation throughout my day to get by. Every moment of boredom or silence, I pick up my phone to scroll on Tik-Tok. It's become so bad that I've found it nearly impossible to have a minute alone with my thoughts. It's too easy to open up my phone and access an endless stream of entertainment and dopamine. In her book *Dopamine Nation*, Dr. Anna Lembke describes smartphones as *"the modern-day hypodermic needle, delivering digital dopamine 24/7 for a wired generation."* Your phone is basically a dopamine slot machine, an endless supply right at your fingertips.

Scrolling on TikTok gives me dopamine, but the more I do it, the more I need to do it. My tolerance level for stimulation keeps increasing, and I require more in order to get that good feeling. This is a classic example of how vices form. Long-term exposure to dopamine-inducing stimuli increases our tolerance for pleasure while decreasing our pain tolerance. Too much dopamine can leave us in a dopamine-deficient state, where our baseline is now tipped toward pain.

Many of us live a life where all our actions and behaviors are motivated by the desire to increase pleasure and decrease pain. Pain in this case could refer to healing from a heartbreak, being scared to move across the country, or leaving a job you love for one that challenges you. We don't want to process any icky, uncomfy feelings, we just want to feel good. This creates a pursuit of happiness that we believe will be the key to our fulfillment. At first glance, this might not seem problematic, but experiencing tolerable pain is actually necessary for living a happy, fulfilled life. Research shows that those who *only* seek pleasure end up less happy.

When I'm chasing behaviors that give me a high injection of dopamine, like impulsive spending and scrolling on my phone, simple pleasures I love—like making my morning coffee, going for a walk outside, or reading a book—no longer have the same effect. Ideally, we want to live a lifestyle where we are in pursuit of our potential. Meaning that instead of only seeking pleasure, we are seeking a greater purpose. This will allow us to create a life with more meaning and fulfillment. In order to pursue this lifestyle, we need to learn how to reclaim our pleasure from our vices and reset our dopamine levels. Take some time to reflect on the following questions:

- Have any of your survival coping mechanisms developed into habitual vices?
- In choosing behaviors that avoid pain, are you missing out on pursuing a greater purpose?

THE PRICE OF YOUR VICE

Now that you have more clarity around the survival resources that have become a vice for you, it's time to explore how they're costing you. My goal is not to shame you or make you feel bad about these vices; rather, I want to help you understand and navigate them. Before we can move on to some solutions, you need to fully grasp the impact of your habitual survival resource, aka the price of your vice. As we move through the next section, exploring a few common vices and their costs, I want to encourage you to be compassionate with yourself and any feelings that may arise. Awareness is the first step in the process of making changes.

1. Phone/Scrolling

Constantly turning to your phone to cope can lead to issues with your sleep, self-esteem, self-control, impulsivity, stress, depression, and emotional instability. The symptoms of harmful cellphone use are actually strikingly similar to the DSM-5's gambling addiction symptoms. Phones can exacerbate other survival resources we may use, such as online shopping or doom scrolling. If being on your phone leads to increased impulsivity and struggles with self-control, you can imagine how that could end up hurting your bank account. You might find yourself spending money on a whim, or choosing to forego long-term saving for a more immediate reward. If your usage is impacting your mental health, this could interfere with your job performance or ability to properly care for yourself.

For a long time, I was in denial that my phone habit was a problem. I would defend my usage by saying I had to be on it for my job and that it was a way to stay connected with people. My phone may have been necessary for my work, but it was leading to unhealthy spending behaviors, mental health challenges, and decreased work quality. If you have a complicated relationship with your phone, reflect on these questions:

- Are you using your phone as a form of escapism from painful or uncomfortable emotions or situations? What specifically are you avoiding?
- How is your phone use robbing your time, money, energy, mental health, and general headspace? In other words—what is the price of being on your phone?

2. Takeout

I am never going to tell you to stop buying coffee and ordering takeout. I personally order out multiple times a week—it's necessary for my partner and me as we both have mental health challenges and work full-time. I've already ranted about this in the mental health chapter so you all know how I feel. Ordering takeout is not bad, but it can add up, and I want to make sure you're aware of that cost. When looking at how much your takeout spending is costing you, context is important. A realistic takeout budget for one person could be detrimental to someone else's finances. It's not about how much you spend on takeout but rather how you feel about that spending and the impact it has on your financial situation as a whole.

If you want to reduce your takeout spending, there are ways to do so without necessarily reducing how often you eat out. One way to cut costs is to order takeout directly from the restaurant and pick it up instead of opting for delivery. Save your delivery orders for the times you're not feeling well enough to leave the house. Here are some questions to reflect on if you're ordering takeout frequently:

- Are you ordering takeout as a type of survival resource? What specifically is ordering takeout helping you deal with or avoid?
- How much are you spending per month on takeout? What percentage of your total monthly income does that amount to?
- Is your takeout spending negatively impacting your financial goals or your mental or physical health? In other words—what is the price of your takeout spending?

3. Shopping/Overspending

We might joke about retail therapy and swipe our credit card in the name of treating ourselves, but there is a real emotional element to shopping. Feelings such as jealousy, low self-esteem, anxiety, depression, stress, loneliness, and boredom can drive emotional spending. Some research has shown that retail therapy can help with feelings of sadness in the short term, but if you're spending money you don't have, or spending in a way that feels out of control, it's time to reexamine the situation.

Just like other vices, shopping exists on a spectrum, and on the more severe end we have compulsive buying disorder. Compulsive buying is where you will feel an irresistible and almost senseless urge to buy on an ongoing basis. Anyone can move from engaging in occasional retail therapy to becoming a compulsive spender, but some risk factors include mental health challenges (especially for those with impulsivity-control issues like in ADHD), family history, and the heavy influence of consumer culture. You get stuck in a loop, shopping for the dopamine high, having an abrupt comedown and feelings of guilt, followed by the urge to go buy something new, only to start the cycle again after swiping your card. If that sounds familiar, reflect on the following questions:

- Are you spending money as a type of survival resource? What specifically are your spending habits helping you deal with or avoid?
- Is your discretionary spending negatively impacting your financial goals?
- How are your spending habits impacting your time, relationships, money, energy, mental health, and general headspace? In other words—what is the price of your spending?

PASSING THE MIC

Chantel's Story: Using Money as a Please Love and Accept Me Fund

The cofounder of the Trauma of Money, Chantel Chapman (she/her), opens up about her journey recovering from financial codependency and shares tools you can use to become an actor instead of a reactor in your life and finances. Chantel has 14 years of experience as a mortgage broker, 10 years as a financial literacy consultant, and has performed extensive research in addiction, behavioral science, trauma, and mindfulness. She developed the Trauma of Money Method after noticing a gap between the finance space and the mental health space. Here is her story:

I was working in finance as a financial literacy educator. I was teaching all the right things you should do with money, yet I wasn't doing them myself. I was overspending and underearning, I was using my money like a "please love and accept me" fund, and I was suffering. I had consistent thoughts like: I'm inadequate, I'm not good enough, I'm not worthy, all this stuff. During this time, I was also going through an experience in my personal life where one of my family members was struggling with addiction and I just threw myself into their addiction recovery. And I asked them, "Why did you use this substance?" They were like "Well, I've always felt so inadequate, I never felt good enough." At that moment it hit me so strongly, and I realized I was using money to turn off those similar thoughts that I had.

This pushed me to start exploring the root of these behaviors, and I arrived at this awareness that I was a codependent. Codependency is a type of fawning trauma response where we essentially people please in order to stay safe. Financial codependency is when we prioritize other people's comforts over our own. For me, a lot of this stemmed from the trauma that I experienced in my childhood.

I now can proudly say I'm a recovering codependent and I've put in a lot of work to get to this point. When I'm in active co-dependency I'll just say or do whatever I need to get acceptance, but in recovery, I have the ability to pause and ask myself, what am I actually feeling in this situation? Learning how to create space between a situation and my reaction has been incredibly helpful. Now I can slow down and choose a different course of action. Something we teach in the Trauma of Money is asking yourself this question: *What's the why of the buy?*

Do you want to buy that shirt because you don't feel like you're worthy and you're going to an event where you feel like you'll be more accepted if you have it? Are you trying to soothe the pain of not feeling accepted somewhere else or not feeling safe? Take a moment, and as you start introducing those layers of mindfulness, you create more ability to become an actor instead of a reactor. This gives you the space to replace your behavior with something that is going to soothe your nervous system in a helpful way that doesn't have negative consequences. Maybe that's going outside in nature, calling a friend and having a laugh, or saying no to buying that shirt but getting yourself a matcha latte instead.

Learning boundaries is also important in the codependency recovery world, because that's something that we often lack. They can be challenging to express in the beginning because you might piss people off that have benefited from your lack of boundaries. I know I'm in recovery because I have this strong rooted feeling that I'm still a valuable, worthy person regardless of what another person thinks about me. If you're on a similar journey, I think it's important to remember that money is way more emotional than it is numbers. It's not black and white. It's layered, it's deep, it's emotional. As you work through your behaviors and trauma, go slow and be gentle.

THE BENEFIT OF YOUR VICE

We only covered a couple examples of vices and how they may be costing you, but you can apply this same curiosity to whatever survival resources you're struggling with. But it's not enough to just look at the price of these vices, we also have to explore the benefits. Yes, I said benefits.

We use survival and creative resources to help us manage stressors. Regardless of how helpful or harmful these resources may be, most will soothe your senses to some degree. You will experience an increase in pleasure and a decrease in pain. Get curious about your vices and think about what "benefits" they provide you. Perhaps they serve as a distraction, fill a void, give you dopamine, provide relief or happiness, or make you feel a part of something. Allow yourself to move through that curiosity without placing judgment on yourself.

- What benefit(s) are your vices providing?
- What need(s) is your vice fulfilling?

For instance, ordering takeout every night is helping you feed yourself when you don't have the energy or capacity to cook. It lessens the mental load because you don't have to think about what meal to make, how you're going to make it, what ingredients you need, etc. It provides more space for you to relax and recover from your day.

The benefits we receive from our survival resources enable us to endure and navigate stressors with more ease. They provide relief, even if that relief is temporary. Assessing these benefits is helpful for recognizing that our vices aren't necessarily always harmful.

WEIGHING THE COSTS AND BENEFITS OF YOUR VICE

In order to properly assess what you may need to change about your behavior, a cost-benefit analysis is crucial. A cost-benefit analysis is a tool that can help you analyze the different outcomes to make more informed decisions.

When doing this analysis, you also want to have a question that you're trying to answer. In this case, the question is: **Should you change or replace any of your survival resources?**

In the simplest form, a cost-benefit analysis involves subtracting one from the other. If the costs outweigh the benefits, you may want to explore a different form of coping or consider using a creative resource instead. If the benefits outweigh the costs, you're probably doing okay. But it's not always that simple. Even if the benefits are greater, you may still want to explore other options.

When doing a cost-benefit analysis, it's easy to overlook the impact of the status quo. **If you change nothing, what potential benefits or risks could occur in the future?** There are factors beyond your control, but others can be somewhat predicted. For example, maybe one of your survival resources is buying yourself a new book whenever you're feeling sad about the state of the world. Let's say you only have $100 to spend from your paycheck after your bills are paid, and you're spending it all on books. You're not currently putting any money into savings or a retirement fund. The cost of buying yourself books isn't hurting you financially right now, but does it hurt you in the long run? As the years go on, you might find yourself more stressed about getting ahead and worrying about not having money set aside for retirement. Somewhere along the line, the cost may begin to outweigh the benefits, even though your behavior hasn't changed.

Some cost-benefit analysis models also consider something called the opportunity cost. The opportunity cost is essentially what other potential benefits you're missing out on due to your current choice. Assessing the additional benefits you could receive from alternative options can help you make a more informed decision. **Would another form of coping give you more benefits?**

It's very likely that your methods of coping are what you currently have the capacity for, and you may not be in a place to change that. When I'm in a situation where I don't have access to a support system and I'm in a deep depressive state, trying to cope in a more "productive or healthy" way isn't possible. For example, being on my phone allowed me to distract myself and keep going, but eventually I noticed that it wasn't working for me anymore. I needed to get more creative with the resources I was accessing.

COST-BENEFIT ANALYSIS
OF GETTING A MANICURE

• BRINGS ME JOY
• SHOWCASES MY IDENTITY
• IN LINE WITH MY VALUES
• BOOSTS MY CONFIDENCE

BENEFIT

COST

• SPENDING GUILT
• LESS MONEY TO SAVE
• $80/MONTH

So far in this chapter we've covered the resources you've been using to cope and how this is linked to your desire for dopamine; we have also explored the costs and benefits of your vices to determine where change would be helpful. You're aware of why you're doing certain things and how your behavior is affecting you. You have all the knowledge—now it's time to implement it. I won't lie to you, now would be an easy time to stop. You feel more educated and aware, and it would be less painful to just skip to the next chapter and sweep this under the rug. But I know you picked up this book because you're ready to face the hard stuff and rewrite your money story. I encourage you to keep wading through the uncomfortable feelings that come with change. Take it one step further and start working toward the behavior modification you want in your life. I'll be right here with you.

HOW TO CHANGE YOUR BEHAVIOR

Why is it so hard to change the habits that may be harming us? To help you better understand how to change your behavior, I'm introducing a tool called the habit loop. Behaviors that are difficult and resistant to change can be defined as habits. Habits aren't a bad thing; in fact, they can provide an advantage by automating our behavior. The automation will essentially shut down the decision-making part of your brain. This allows us to operate on autopilot and direct our energy to other tasks. Though many habits are helpful and valuable, our vices may not be giving us the benefit we want. In this section we'll explore how to work with our brains to reprogram these kinds of habits.

Habits consist of three parts: the cue, the routine, and the reward. The cue is the trigger that will initiate the behavior. Cues can be a location or time, an emotional state, the people around you, or a preceding action. The routine, also referred to as the response, is the actual habit, the repeated behavior that follows the cue. The final piece, the reward, is what you get from the routine. In most cases, this reward will include dopamine, along with any other benefits. The reward and the repetition reinforce the routine and eventually turn it into a habit. The author of *The Power of Habit*, Charles Duhigg, states that *"the weird thing about rewards is that we don't actually know what we're actually craving."*

I previously shared that I struggled a lot with impulse spending because of my ADHD and the lack of dopamine in my brain. I formed a habit around spending money because every time I swiped my card, I got an increase in dopamine. What I wasn't aware of at the time was the cue that drove this behavior. Here's how the scenario usually went down. After finishing up work for the day, I would lie down on the couch and start scrolling. At this point, I would be really bored and understimulated, now that I wasn't working on the computer or engaging with other people. To stimulate myself, I would start online shopping. As soon as I bought something, I would feel good. Then the next time I found myself bored or understimulated, I would immediately turn to shopping because *subconsciously* I knew it gave me the dopamine hit my brain was craving.

HABIT CYCLE

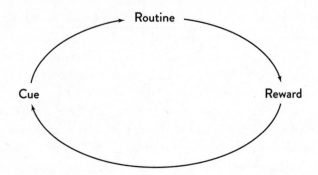

The cue: feeling bored, lying down on the couch right after work
The routine: spending money via online shopping
The reward: dopamine, excitement, anticipation of a package coming

Habits that give you pleasure are more difficult to break than others, because every time you engage in that behavior, your cravings strengthen. But we don't necessarily have to break our habits. Instead, we can make changes or replace the behavior. Taking a mindful approach to vices can be helpful when attempting to redirect them. I knew that my spending habit was costing me, and I was ready to make some modifications. If you're generally unhappy with the control dopamine has over your life or with the price of your vice and are ready to make a change, here are some ways to do that.

1. Break the Habit (Interrupt the Loop)

One option, and perhaps the most challenging one, is breaking your habit. To do this, you need to interrupt the habit loop. Oftentimes we aren't aware of exactly which cues trigger a response and what reward(s) enforces the behavior. You need to fully understand your habit before you can break it. Consider the behavior you want to change and determine the cue, routine, and reward. This might require you to engage in that behavior and pay close attention to the various cues present, like your environment, time of day, or emotional state. If you can't pinpoint the cue that is triggering your habit loop, it'll be more difficult to break.

Once you have the mindfulness piece, it becomes easier for you to disrupt the loop. In his book *Atomic Habits*, James Clear suggests making the cue invisible, the response more difficult, and the reward unsatisfying when trying to break a habit.

Make the Cue Invisible

Making the cue invisible involves limiting your exposure to any behavior triggers. Now, making your cues completely invisible might be next to impossible, but see if you can make them less obvious or common. Remove visual triggers from your space or change up your environment. If your cue is an emotional state, this is much harder to control, but pay attention to what initially sparks that state. Clear also observes that instead of having a single inciting event, the entire context can lead us into a habit loop, and the cue can become the context itself. If you can disrupt the context of your behavior—the situation in which the cue takes place—this will effectively poke holes in your habit loop. Here is an example:

My impulse shopping often started with me lying down on the couch after work, so, what if I didn't go to the couch? Maybe I could rearrange my living space so that I had to pass by a chair before getting to the couch. Or, instead of throwing my keys down and beelining for my living room, I could go get changed into comfy clothes first. Even a small disruption of your behavior could be enough to limit the effect of your cues. Examples of removing cues for impulse spending include:

- Unsubscribe from marketing emails
- Unfollow or mute brands/creators/influencers that tempt you to buy things

When it comes to scrolling on my phone, I was always picking it up when I wanted to avoid work, and just seeing it or hearing it vibrate was enough to start the cycle. I could remove this cue by keeping my phone in another room or by turning it on silent when working.

Make the Response More Difficult

Making the response more difficult involves putting up barriers for yourself so it's harder to execute the routine. Work on increasing the friction involved in completing the response so that it's harder to achieve on autopilot. The more steps required to carry out the behavior, the less desirable it will be. Examples of barriers for impulse spending include:

- Remove auto-filled credit cards from your web browser
- Stop using Apple Pay on your phone
- Only carry around the physical cards you feel comfortable using
- Delete apps like Uber Eats or SkipTheDishes from your phone
- Make "rules" for yourself around spending, such as waiting 24 hours before purchasing, or texting a friend for approval first

Another thing you can do when it comes to any of the habits you're trying to break is to simply take a pause. If possible, take 3 deep breaths or count to 20 before you complete the response. This gives you time to reflect on why you're making this particular decision. When it comes to a habit that involves spending money, ask yourself these questions:

- Why do I want to buy this?
- Can I wait to buy this?
- Does this purchase support my values and goals?
- What value will this purchase add to my life?

Examples of barriers for scrolling on your phone include:

- Put limits on apps so they lock after a certain period of time
- Keep your phone in a separate room 1 hour before bed and 1 hour after waking
- Put your phone on silent
- Delete apps that are consuming your life
- Turn off facial recognition and instead use a long password
- Set alarms for scrolling time

FINANCIAL SIDEBAR

One of the issues that exacerbates impulse spending is not having your accounts organized. Raise your hand if you use 1 or 2 bank accounts for all your financial activities. It's the account your paycheck goes into, the one you pay your bills with and use for daily spending. As a result, you're always doing mental math to figure out if you have enough money to spend on those concert tickets you want, or if that bill has been paid yet, and constantly feeling stressed and anxious about it.

If your hand is up right now, that's why I created my 5-account system that will help keep your money organized! This system provides structure to help keep your finances on track but also has room for freedom and customization. Here are the accounts you'll need:

1. **Hub account:** This is where your paycheck or income is deposited, and it serves as a sort of holding account until the money can be transferred out. You can transfer money to each of the other accounts we are about to go over every time you get paid, biweekly or once a month. This can be done manually or automatically, which we will cover later in this book!

2. **Bill payment account:** This is the account you will use to pay all your monthly expenses. Alternatively, you could opt to use a credit card to pay all your bills—and *only* use that card for your bill payments.

3. **Spending account:** This is your allowance, which we covered back in Chapter 4.

4. **Short-term savings account(s):** These accounts are for your safety fund as well as anything you're saving for in the next ~5–7 years.

5. **Long-term savings account(s):** These are the investment accounts for long-term saving and retirement.

The 5-account system allows you to keep your money organized based on its purpose and reduce some of that mental math. As always, this is just a suggested starting point! Feel free to keep your single bank account if it's working for you or adjust this system to be a 3- or 6-account system. Consider how your bank accounts are currently serving you (refer back to your Financial Audit), and whether or not a change is warranted.

Make the Reward Less Satisfying

This is the most challenging one because the reward is often a dopamine hit, which feels amazing in the moment. You want to be able to remind yourself of the long-term negative effects of your vice. The best way to do this is by having someone who can hold you accountable. This should be someone who you don't want to disappoint or let down. Or go online and share what you're trying to accomplish so you have a community following along on your journey.

You can also make the reward unsatisfying by adding some sort of "cost" onto it. In the case of the vices that are impacting your finances, I suggest routinely reviewing your future financial goals. Display a vision board of what you want to achieve and go look at it whenever you slip up on your behavior change. Keep a wish list or Pinterest board of all the items you'd love to buy one day that you can browse when you're feeling tempted by the dopamine craving.

2. Reduce the Craving: Dopamine Fasting

Dopamine is a powerful force in our lives—if anyone ever gives you the advice to "just quit" your vice, they probably don't understand that fact. However, we're not completely at the mercy of this brain chemical. We can work on resetting our relationship with dopamine. Dr. Anna Lembke suggests engaging in a dopamine fast using a framework she developed. If you attempt a fast, you must be prepared to move through those uncomfortable feelings and emotions without relying on your vice. The framework uses the acronym DOPAMINE:

Data = understand how you're getting dopamine, when, and how often

Objectives = reflect on why you are engaging in that behavior

Problems = consider the price of your vice, any consequences related to use both now and in the future

Abstinence = fast from your dopamine source for 4 weeks

Mindfulness = observe how you respond without judgment, have compassion for yourself

Insight = get clarity on how your behaviors are affecting you

Next steps = decide where you want to go after fasting, make a plan for yourself

Experiment = explore different strategies for maintaining your new dopamine set point

Disclaimer: This framework is only suggested to be used by folks struggling with nonclinical addiction. If you are struggling with any sort of substance abuse, this is not recommended, as withdrawals could be life-threatening.

3. Redirect the Habit

Replacing your habit is often easier than breaking it. By redirecting our response to cues, we can change the outcome with less effort than it would take to eliminate the behavior altogether. This is where our creative resources come back in. Implementing a creative resource instead of a survival one will divert the habit and change the response. Spend some time figuring out which types of creative resources work best for you. Choose from the list of examples below or try out your own.

- **Relational:** group activities, relationships with partner, friend, family, pets, hugs, cuddling
- **Artistic:** music, dance, writing, drawing, painting, building, crafting
- **Somatic:** walking, dancing, running, lifting weights, massage, stretching, deep breathing, sensory elements, weighted blanket
- **Emotional:** accessing all emotions, being able to regulate emotions, support system, crying, laughing, therapy

- **Intellectual:** problem-solving, learning new things, crossword puzzles, reading, language courses, informative TV
- **Material:** financial security, safety fund, a safe home, comfy bed, cleaning and organizing, decorating your space
- **Spiritual:** meditating, praying, connecting with nature, higher power, church, temple, mosque
- **Natural:** fresh air, watching the sunrise, feet on the ground, houseplants, gardening, bird-watching
- **Psychological:** therapy, self-help books, journaling, safe spaces, medication

MINDFUL MOMENT

Let's be honest, changing your behavior is not easy. And it's not always realistic or possible because of your mental health challenges. As someone with ADHD, I especially struggle with creating and sticking to habits. I could have a habit of doing something for 3 years straight and then one day get tired of it and never do it again.

So first off, I want to remind you that all you can do is your best, and that is enough. Our brain likes to convince us that habits should be "all or nothing" and that you have to do it every day in order to be successful. But that's not true, and in this book, we are aiming for "all or something."

Your goal is consistency, but not in the sense of doing something every single day. Rather, work on consistently improving your behavior. If you've never meditated in your life, then meditating once a month is consistently better than before. If your current savings strategy is transferring extra money at the end of the month into your account, then intentionally transferring $5 per week is an improvement.

If you're struggling to replace your survival resources or implement a new habit, start with small wins. Aim to be 1% closer to where you want to be. Most importantly, practice self-compassion. If an episode of depression or an exhausting week at work throws you back into your old patterns, give yourself some grace. Try to imagine what you would tell a friend or loved one who was feeling the same way. You deserve nothing but kindness and love, my friend. Oh, and in case you haven't heard this lately: *I'm so proud of you.*

4. Have Dopamine on Deck

When trying to redirect survival resources and implement creative resources, it's important that we reduce as much of the friction as possible. If your brain is set on autopilot to go spend money when you're sad, it's not going to be easy to convince yourself to do something else instead. You'll likely take the path of least resistance. You can reduce some friction by making it easier to engage in creative resources.

My favorite tool for this is the Dopa-menu, an approach I learned from Eric Tivers and Jessica McCabe. This is essentially a list of sources of dopamine that you can easily turn to in a pinch, but they are categorized, just like items on a menu.

Appetizers: These are quick and easy activities that will give you a quick hit of dopamine but won't suck you in. Aim for things that take no more than 10 minutes to execute.

- Breathe deeply
- Go for a walk
- Sing a Taylor Swift song
- Read a couple pages in a book

Mains: These are activities that are longer and more fulfilling. They may take more time and energy, but they will give you more dopamine.

- Meet a friend for coffee
- Work on an art project
- Go on a date
- Exercise

Sides: These are things that you could easily add to other activities to make them more fun and enjoyable.

- Listen to music or a podcast
- Have your favorite beverage
- Wear comfy clothes
- Body double with someone

Dessert: These are the activities that are your typical go-tos for dopamine and that you ideally don't want to engage in all the time. Sometimes this might be your only option when you don't have the capacity for much else, but overall, we want to make sure to eat dinner before dessert.

- Watch TV
- Scroll on your phone
- Play video games (I'm currently loving *Tears of the Kingdom*)
- Shop online

WRAPPING IT UP

As you've learned, dopamine is a driving force in shaping your behaviors and habits, which can have an impact on your finances. As we naturally try to avoid discomfort in our lives, we turn to survival or creative resources in hopes of tipping the scale back toward pleasure. Unfortunately, your desire for dopamine can end up hurting your bank account. Now that you understand the relationship between this "feel good" hormone and how you cope, you can begin to take steps to develop healthier financial habits and behaviors. Remember that you want to embrace a lifestyle where you are in pursuit of your potential, not simply in pursuit of pleasure. And the change begins with you, right now, learning to sit in discomfort, developing new creative resources, and prioritizing your financial future. You've got this, my friend!

PUTTING IT INTO PRACTICE

1. Conduct a cost-benefit analysis of your vices or survival resources. Remember, the question you're trying to answer is: **Should you change or replace any of your survival resources?**

- **Start with the costs:** How is your survival resource robbing your time, money, energy, mental health, and general headspace? In other words—what is the price of your vice?
- **Next, the benefits:** What need(s) or benefit(s) is your vice fulfilling?
- **Then, potential future or opportunity costs/benefits:** What potential benefits or risks could occur in the future? Would another survival resource give you more benefits?
- **Compare the costs and benefits:** What is the value of each to you? Does this behavior support the person you want to become?

Decide whether you're okay with keeping that survival resource, or if you'd like to try replacing it. Remember that this is just one tool you may use to help you make a decision. Make sure you consider your values and goals before committing to anything.

2. Create your own Dopa-menu! You can find a template in the resource section. I recommend putting it up somewhere you can see it, whether that's on your fridge or set as your phone background. This way, next time you need dopamine, you can easily refer to your Dopa-menu. Set yourself up for success by preparing as much of the materials you might need on your Dopa-menu as you can ahead of time—remember, we want to make the cue more visible and reduce any friction.

CHAPTER 7

Mother Knows Best

HOW FAMILY DYNAMICS
AND CULTURE FORM
YOUR MONEY VIEWS

The most exciting part about going back to school in September as a kid was the back-to-school shopping. My sister and I would sit down and take inventory of all the school supplies we could reuse from the previous year and make a list of everything we required for the new school year. We also got to do the same with our clothing, to see if there was anything that needed replacing, or that we'd grown out of. When I was younger, there wasn't much extra money, but as we got older and my dad started to make more, there were a couple years that my mom took us on a back-to-school clothes shopping spree. Ah, the good old days.

She would tell my sister and me that we each had $100 to spend on new clothing and that we could spend it however we wished. We would drive into the city to hit up the mall and shop until the stores closed. My sister would try on a huge pile of clothes in every store and always ended up buying something. If she liked it, she would buy it. Halfway through the day, she had burned through her money. In contrast, I would come prepared with a list of specific items I was looking for, pick out a select few to try on, and then struggle to make a decision. Even if I found something that I was looking for, that fit perfectly, I would hem and haw about it. Was it too much money? Would I wear it a lot? Did I really love it? At the end of the day, my sister would leave with full shopping bags and no money left, and I would leave with 1 or 2 items and most of my money.

Even though we grew up in the same household, my sister and I had wildly different spending behaviors. But when you take a step back and look at my parent's spending behaviors, it makes a lot more sense. My dad has no problem spending money. If he wants something and has the money for it, he will buy it. He knows what he likes, and he never feels guilty spending money on those things. My mom, on the other hand, struggles to spend money on herself. If she wants something, she will probably convince herself she doesn't need it. We grew up with parents who had two contrasting spending behaviors and beliefs, and as a result, my sister and I also had opposing spending behaviors. Thankfully, as an adult, I've found a happy medium. If I hadn't found a career in finance and really put work in to change my money story, I might still constantly struggle to spend money on myself without feeling guilty. My sister, on the other hand, still wants to buy everything she tries on (Rachel, if you're reading this—I love you, please don't be mad).

The beliefs you hold around money, debt, saving, and wealth can probably all be traced back to your childhood experience. What your family taught you, what you observed or experienced as a child, and the culture you were raised in will form the foundation of your story around money today. What's most fascinating about this is how varying the outcomes can be from person to person. Like with my sister and me, two siblings could grow up in the same household together and develop completely different behaviors around money.

As a child, you are like a sponge, and you soak up everything around you: the words you're told, what you hear from behind closed doors, the actions you observe, even the energy you feel. By age 3, children can understand simple financial concepts, and by age 7, habits have already been formed. By the time you are old enough to really think about your money behaviors and patterns, they've already been created. Just like your parents teach you to say "please" or "thank you" or give up your seat on the bus for a senior, they also teach you (often unknowingly) how to manage and spend your money. This process is called financial socialization. Many of us probably don't even realize how much of our childhood experiences are dictating our finances today. You might feel a little helpless after hearing that you're already essentially fully baked financially once you reach adulthood, but don't worry, your behaviors aren't set in stone. This chapter will help you make those connections, rewire those patterns, and rewrite your inherited money story.

THE INHERITANCE OF FINANCIAL "RULES"

Before we get into your childhood experiences around money, I want to remind you that your caregivers were simply doing the best they could with the tools they were given. While this chapter will explore how some of the narratives you learned could be harming your finances, I urge you to extend compassion to your caregivers, as they were dealing with their own trauma. Your current situation is nobody's fault, but now it's your responsibility to choose how you'd like to move forward.

Someone once asked me what my first money memory was, and I didn't have an answer. I can remember a lot of moments after around age 10, but before that is fuzzy. I truly don't have very many early money memories because my parents simply did not talk about money. Money was a taboo subject in our household. The main things my parents explicitly taught me about money were (1) never go into debt; (2) save every penny you can; and (3) you need to go to college to get a good job. They didn't sit down and explain financial concepts to me. They didn't argue or fight about money. I never heard them discussing finances. When I applied for student loans in university and had to put in my parents' income information, my dad literally took my laptop into another room to enter his income so that I couldn't see it. Conversations around money were actively avoided. Even though I wasn't taught financial literacy by my parents, I learned how to understand, view, and spend money from them.

What Was Your First Money Memory?

Content creator Zoe Potter shared in a podcast interview with me that a money memory that really stood out was her dad saying her allowance was "just burning a hole in your pocket" and that she should spend it right away. From a young age, she knew how to spend money but reflected that she never was taught how to save it instead.

After identifying your first money memory, think about how that might play a role in your finances today. Maybe your earliest memory is hearing your parents fight about money. This may have taught you that money is stressful, that money ruins relationships, or that talking about money is bad. You may now struggle to have money conversations in your own relationship.

In these childhood scenarios we experience, we often lack the context to understand what is actually going on or to grasp the nuance and full scope of the situation. As a result, our brains will fill in the gaps and form beliefs around them. This creates unspoken "rules" that begin to dictate how you make decisions. You need a system to sift through all these rules to see what you've subconsciously and unknowingly built into your life so that you can be more intentional moving forward. Once you understand that—that's where the magic happens. It can be overwhelming to try to think of all the ways your caregivers impacted your money story, so let's break it down a little with a reflection exercise.

As you're going through this exercise, I want you to also think about how your caregivers influenced your beliefs around work and career, as these heavily tie into money. For each of the following sections, try to list as many examples as you can think of from your childhood.

What They Taught You

This is everything your caregivers explained about money and financial literacy. This doesn't include random remarks they made about money, only what was explicitly taught. Examples:

- Gave you a piggy bank and taught you how to save money
- Told you all the reasons credit cards were dangerous
- Helped you open your first bank account
- Taught you how to count your money

As a kid, I remember rolling all my dad's change to take to the bank. My dad taught us how to count the coins, put them into the tube, and roll them up. A past client shared with me that their mom used to look over their credit card statements and tell them why every single purchase was either a good or bad choice. Another client had parents who sat down and walked them through in detail how student loans worked and how they could pay them back. You might have examples of being explicitly taught a concept or you may have been educated more casually. Some of these might be more positive memories, and others more negative. Even if what they taught you was ultimately incorrect or harmful, I want you to come up with as many examples as you can remember.

What They Said *to* You

This is different from what your caregivers taught you, because in this case they weren't teaching you but rather making comments or remarks about money. Examples:

- We can't afford that.
- Money doesn't grow on trees.
- I deserve to buy this.
- Rich people are evil.
- Money can't buy happiness.
- Let's save up for that.

Reflect on the narratives your caregivers had around money that they openly shared with you. **How did conversations about work and career play into these narratives?**

Maybe you had a parent who preached the importance of working hard to provide for the family, which in their case meant never being home. As a child, you might interpret that as hard work equals more money. Or that having enough money to pay the bills equals working all the time. While this is the reality for many people, as children we don't understand the deeper nuances to the situation. We just think that's the way the world works. Did your father have to work 100+ hours a week to cover your family's bills? Yes. Does that mean that the *only* way to survive is to work 100+ hours a week? No.

What They Said *Around* You

Now that you've reflected on what your caregivers said to you about money, let's think about how they spoke about money when they didn't know you were listening. If you grew up in a two-parent household, these could be things they mentioned to each other behind closed doors. This could also be how a parent spoke with other adults or even over the phone. Examples:

- Hearing your caregivers fight about finances
- Listening to a caregiver arguing with someone on the phone about money (maybe a service provider or the bank)
- Hearing your caregivers discuss the cost of a family vacation
- Overhearing a caregiver and their friend talk about what they would buy if they won the lottery

What You Observed or Felt

This might be a little harder to pinpoint, but I want you to try to think of situations you witnessed, or energy you felt from your caregivers as a child. Examples:

- Seeing a parent always coming home stressed and angry from work
- Knowing your caregivers were worried or upset about money during a certain time of year (tax season, holidays)
- Watching your caregiver compare prices at the grocery store
- Witnessing caregivers celebrating winning money from a lottery scratch ticket

Every day, when my dad came home from work, he would give my mom a hug and a kiss. He was always excited to see all of us, even if he was exhausted. This positive memory has always stuck with me. Reflecting on that memory as an adult, I think I understood that my dad genuinely enjoyed his job (which he did) and that his family was still a priority for him. I've always held onto the idea that your job shouldn't be so draining that you don't have the energy for your home life. Let's hope this story will help my dad forgive me for exposing his financial secrecy earlier on in this chapter.

HOW CHILDHOOD EXPERIENCES IMPACT
YOUR PRESENT FINANCES

Everything that came up during this reflection exercise makes up a large part of your money story. Our next step is figuring out how these childhood experiences show up for you today.

Earlier in this chapter, I mentioned that your childhood experiences can create subconscious rules that will then influence how you make financial decisions. Looking at all the examples you just identified—**what financial rules were informed by your childhood experience?** Or, in other words, **how do these experiences show up or play out in your finances today?**

Let's take the example of hearing phrases such as "we can't afford that" or "money doesn't grow on trees" as a child. This might have been something

you heard when you begged your mom to buy you that toy at Walmart or when you asked if you could get hot lunch at school like the other kids. The underlying messages behind these phrases are that money is hard to come by, you have to work hard for it, and you have to be careful what you spend it on. You might begin to believe things like you should only spend money on essentials, money is scarce, or you don't deserve to spend money on enjoyment. As an adult you might struggle with guilt around buying anything for yourself—even if you need it. You might either overwork and hoard your money because you're not sure you'll have enough, or spend it all quickly for the same reason.

List as many connections between your experience growing up and your current finances as you can. As you do so, take note of the rules that support or help you, and those that are unhelpful or harmful. Pinpoint the beliefs that are no longer serving you. If you're writing these out, star or highlight the financial rules that you want to reframe. Consider adding your list of connections to a note on your phone, so you can reference it when you need clarity around why you made a certain financial decision.

For example, you could reframe the belief that "money doesn't grow on trees" to something like "there is enough money to go around, money is not a finite resource." When you feel that scarcity mindset creeping up, you can remind yourself of the rewritten belief.

Whenever I've done this work with my clients, they've always had life-changing epiphanies about the root of many of their financial decisions. If you're having one of those moments right now, try to hold some space for yourself. Take a couple minutes to stand up, stretch, or drink a glass of water. Use some of the tools provided in Chapter 5 to return to your Window of Tolerance if you find yourself getting triggered. Regardless of how you would describe your childhood, all this deep reflection is hard on the nervous system.

I often ask guests on my podcast about the messaging they received from a young age around money and how that impacts their lives as adults. Here are some of those stories:

 QUEERD CO. COMMUNITY COMMENTS

"We didn't talk much about money apart from the standard allowance, getting little amounts of money for chores, getting gifts of money, things like that. I didn't really learn much about savings or bank accounts or anything like that until I was much older. I had no concept of credit whatsoever."

—Zoe

"I grew up in a family where we didn't talk about money, especially if you were really struggling with it or if you had debt, you just figured it out, pushed it under the rug, pretended everything's okay. And because of that, when I went off and went to college and started managing my own money, I didn't know how to do that."

—Lexa

"My mom always told me that she was the person that was really in charge of keeping our money. My dad wasn't a big spender either, but she was really on top of not spending frivolously and making sure that we had enough money saved to invest in me and my brother's education and this house that my parents bought. And so, she taught me the importance of saving, which I really am so grateful for, as annoying as it was to have her drill it into me every single day."

—Nina

Do any of these stories resonate with you?

We've talked about how your childhood experience contributed to your financial socialization and built the foundation for many of your money beliefs today; now it's time to dig deeper. Imagine your money story is an avocado. The tough exterior of the avocado represents your money beliefs and behaviors today as an adult. The green inside represents the underlying childhood experience that formed those beliefs. But the pit of the avocado is really what's at the core of everything. In your life, the pit is the intergenerational trauma and cultural systems of your family. Your family systems planted the seed that grew into your money story.

To be clear, there are very real barriers many people face, such as those due to poverty, systems of oppression, and inequity. Our beliefs around money are just one piece of the puzzle, but they are within our control. While upheaving the entire capitalist system is going to take some time, you can start rewiring your brain and reframing the financial stories that you tell yourself now. You cannot "money mindset" your way out of poverty, but you can begin to rewrite your money story and start to view your finances in a more positive way.

CHILDHOOD EXPERIENCES WITH MONEY

MONEY BELIEFS & BEHAVIORS

FOUNDATIONAL FAMILY SYSTEMS

YOUR MONEY STORY

(AS AN AVOCADO!)

THE ROLE OF FAMILY SYSTEMS
AND CULTURE

The first time I realized that my classmates didn't all have the same financial situation as my family was when we had a scholastic book fair. I have the fondest memories of the book fairs because I loved books and I loved to window shop. Most of the time the books I read would all be from the library, but at book fair time I was allowed to pick out 1 or 2 items to purchase. I would pore over the catalog before the fair and spend all of recess walking around and looking at everything. Over the course of the book fair, I began to notice that not all my classmates got to purchase something. Some of them didn't bring any money to school while others were buying up everything they wanted. Although I understood that other kids had different home lives than me, this was the first time I realized how privileged I was.

It's easy to get wrapped up in our own little bubble and forget that there are many different family dynamics and cultures out there. Where you grew up, and who you grew up around, will influence what money means to you. Ideas of wealth and the value of money differ across cultures. When I started working with a variety of financial coaching clients, I began to see just how much these different cultures impacted their finances. Let's explore how your family's culture plays a role in your money by considering some different examples.

Jenny, the daughter of Sri Lankan immigrants, shared that gold has a lot of value within her culture and is often involved in celebrations as a symbol of prosperity and abundance.

Nina, a child of refugee parents, grew up in a household where money was stressful and scarce, which impacted her money mindset as an adult. She shares that a lot of pressure is often put on children of immigrants to make good money and support their parents, who sacrificed so much for them.

Jane, a Latina woman, reflected on the challenges of trying to apply for financial aid and translate the related jargon to Spanish for her parents. She acknowledged that the language barrier made it hard for her parents to learn about the financial system, and as an adult she had to figure out most money concepts on her own.

In Western culture, we place a lot of value on money and building wealth. It is the driver of our capitalist system and dictates a lot of families' financial goals. The goal is to become wealthy (or be perceived as such) and create generational wealth. In other cultures, the value of money is different. How you value money also influences how you choose to spend it. In some cultures, it's common to pitch in cash to help pay for events like a wedding. This is known as Kuri Kalyanam in India and Harisma in Greece. Some Caribbean cultures will practice Susu, a form of community funding that allows friends or family experiencing financial need to access money and support. There's also Harambe, a similar practice in Kenya, where funds are pooled but go to support the community instead of a household.

PASSING THE MIC

Parween's Story: Finding the Balance Between Supporting Yourself and Your Family

I spoke with Parween Mander (she/her) about her experience with money as a South Asian woman and how to balance cultural expectations while living in a capitalist society. Parween is an accredited financial counselor, certified Trauma of Money facilitator, and the founder of the Wealthy Wolfe. She's passionate about helping women of color from immigrant upbringings reclaim their financial independence and build generational wealth. Here's her story:

My first real job was working at Burger King when I was 15. Over that summer, I was able to save up $800, and I was so proud of myself. But then my parents needed to go to India, and I had to give them all that money. I didn't feel like I had a choice, and I didn't really realize what it meant to do that at the time. Although they did eventually pay me back, that was the beginning of me providing for my parents.

When I was in high school, we almost lost our house, and I was suddenly overly exposed to adult financial matters. I remember going into the counselor's office and telling her about the situation and how I made a budget for my parents so that we could save the house and be okay. The counselor, who was white, looked at me and said, "That's not your responsibility." But I was a part of it, I was translating information from the bank for my parents, and I couldn't just ignore it and turn my back on my family. That really highlighted the disconnect between the individualistic values of Western culture and the collectivist values of my culture.

In Western culture, if you can't afford to help someone, you shouldn't do it. You're told you need to participate in capitalism and work and earn money and do all these things for yourself. Within my culture, we are taught that you take care of your family. If someone needs help, you just do it and figure it out later. So financially, there's more burdens and expectations and we feel like we are constantly failing because we aren't doing what Western culture is telling us to do.

When you're juggling these cultural pressures, I think you need to learn how to bend the rules and expectations to find what actually works for you. So yeah, I am saving for my retirement, but I'm also setting money aside for my parents' retirement, and I'm in a privileged position to be able to do that now. When I was younger, I was giving money out of survival; they needed it, so I gave it. Now I'm giving it by choice and using money in a way that's authentic and meaningful to me.

When you're making financial decisions, the cultural context matters. Let's dig deeper into how your culture impacts your money with some reflection questions.

What Role Does Your Family Play in Financial Decisions?

Maybe you make big financial decisions as a family. Maybe your family doesn't factor into your thought process at all. Or maybe your parents and/or culture have already made the decisions for you.

What Traditions or Values Does Your Family Have Around Money?

Vanessa, a Latina woman who moved abroad, described the struggle of not being able to sustain the cultural expectation of financially giving and supporting her community. Birthdays, weddings, and holidays for extended family and friends are highly valued and seen as important to spend money on. She added that she could be perceived as selfish, or not caring enough, for not contributing to baby showers, funeral funds, or families in need—even if it meant sacrificing her own financial stability.

What Attitudes Toward Money and Financial Institutions Does Your Family Have?

If your family has a background of trauma related to financial institutions, there may be a general distrust toward banks. Candace, an Illilliew Cree woman who grew up on a reservation, shared that there's a lot of red tape from the Canadian government that prevents these communities from expanding. She went on to say that Service Canada controls the policies and the amount of money they are willing to provide. If your family had a negative or positive experience dealing with these systems, that can carry onto you and become part of your money story.

How Do Your Family's Religious Beliefs Play into Money Management and Financial Decision Making?

There's an interesting intersection between money and religion in Islamic finance. Financial interest—whether it's losing money in interest from debt or earning money in interest in investments—is categorized as "riba," which is prohibited under Islamic law. One line of reasoning behind this system is to protect people from an imbalanced system that goes against the goal of fair distribution of wealth. This law has been interpreted in different ways, and there is discussion around how to participate in Western financial systems as a Muslim. This is a great example of how culture and money can collide in complex ways.

In answering these questions, you might feel empowered by the role your culture plays in your finances; alternatively, you might feel inhibited or constrained by it. There is no right or wrong. The collision of culture and money, especially if you're surrounded by people who have different beliefs, is difficult to navigate. Your culture plays an important role in your money story and should not be erased. However, if there are aspects that are no longer serving you, or are harming your own financial future, it might be time to shift the narrative. Reflect on your family systems, religious expectations, and cultural influences and consider how you'd like to move forward with your money.

For me personally, the only culture I really have is the puke bowl, aka the popcorn bowl, aka the Halloween candy bowl (iykyk), and this doesn't impact how I make my financial decisions. I'm not going to pretend to understand the complexities of what folks with other cultural backgrounds might be dealing with. Instead, I'm going to bring back the voices of Nina, Jenny, Jane, Parween, and Vanessa to share some of their advice on embracing their immigrant and cultural identities within finance.

 ## QUEERD CO. COMMUNITY COMMENTS

"Your family is so important to you, and you don't want to push them away, but if that relationship is directly harming you, it might require you setting boundaries to protect yourself and your bank account. It's not uncommon for a lot of guilt-tripping to happen, and that makes it hard to uphold boundaries. I don't think people realize that sometimes there is no choice, you might have to give in when you don't want to. Just do your best and be kind to yourself."

—Parween

"You deserve to invest in yourself and you deserve to be happy, whatever that means to you. It's amazing that you want to help your family do that [retire], but also you are important and your happiness is important."

—Nina

"For anyone who's a child of immigrants especially, find ways to spend time unpacking the complexity around security that so often immigrant parents want for us. The true reason why so many immigrant parents, especially in the South Asian or Asian communities, push for their children to be a doctor, lawyer, engineer is not necessarily because of the prestige of those jobs, but because of the security that is perceived to come with it. I think the more you can spend some time considering what security actually looks like for you, irrespective of what your family or the people in your culture may perceive, and deciding how you want that to show up, the easier it gets to navigate the complex feelings of pressure or of feeling guilty for not doing what someone might tell you."

—Jenny

"The more that I learned about other people's cultures and perspectives, the more I was aware of my own, which made it really cool to experience. It felt like I was learning about my culture from a brand-new lens, the role that it played in my decisions and how I carried myself or in my work ethic or in my leadership approach and all of those different components of it."

—Jane

"I financially could not sustain [the celebrations] because our culture demands generosity and a lot of family and community inclusion. We often sacrifice our own personal finance goals to make sure that we're adhering to those cultural expectations. I moved abroad so I would be my only responsibility, so that I could figure out what's important to me and what I need to do and how I can release that additional expectation that I need to take care of everyone else."

—Vanessa

FINANCIAL SUPPORT (OR LACK THEREOF) WITHIN YOUR FAMILY

The intersection of culture and money may also come with either the presence or absence of support. Families can be wonderful and powerful support systems (both financially and otherwise); alternatively, they can be inequitable and draining. Family support systems could be the reason you are able to get through tough financial situations or afford opportunities you otherwise couldn't. On the other hand, if you're the one providing support without anything in return, that could put you in financial distress. It's important for you to reflect on the support you give and receive and how that impacts your money.

- In what ways does your family support you?
- In what ways do you support your family?
- Most importantly, how do you feel about the support you're giving and receiving?

For some of you, it might feel good to support your family without any expectation of receiving support back. Conversely, you might feel resentful about the support you're giving. You may notice that any support you receive has strings attached. Or you might believe that your family has the means to support you more than they currently are. What's key here is how *you* feel about the situation, not what society or anyone else has to say. Think about how your family patterns have informed your money story up to this point. Once you're able to organize your thoughts, consider whether changes need to be made around family financial support moving forward.

Providing Financial Support

If you're considering lending money to family or supporting someone financially, make sure you evaluate the potential repercussions. Money can create a unique power dynamic that may change your relationship. I personally believe that if you are giving money to close friends or family, you should do so without any expectation of receiving that money back. If your acts of giving are laced with conditions, this could lead to resentment in the future. Instead of approaching it as a loan, consider it a gift. If you get paid back, it's a bonus. This approach also allows you to realistically assess if you can afford to give that money. If doing so would jeopardize your ability to meet your own needs, I would urge you to say no. To show up and financially support others, you first need to ensure you're taking care of yourself.

FINANCIAL SIDEBAR

We are going to hear from Parween again, who will share some practical tips for retiring or financially supporting your parents. She told me, *"When it comes to financial education, there isn't much out there that accounts for cultural expectations. Nobody ever talks about how to plan for two retirements AND your children."* Here's what she suggests:

1. A savings account specifically for family

Open up a savings account (ideally a high yield savings account) and start setting aside money each month that is separate from your safety fund and other financial goals. When your family asks you for money, you can give them what you've saved up.

2. Future projections

If there's the expectation that you'll need to financially support your parents in retirement, you'll want to crunch some numbers to figure out exactly how much money to save for both your own and your parents' retirement. Think about what you're currently bringing in now as well as what you're projected to be earning in the future. To understand what it's going to cost your parents to live in retirement, here are some questions to think about:

- Do they have a mortgage and will they still be paying it in retirement?
- What monthly bills will they have? (housing, transportation, groceries, utilities, medication)
- Are there any medical expenses that you'll need to cover?
- Will they need any additional support or care in the future? What would that look like?

These are obviously really big, overwhelming questions, but starting that process now, even with just a rough estimate, can help ease the pressure down the road. Plus—it stops the overthinking and gives you a jumping-off point.

3. Parent retirement fund

This is also a savings account, but you're putting this money away for your parents' future retirement. You could also invest this money in a nonregistered account (i.e., not an IRA, TFSA, etc.) if that makes more sense for your situation. Your monthly contributions would be based on the future projections you just calculated and what's doable within your current budget and income.

Overall, think about how you can create a little bit more flexibility in your budget by either bringing in more income (salary negotiation, pursuing higher education, increasing skill set) or lowering monthly expenses. Increasing the gap between what's coming in versus going out will help you be less stressed while supporting yourself and your family.

Asking for Financial Support

It's really freaking hard to ask for money and sometimes even more challenging to accept that money. Often our shame, guilt, or pride gets in the way. Capitalism promotes hyperindependence and individualism, so let me tell you that accepting help and support is one of the bravest actions you can take. If your family is able to financially support you, that is a privilege you can take advantage of should you need it.

The tricky part about accepting help from our family is the potential expectations or "strings" that come along with it. One of my client's parents offered to pay off their student loans but didn't openly communicate that they expected to be paid back for it. My client was overjoyed, thinking her parents just helped her out, only to be asked to begin repaying them a couple months later. Other parents will pay for their children's education with the caveat that they go into a specific field of study. This is often what the parent deems as an "acceptable" major but not necessarily what the child wants. This can lead to both parties feeling upset and confused. Although my belief is that money from family should be given with no conditions, I know that not everyone will agree with me on that. In that case, I would suggest approaching this situation as if you are borrowing money from a bank. Sit down and discuss exactly what terms are going to apply. Write down or record what you've agreed on, so both parties are crystal clear on the situation. Here are some questions you can ask to get on the same page:

- How much money are you willing to give me?
- Do you expect this money to be paid back? If so, what is your timeline for paying it back?
- Based on your timeline, how would you like to receive payments? (e.g., monthly, weekly, by check, cash, etc.)

- If I miss a payment, or don't have the means to continue making payments, how would you handle this?
- Are you open to renegotiating these terms if needed?

HOW TO SET AND RESPECT BOUNDARIES

If you have identified that your interactions with your family around money need to shift, you most likely will need to set some boundaries. Boundaries get a bad rap as a big, scary, and even selfish thing to enforce with loved ones, but in reality they benefit everyone involved. Boundaries clearly communicate how you deserve and expect to be treated. In the same way that your family may assume you can or will support them, and be hurt if you don't, they might not be able to offer the support you expect or want. Just as we would want our boundaries to be respected, we need to be mindful and respectful of others'.

RESOURCE

Boundary-Setting Resource, page 314

MINDFUL MOMENT

Boundaries can be difficult to set within cultures and families that don't have strong communication skills to begin with or hold strong collectivist values. If you've never set boundaries with your family before, this might be uncomfortable, but I promise it's worth it in the long run. It's important for you to figure out what works within the context of your culture and values. Here's how to start setting boundaries:

1. Identify what your boundaries are

Boundaries can be physical, mental, emotional, spiritual, and of course, financial. Examples of financial boundaries could be not financially supporting family, giving X amount of money a month, certain topics or questions are off-limits, separating finances from partner, etc.

Think about the areas in your life where you may need to set a boundary and what that boundary would look like. Be as specific as possible about how you will expect yourself and others to uphold this boundary, and how you will respond if/when that boundary is not respected.

2. Give yourself permission to set those boundaries

Many families don't practice or teach setting boundaries with their children, so don't feel bad if this is your first time. It's normal to have feelings of guilt or worry about letting others down when setting boundaries. Remember that all boundaries don't necessarily need to be communicated fully or at all to the other person if you feel it's an unsafe conversation. You can set them for yourself, just like Vanessa did by moving abroad.

3. Be kind to yourself

Setting boundaries is not easy, so give yourself some grace as you navigate them. When working with boundaries inside cultural and family systems, it might not always go the way you hope. Sometimes you will give in, or let a boundary be crossed, and that's okay. Give yourself and your family some time to adjust and forgive yourself when you slip into old patterns. You've got this!

WRAPPING IT UP

I know for some of you this has been a challenging chapter. You've heard some suggestions from me and folks with different cultural backgrounds, but ultimately it's up to *you* to decide how to proceed. You know your family best. You need to assess your comfort level with approaching these conversations and decide what makes sense for you. This is your permission slip to let go of anything that isn't working for you. You deserve to prioritize your own happiness and financial future.

PUTTING IT INTO PRACTICE

Since we covered **a lot** of reflection questions in this chapter, I've included those questions here, along with one additional prompt to help you start rewriting your financial rules.

1. Reflect on your childhood experiences around money. Write down as many examples as you can remember, positive or negative!

- o   What were you taught?
- o   What was said *to* you?
- o   What was said *around* you?
- o   What did you observe or feel?

2. Write down all the financial rules you hold that were informed by your childhood experiences.

- o   How do these experiences show up or play out in your finances today?

3. Clarify your connection between family, culture, and money.

- o   What role does your family play in financial decisions?
- o   What traditions or values does your family have around money?

o   What attitudes toward money and financial institutions does your family have?
o   How do your family's religious beliefs play into money management and financial decision making?

4. Create your own money manifesto. Rewrite the financial "rules" you have that are no longer serving you.

I choose to believe _____ regardless of _____.

For example, I choose to believe that money can buy happiness, and rich people are not evil, despite what my mother taught me.

I will do _____ regardless of _____.

For example, I will continue to financially support my family regardless of what other people think, because it's important to me.

Find the compromise between family, culture, and money that you can confidently use as your financial rulebook moving forward.

CHAPTER 8

Uphill Both Ways

THE TRUTH ABOUT THE
GENERATIONAL DIVIDE

I like to think that I'm pretty cool and "with it" (that phrase alone exposes my age and the evidence that I am, in fact, not very with it), but being active on TikTok has taught me how delusional I am. Just the other day I learned that I've been using the wrong laughing emoji when texting. Apparently that emoji is "out" and a different one is now "in," and I should just know that??

I grew up on the cusp of the millennial and Gen Z generations, and I believe I got the best of both worlds. I learned to be patient while waiting for the dial-up internet to connect. I listened to music on my Walkman, then MP3, and I distinctly remember the very first iPod coming out. I've moved through MSN messenger to T9 texting to BBMing to iMessaging, all before graduating high school. I rocked skinny jeans and a side part for way too long. These examples are all quintessentially millennial. That's where most of me fits, but I also relate to Gen Zs. I pick up new social media platforms with ease, I'm entrepreneurial, and I resonate with Gen Z's approach toward grassroots social activism.

Imagine me going up to a Gen Z person and trying to convince them that an MP3 player is the best way to listen to music. Or that MySpace is the best form of social media. It would be comical and ridiculous. Just as styles, devices, and social media platforms have come and gone out of style, so have financial advice and systems. But switching how you bank or where you invest your money isn't quite as simple as swapping out the cut of your jeans. This is why the rapidly changing financial landscape is often met with a lot of resistance from older generations, and as a result, the financial advice stays the same. In this chapter we are going to explore why financial systems have changed, how we can learn from past experiences, and the approach we should take moving forward. The generations that we will focus on are:

Baby boomer: born 1946–1964
Gen X: born 1965–1980
Gen Y/millennial: born 1981–1996
Gen Z: born 1997–2012

When I refer to the "older generation," this will refer to baby boomers and Gen X and the "younger generation" will refer to millennials and Gen Z. Let me be clear, this is not a chapter meant to tear down boomers or Gen X, or place blame; rather, I intend to help *all* generations understand why these intergenerational differences exist and how we can navigate them.

THE GENERATIONAL DIVIDE

You may have picked up this book solely because you're tired of being told by older generations that being good with money involves cutting all joy out of your life.

Stop buying expensive coffee and avocado toast.
Don't go out to eat until you're debt-free.
Work harder.
Save more.

This "advice" paints a depressing (and to be honest, boring!) picture of what it means to be financially stable. If you're a millennial like me, most of the financial advice or education that you're exposed to likely comes from the baby boomer generation, not only because they raised us, but also because they've accomplished all the things younger generations are working toward. Most of them are in retirement now, proud of how they built their wealth, and eager to share their wisdom with the younger generations. Initially it might make sense that we would learn from them, but when we step back and look at how the world has changed, it becomes clear they should not—and cannot—be our *only* teachers. While they have gathered invaluable knowledge from their experiences, we shouldn't be blindly applying their formula for success. Instead, we must learn to take the important lessons, and then adapt them to fit our current reality.

Like previous generations, many millennials and Gen Zs were taught that the key to financial success is to get a degree, a good job, and buy a home. If you were taught any financial literacy in school, it likely came from people like Dave Ramsey, who urged you to avoid debt, pay for everything in cash (including your house, and yes, he really preaches that), and basically not enjoy life until you're retired. I will acknowledge that Dave Ramsey has helped thousands of people get out of debt (and if he's helped you, that's great!), but his method is very restrictive and doesn't match the reality of current financial situations. We are stuck dealing with the consequences of trying to use strategies that just don't work anymore.

Across generations, society and the systems within it have changed, and advice that used to be effective can no longer be applied in the same way. The problem is that because these practices shift over time, we don't actively see the divide that's being created. As a result, we go through life thinking something is wrong with us. There's an expectation that we achieve everything our parents did, using their systems, and when we fail to do so, we are left feeling inadequate. So, what exactly has changed that has led to such a divide between generations? Why don't the systems we've been taught work anymore? And how do we figure out the systems that will work?

THINGS AREN'T LIKE THEY USED TO BE

Every generation will experience changes from the last, but the changes that occurred in the last 50 years have been immense. Almost everything about the way the world works has shifted, from laws to new financial products that didn't exist for our parents. We see macrolevel changes to policies and economic systems, as well as lifestyle changes involving how we approach our careers, marriage, and kids. Let's walk through some of those shifts now, so you can get a better idea of how much things have changed.

Family Life

The younger generations are taking a different approach to family life than their predecessors. We are waiting longer to get married, or not getting married at all. In 2019 the average woman was marrying at 28, which was 7 years later than the average woman in 1968. Historically, women could not open a bank account, access credit, or own a home, and many would marry out of necessity. Just as financial and legal considerations have changed, our social expectations have shifted too. One example is that the judgment around sex and living together outside of marriage has eased considerably. These expectations and potential incentives around marriage still vary by culture, region, and religion.

More and more people are choosing to not have children and instead embrace the "DINK" (dual income, no kids) lifestyle. (I can't wait to live my best DINK life with my partner. We are going to be the cool rich aunts who travel a lot and treat our pets as our children.) Those who do want kids are waiting longer to start their family. This is partially due to the cost of having children and the need for more time to financially prepare.

Millennials are less likely to live with a spouse and child and more likely to live at home with parents or family. I guess the stereotype of us living in our parents' basement till we are 30 does have some truth to it. (Remember, though, for many cultures, multigenerational living is the norm.) This statistic highlights the fact that fewer millennials are financially able to support themselves living alone and therefore need to live at home or with roommates.

Taken together, we have more freedom now than ever when it comes to marriage and children, but we also are struggling more with the financial cost of those decisions. I want to acknowledge that most of the research out there still focuses on the "traditional," heteronormative, two-parent, American family, but there are many unique ways to create your family life. Platonic partnerships, which involve committing to building a life together but without romantic feelings involved, have grown in popularity over the past few years and provide a unique alternative to traditional marriage or partnership. There's also been a rise in communal housing options, a sort of blend between a hostel and apartment with shared living spaces and community support. Although some might view these options as a step down from past dynamics, I personally find it to be a step toward collective support. Capitalism taught us to be hyperindependent, but often what we really need to survive is community.

- What does your ideal family life look like?
- Do your finances support that family life? If not, what needs to change so your ideals can become reality?

Work Life

Millennials pay more to go to college, graduate with more debt, get paid less when entering the workforce, and are less likely to have a pension plan than boomers. Yeah, it's brutal out there.

The cost of education rose over 3,700% between 1964 and 2015. Adjusted for inflation, boomers' average *annual* tuition at a public institution was $1,031 compared to the average of $9,970 millennials are paying today. Before anyone tries to say that our parents are paying for it, only 9%

of students received the majority of their college funding from their parents, and 45% didn't receive any financial help at all. As you might guess, this dynamic leads to higher student loan debt, with over 40% of millennials graduating with student loan debt compared to only 13% of boomers.

Okay, so that's depressing, but turns out it might be worth it to land a higher-paying job. College graduates continue to earn more than those without a degree, and job opportunities for the latter are declining in quality. What's really unfortunate is that while millennial college graduates may be earning more than those without a degree, their income is still comparable to that of boomers without a degree. On average, we are earning $10,000 less than our parents did at our age. When it comes to actually securing a job, it turns out all generations have struggled with that in some sense. Boomers dealt with factories being moved overseas, millennials entered the workforce right around the 2008 financial crisis, and Gen Zs graduated college during the COVID-19 pandemic.

I'm reporting on the numbers, but I'm still a firm believer that you don't need a degree to find a high-paying job and fulfilling career path. I do, however, believe that education is key. Education can take the form of reading a book, watching videos or podcasts, going to a free local seminar, having meaningful conversations, or exposing yourself to new food, places, and people. Research more about your industry, work on your craft, network, and never stop learning. This is crucial, as one of the single most important indicators of building wealth is your income. In your twenties and thirties, focus on increasing your income as much as possible by continuing to expand your skill set.

Owning a Home

Younger generations have an easier time buying a home! *Just kidding*, of course. Considering we have more debt and are getting paid less than previous generations, millennials are less likely to own a home. Debt has continuously been reported as one of the factors preventing younger generations from achieving other financial goals such as home ownership. In addition to all that, the housing market is still recovering from the pandemic housing bubble, and the cost of living continues to rise.

Over half (51%) of boomers owned a home by the time they were 25–34 years of age compared to 37% of millennials ages 25–34 who own a home.

Next time you find yourself in a heated discussion with your parents or grandparents about why you still don't own a house, let them know that housing prices have increased 250% since 1980. We are going to talk more about the barriers that currently exist around buying a home—for all generations—in Chapter 11.

Okay, so things have changed, you get that. What you might not understand is *why* they've changed. Some of these systems change over time, a natural progression of economic systems. Other changes needed a catalyst, something that sparked an investigation into the effectiveness of our systems. Let's use my oral hygiene as an example. I went four years without going to the dentist and never saw a problem with that schedule until I chipped my tooth while flossing, which prompted an emergency dental visit the next day. Without this happening, I would have continued not going to the dentist. Unfortunately, our financial systems often need a chipped tooth in order for us to realize that maybe we need to do something differently. One of the only things strong enough to chip society is traumatic events, which become the catalyst for societal change.

CATALYSTS FOR CHANGE

In March 2020 I had just returned from a trip celebrating my birthday, when the world closed down due to the COVID-19 pandemic. A few days later, I was laid off. Oof, okay, that is a painful chipped tooth. The pandemic caused (and is still causing) collective trauma. Collective trauma is when a group of people all experience trauma as a result of being exposed to the same intense event. (Refer back to Chapter 5 if you need a refresher on trauma and how it impacts your finances.)

The collective trauma is not just from the pandemic itself but also from all the events that took place around that time. The world watched the murder of George Floyd, which ignited worldwide protests in support of the Black Lives Matter movement. (It should be noted that the Black Lives Matter organization started well before this and was already building national conversation, but George Floyd's death was when it became visible to more white people.) America mourned the death of Ruth Bader Ginsburg and experienced unease with the confirmation of Amy Coney Barrett to the Supreme Court. The 2020 US presidential election took place in the midst of civil unrest, unemployment, and an out-of-control global pandemic. That was followed by the January 6 attack on the United States Capitol. Let's also mix in the overturning of *Roe v. Wade*, a coronavirus death toll of almost 7 million, the so-called freedom convoy in Canada protesting mandatory vaccines, and multiple horrific natural disasters. Seriously, ARE WE OKAY?

Since the beginning of the COVID-19 pandemic, the back-to-back exposure to numerous traumatic events has left little time to recover in between. This will leave a lasting impact on our economy, finances, politics, social security systems, communities, and our own identity as individuals. During these times we begin to question the status quo and reevaluate the existing systems. Collective trauma is decontextualizing; it will remove you from any cultural and social contexts you've built or that have been built around you, allowing the trauma to become a catalyst for social change. Any time we are forced to adapt and change in light of these moments of collective trauma, it highlights the gap between generational systems. This is because the way that each generation experiences these events will be different, eliciting varied reactions.

THE iMPACT OF COLLECTiVE TRAUMA

As I write this book, we are still actively experiencing a traumatic event and do not know the full extent of the impact. We are stuck in limbo, unsure of what the healing process will look like. The only thing we have to base this experience on is other catalysts for change, such as 9/11 or the 2008 financial crisis. By understanding the impact of our collective trauma, we can understand how such events spark change in our society, begin to appreciate our generational differences, and create a plan for moving forward together.

CASE STUDY #1: THE 9/11 ATTACKS

I don't need to spend time explaining the tragedy that occurred on September 11, 2001. What I do want to focus on is how this traumatic event was a catalyst for change—specifically when it came to finances. The 9/11 attacks made everyone question the stability of their world. It left North America devastated and afraid, and because of this act of terrorism's prominence on the global stage, the impact spread to much of the rest of the world. The events of 9/11 served as a reminder that life is precious and short and that each day does not come with a guarantee. People's individual sense of identity was impacted, as was the nation's sense of power.

> *"Terrorism, by its very intent, shatters people's beliefs in a benevolent and predictable world, and witnessing a terrorist attack on one's own soil may similarly erode one's sense of invulnerability."*

As a result of such an event, whether they realize it or not, people will alter their financial decisions. They may become more conservative with their finances, or more wary of financial institutions. They may also go in the opposite direction and stop their retirement contributions in order to live for the moment. After 9/11 the economy as a whole was impacted: the stock market dropped 7.1% that day and 143,000 people in New York lost their jobs in the wake of the attacks. The cost of cleaning up debris and repairing the World Trade Center was in the billions.

I was only in second grade, living in Canada, far away from New York when 9/11 happened. My experience and memories of 9/11 are much different from, say, those of a boomer who was living in New York at the time, or an Islamic citizen living anywhere in America. I think it's powerful and important to recognize the various ways these traumatic events affected people across generations and globally. Here's how 9/11 impacted different generations of the Queerd Co. community:

QUEERD CO. COMMUNITY COMMENTS

Boomer
"9/11 pushed me to quit university, which ended up being the BEST financial decision."

Gen X
"9/11 taught me to not panic, and just wait and see how the stock market will respond."

Millennial
"My dad was in the military and deployed after 9/11. The support we received was incredible, but I definitely felt helpless, like a charity case. I think that period of time, among other things, has contributed to the shame and helplessness I feel about my finances now."

CASE STUDY #2: THE 2008 FINANCIAL CRISIS

The 2008 stock market crash is defined as a financial crisis, and the aftermath is still present today. I'm going to explain the basics of what caused the crash, as I think it's important to understand why this happened and how we can prevent it from happening again. The root of this crisis was planted in mortgages. If you want to buy a home, you first must get approved by a bank for a mortgage. Banks will evaluate your finances to assess how much they can "risk" lending you and calculate what you're able to afford to pay back. Once you get approved, you can get a loan of hundreds of thousands of dollars from these lenders, and the bank owns your mortgage. Each month you pay back a portion of this loan plus interest until you pay everything off.

Now, in the early 2000s investors were making money through a type of investment called bonds, but they wanted to earn more interest. The housing market was doing well in the United States, and they saw this as an opportunity. The banks also saw a way to profit off this situation, so they packaged up bundles of mortgages and sold them off to investors as mortgage-backed securities. Nothing changed for the individual who took out the mortgage, they continued to make their monthly payments, but now the payment went to the investors instead of the bank. Well, this worked wonderfully for a while, and everyone was happy and making money. But investors were demanding more mortgages (to make even more money), so lenders began to be more lenient with their approvals. They started approving folks who had low credit scores or inconsistent income for mortgages. These were known as subprime mortgages. Subprime mortgages often have a low interest rate and lower monthly payments at first, but the payments skyrocket after a couple years, often beyond what the homeowner can afford.

Let's pause here for a moment to acknowledge how predatory this is. These lenders saw how much people wanted to own a home, especially low-income households, and they took advantage of their dream. While some of the blame does fall on the homeowners, I would argue that most of the blame still falls on lenders approving these mortgages. It's also important to note that subprime mortgages were disproportionately given out to Black families who actually met all the requirements to be approved for a regular mortgage but were denied due to discrimination (more on this later!).

As more people were able to get approved via subprime mortgages, this increased the demand for homes, and housing prices went up. Not long after the initial lending spree, many homeowners struggled to make their monthly mortgage payments. People began to lose their homes, which meant that possession of the homes defaulted to the investors who had bought these mortgage bundles from the bank. Investors would try to sell these houses, so more homes became available on the market; supply went up and demand went down. This caused housing prices to fall, and as a result people were stuck with a mortgage that was higher than the value of their home. More people defaulted on their monthly payments and housing prices plummeted.

The negative impact spread like wildfire. Investors stopped buying these mortgages, and banks got stuck with all these subprime mortgages people couldn't pay anymore. On September 15, 2008, Lehman Brothers (a large investment bank) declared the largest bankruptcy in US history. People began to panic, their trust in the government and these institutions eroded. This caused people to instinctively pull their money out of the stock market (referred to as "panic selling"), and we saw a big drop. Absolute chaos ensued. Millions of jobs were lost, America was hit with the worst recession to date, and the ripple effects were seen worldwide.

That was a lot of financial jargon, so let's compare the 2008 crisis to buying concert tickets. Imagine there's a popular artist going on tour, and you desperately want to get tickets. You wait in the online queue for hours, only to get to the front and realize the tickets are sold out. There is no way you're missing this show, and you finally manage to secure tickets from a scalper for 5x the original ticket price. You can't really afford those tickets, but you figure you could always resell them before the concert if you really need the money. But then, this artist adds a second performance. You snag some cheap tickets and go to resell the other ones, only to discover that nobody needs to buy them anymore. As a result, you're stuck with these expensive tickets that you overpaid for, forced to sell them at a loss. Meanwhile, the scalper who sold the tickets to you benefited from this exchange. This is a very simplified example of what happened with the housing prices and values that led to the 2008 financial crisis.

The 2008 stock market crash and following recession had a widespread impact. People's confidence in financial institutions and systems was broken. Millions of dollars were lost in the stock market crash. Mass layoffs occurred. 10 million Americans were displaced due to foreclosures. The "American dream" was shattered for many and tainted for the younger generations. Boomers lost jobs they had held for much of their lives. Millennials were just entering college and the workforce at the time and were unable to find good jobs. This had a catastrophic impact on the job market and, of course, the housing market. Here's how the 2008 financial crisis impacted the Queerd Co. community:

QUEERD CO. COMMUNITY COMMENTS

Boomer
"I felt I wasn't educated enough. After many hard hits, things felt impossible, including retirement."

Boomer
"I lost my job in 2008 and decided to start a property management business with a friend. It failed, and I ended up declaring bankruptcy. However, I ultimately ended up retiring early with my wife at 60, and we are living comfortably."

Millennial
"I graduated undergrad in 2007 and had a terrible time trying to find a job in the town I lived in. I chose to go to grad school to acquire more skills but took on another $40K in loans to do so. Sure, I gained earning power, but I feel like I'll never dig out of my $74K in total student loan debt."

Millennial
"My family went from upper-middle to lower-middle class, and our house was worth less than the remaining mortgage. My mom continued to spend like she had prior to the crash, and this created a lot of fear and instability for me as a teenager that is still affecting me today."

> "I felt a sudden shift of my parents' behavior from frugal to extreme penny-pinching. A lot of the strain came from still sending money back home to relatives, even while they were struggling. That sense of scared survival never left."
>
> — Gen Z

CASE STUDY #3: THE PANDEMIC (AND ALL THE OTHER CHAOS THAT OCCURRED WITHIN IT)

The COVID-19 pandemic was a true lifting of the veil and a wake-up call revealing the flaws in our system. The unique defining factor of the pandemic compared to the other events we've explored is that it led to isolation for an extended period. This enforced isolation allowed some of us to step back, stop working, and slow down, which gave us the time and capacity to really reflect. (Let's not forget all the essential workers who weren't afforded this luxury.) People began to question systems—especially around the workplace. As a society we transitioned to working from home and realized that companies could still be productive even if workers didn't go into the office. We woke up to the fact that calling in sick should be taken much more seriously. Career paths and salaries were questioned. This prompted the Great Resignation, an economic trend characterized by voluntary resignation due largely to inadequate wages, high cost of living, hostile work environments, lack of benefits, inflexible remote work, and overall job dissatisfaction.

We also started to question ourselves. Who are we really and what do we care about? I know I'm not alone in the experience of "finding myself" during this time. I came out publicly as queer and was diagnosed with ADHD. Everything I knew about myself was challenged, and although that was lonely and painful, it led to more clarity about how I want to live my life. I know a lot of relationships didn't survive the quarantine, while other relationships thrived or blossomed.

It also forced people to look at their financial situation, which is part of the reason my business grew the way it did. I began sharing career and financial tips on TikTok because I knew that's what people needed to hear. The initial period of quarantine helped many people save more money or pay off debt because they weren't able to go out and spend that money. Other people greatly suffered as a result of being laid off and not being able to receive unemployment insurance. The financial impacts you experienced may have been direct, such as losing your job, or more indirect, such as slowly starting to save money because you were spending less. Interest in financial literacy grew as people became determined to change their situation. Let's hear how the pandemic financially affected the Queerd Co. community:

 ## QUEERD CO. COMMUNITY COMMENTS

Boomer
"While it was anxiety inducing because of the health risks and the inability to connect with others, my husband and I are financially secure, retired, and own our home, so we felt much more at ease compared to past traumatic events."

Millennial
"I was laid off from a $70,000 job in 2020, ended up job hopping, then landing where I am now at a $25,000 job. I took a job where the pay sucked but I had more days off because I realized my time and peace of mind is worth more money than any job will pay me."

Millennial
"I overextended myself financially, buying things that brought me joy because for a while, that seemed like the only way to feel happy."

> **Gen Z** "All my work experience has been remote with flexible hours because of the pandemic. I don't know if I can hold down a regular 9–5."

> **Gen Z** "My finances completely went out the window; I was never in debt until now."

> **Gen Z** "Graduated college in 2020 and never met my coworkers at my first job out of college. I quit after 7 months because I didn't know anyone and the pay wasn't enough to make up for it."

The different ways that generations experience these traumatic events illuminates the fact that what worked for past generations won't necessarily work in the future. The older generations have lived through recessions, they have seen the stock market crash and then soar, and they have survived past traumatic events. It can be reassuring for younger generations to hear that there is hope of making it through tough times. If you are someone from an older generation reading this, consider how you can provide encouragement and wisdom without prescribing one path to success. While I think we can learn a lot from these past experiences, we need to apply those lessons to our current situation. The divide between generations still exists, and we cannot simply default to what has worked before. Instead, take the important lessons, adjust these based on your current reality, and forge a new path forward.

MINDFUL MOMENT

Knowing what to focus on when you're experiencing collective trauma is challenging, so I wanted to provide you with a starting point. Here are some suggestions on what you can focus on during the different stages of a crisis.

If the traumatic event is currently happening:
- Focus on your immediate safety and making sure your basic needs are met
- Prioritize your mental health
- If possible, connect with loved ones
- Limit the amount of news/media you consume
- Try to avoid making any big financial decisions

Think back to our lessons on trauma and the impact that it has on your brain and nervous system. You might be in an ongoing trauma-activated state without even realizing it. Take a moment to gauge where you're currently sitting in reference to your Window of Tolerance. If you find yourself outside it, employ the Trauma Evacuation Plan from Chapter 5.

Once you've achieved some stability and safety:
- Begin to address and process your experience
- If possible, talk to a mental health professional
- If possible, return to usual daily activities
- Focus on keeping your nervous system regulated
- Offer support to others if you have the capacity

Once the crisis has ended or slowed down significantly:
- Resist the desire to "move on" and return to normal
- Continue to share your story and experience
- Be honest about the trauma you've faced
- Reflect on how this experience has impacted your career, finances, mindset, and life

At this stage you can begin to make large financial decisions again, as long as you're not in a trauma-activated state.

Once significant time has passed:
- Continue to work through your trauma
- Lean on your community
- If possible, engage in trauma-informed therapy
- Start to plan and set goals that align with your shifted values and behaviors
- Reevaluate how your life may need to change as you move forward in a new way

Take it slow and be gentle with yourself.

FORGING A NEW PATH FORWARD

Large-scale traumatic occurrences such as a pandemic or recession can put a strain on your finances. I want to help you navigate potential financial challenges, in any current and future experiences you might live through. To that end, I've compiled some of the most important lessons and tangible tips we've learned from past traumatic events. These can be adapted to fit any generation's approach to financial security.

1. When it comes to buying a home, don't just rely on the professionals to tell you what you can afford.

Although the process of getting approved for mortgages has greatly improved since the 2008 financial crisis, there are still many issues with the system. Ultimately, the more people that are approved, the more money mortgage brokers make. I recommend doing your own mortgage affordability test to get a better idea of what you can actually afford. You can find some calculators in the resource section.

RESOURCE

Mortgage Calculators, page 314

But don't stop there: you also want to think logically about how a mortgage payment and owning a home will impact your life. Mortgage brokers look at your numbers, but they don't see all the emotional factors that are at play too.

2. When living through a recession, or period of unemployment, one way to offset the strain is by lowering your cost of living.

This is not always possible and can be incredibly difficult, especially with rising living costs in major cities, but here are some steps to consider.

Step 1: Remove any unnecessary expenses

Look at your subscriptions and explore why you have them and what value they bring. This can include subscriptions such as Spotify, Netflix, Amazon Prime, gym or fitness membership, meal kits, phone apps, etc. If they are currently not being used, or you feel that you could go without them, cancel them!

Step 2: Negotiate expenses

Many expenses are open for negotiation, such as your phone plan, internet, TV services, rent, and even your credit card interest rate. Many people were able to secure lower rent and a reduced credit card interest rate during the pandemic. Even if it's for a limited time, it still helps. If you're like me and you hate talking to people on the phone, you can try negotiating using online chat features. It doesn't hurt to ask if they can offer you a better deal!

Bonus tip: Optimize your expenses by aligning your bill due dates with your income. You can generally request that the due date for a bill be moved by reaching out to the company or simply logging online to your service account. For example, if you get paid on the 1st and 15th of the month, split up your bills so that they are more evenly distributed in relation to your paycheck(s). It's common to pay rent on the 1st of the month, which is often a big expense, so try to avoid having your other bills due at the same time.

3. You can prep for tight financial times by padding your safety fund to include 9–12 months' worth of expenses.

In Chapter 3 we talked about having 3–6 months' worth of expenses in your safety fund: having extra money in there can help protect you if you get laid off and give you more freedom of choice.

4. Keep cash on hand in case of any large-scale impact to financial systems.

In 2022 a massive network outage in Canada caused the Interac payment system to go down, meaning people could not use their debit card across the country (yikes). I recommend having $500 to $1,000 of cold, hard cash that you can use for emergencies.

5. Protect yourself and your loved ones by making a will.

I know, I know, this sounds morbid and unnecessary, especially if you're young, but it's so important. Accidents happen, horrible events happen, and having a will gives you peace of mind. Your will is an opportunity for you to express how you would like decisions to be made and ensures that any wishes are fulfilled. Creating a will forces you to really think about where you'd like your money and assets to land, which is important at any age. I've added some of my recommendations for will services in the resource section.

RESOURCE

Recommendations for Will Services, page 314

6. The crises discussed in this chapter all demonstrate the importance of investing and diversifying your investment portfolio.

Large-scale traumatic events often can have a negative impact on the stock market, but if you have an investment portfolio made up of a diverse range of investments, you won't need to stress as much. If a single industry takes a hit, and you only hold investments from that industry, you'll be greatly impacted.

Investments such as index funds and ETFs are great because they are a "package" of investments across industries, meaning it's already more diversified and less risky. They are typically more cost-effective and one of the easiest ways to build a diversified portfolio.

This book won't go into investment strategy in detail, but you know where to find some resources on where to start. I want to encourage you to seek out the education, because it will be the best investment into your future.

RESOURCE

Investing Educational Resources, page 314

7. Don't stop honing your skill set when it comes to your career.

These past traumatic events showed us that even "stable" jobs can be lost in an instant. The best thing you can do to prepare, besides having a safety fund, is to continually work on upgrading your skills. Focus on transferrable abilities that will give you a competitive edge.

WRAPPING IT UP

The shifts that have occurred, both from small changes over time and from traumatic events that acted as catalysts for change, create a division between generations. The systems and tools that we have been taught by our parents aren't cutting it for us anymore. Lifestyle changes have occurred, altering the way we choose to work, live, and raise families. It's not as simple as "I did it, now you can do it too" when it comes to financial success. I hope that this chapter illuminated the divide that has occurred from generation to generation but also opened your eyes to the lessons we can still learn. Let the past be your teacher but have the courage to explore your own path as you figure out what works for the lifestyle you ultimately want to live.

PUTTING IT INTO PRACTICE

1. Based on past traumatic events you've experienced (as a child or adult), write out 5 of the most important lessons you've learned. Reflect on the following questions:

- How did that lesson change the way you view your finances and/or career?
- How can you apply that lesson to your finances and/or career in the future?

2. An important part of forging a new path forward involves looking at where we came from. Take the lessons you just identified in the first question and share them with loved ones from both an older and younger generation. Talk to your grandparents, parents, children, or friends about how you each experienced these events. Here are some conversation starters:

- What lessons have you learned from living through past traumatic experiences such as 9/11 and the 2008 financial crisis? (include other events that are relevant for your culture/ family/location)

o How have your financial/career/life goals changed because of those events?
o How has your life changed since the beginning of the pandemic?
o How do you think we can heal and move forward from these traumatic experiences?

CHAPTER 9

Banking on Beliefs

THE POWER OF VALUES-BASED SPENDING

I dig my toes into the soft white sand, gaze out at the turquoise water before me, and breathe in the salty air. It's just after lunchtime and I'm sitting alone on a beach in El Nido, in the Philippines. This has become my routine the last couple of days: after eating lunch at my favorite café and using their Wi-Fi to reassure my parents that I am still alive and healthy, I make my way down to the beach. I spend my afternoons sitting on my tiny travel towel and either reading, journaling, or napping. Today I have been journaling and thinking a lot about the life at home that I've left behind.

When I told my friends and family that I was taking a semester off from college—during what was supposed to be my last year—I was met with shock. You see, I got stuck in the career path laid out by my parents. Get good grades, get into a good university, and then land a good job. You know the drill, right? I went to school for kinesiology with the intent of pursuing a master's in physiotherapy upon graduation. My dream of being a physiotherapist dictated all my decisions. Everyone close to me knew this was the dream I was chasing, so when I began to question it, I felt ashamed. I ended up realizing in my fifth and final year (are you even a millennial if you don't take a victory lap?) that even though I had the desire to help and impact others, I didn't want to do that through physiotherapy. No longer holding the identity of "future physiotherapist," I was lost. So, I did what any reasonable person looking to make a big life decision would do: I booked a trip. That's how I ended up on this beach. Here is an excerpt from my journal that day:

> "In a way, leaving [home] was much easier than staying. At home I feel suffocated, trapped, and helplessly lost. I don't know what I'm doing, or what I want to do. I have no future planned out and no motivation or drive to get there. I have yet to discover my calling. I am praying that it will come. That I will find something I am drawn to, passionate about, and ready to work for. Or maybe I am just supposed to pick something and hope I fall in love with it later. For now, I'm sitting on the beach in El Nido. It has just begun to rain but I don't feel much like leaving. Every time I travel it reminds me how much I have to learn. Not only about the world but about myself."

This was the trip where I was forced to face how little I understood about myself. This was the trip that began my journey to discovering my personal values.

THE IMPORTANCE OF PERSONAL VALUES

At the beginning of this book, we discussed identity economics, which refers to the idea that the financial decisions you make are influenced by who you are. That includes your personal values, which play a role in how you choose to spend or save your money. Personal values are the basic and fundamental beliefs that guide, motivate, and determine what is most important to you in life. They act as a compass, guiding our behaviors, actions, and decisions. Your values might be things like freedom, creativity, loyalty, and equity but are different from emotions like happiness or pride. When you are clear on your personal values, it's easier to live your life in alignment. When you are unsure of your values or are living by those that others dictated for you, it can cause resistance in your life.

Think about a time when you felt conflicted making a big life decision. You may have found yourself asking everyone in your life what they thought you should do. Or you stayed up late at night googling "should I go back to school or keep working?" hoping strangers on the internet would sway you one way or another. Without a compass, it becomes hard to make important decisions with confidence, because you don't know what direction it will take you.

My core personal values have always been blurry for me. I grew up going to church every Sunday, saying grace at every meal, and hearing about God on a regular basis at home. For much of my life, my values were dictated by the church—love your neighbors, put others before yourself, treat your body like a temple, and put God above all else. As I got older and began to separate myself from the church, I had a really hard time separating my own values. I was living my life according to the values everyone around me was following, the values I had been taught. For years I felt lost, not understanding what I wanted or how to make decisions. I was living my life out of alignment.

Close your eyes and think about how you feel when you go out in public in an outfit that doesn't feel good. It might be uncomfortable, or not fit right, or just not really represent your style. Notice how your body reacts to this memory. I'm remembering how I felt when I had to wear a blush pink bridesmaid dress. It was a beautiful dress, just not an item of clothing I felt comfortable or confident in. Now I want you to imagine going out in an outfit that you feel "hot" in. Clothing that fits you the way you want, feels good, represents your style and identity, and that you just know you are embodying. Take note of how your body language changes. Those two feelings demonstrate the difference between living in alignment versus out of alignment. When you're living your life in the first outfit, something just feels off. In the second outfit, you feel good, and nobody can tell you otherwise. You don't need the approval of others, because you just know that it's right.

So how do money and values intersect? If our personal values are not being upheld within our financial habits and behaviors, this can cause resistance, avoidance, guilt, shame, and internal turmoil. If we *are* upholding our values, that can set us up for achieving the things we care about, like traveling the world, buying a house, or supporting loved ones. Now don't worry, I am going to walk through all this with you, so that you can identify what areas of your finances are operating out of alignment with your values. First, we need to understand what exactly your core personal values are.

HOW TO IDENTIFY YOUR CORE VALUES

Before we dive into this exercise, it's important that you feel ready for this work. Settle into your favorite comfy spot, or if you're out in public, pop in some headphones to quiet the noise around you. Make sure you have either a notebook or a device to jot down your answers. Take a couple deep breaths. Remember that these pages are a safe space to get vulnerable.

Step 1

Sometimes it's easier to pinpoint what we don't like rather than what we do like. So, let's start with writing down some of the times you felt like something just wasn't right. One example for me would be pursuing a career in physiotherapy. These can be less significant too, moments that you felt like you were wearing clothes that didn't fit. Here are some more examples:

- Taking a job that has practices you don't agree with
- Not speaking up when your uncle uses a racial slur at the dinner table
- Staying in a relationship with someone you love who has incompatible beliefs

Once you have some examples, think about what value was being suppressed in that situation. Sometimes we don't recognize the values that are important to us until they are taken away or directly challenged by the situation. Completing college when I didn't feel like I belonged felt like a suppression of freedom, creativity, and growth. This can give some indication of what values might actually be important to you. **What was the core principle or value in each experience that was being challenged or suppressed?**

Step 2

Next, I want you to think of experiences that made you come alive. Moments where you felt like yourself, you felt confident and happy. Perhaps a time that you felt proud. Here are some examples:

- Sitting on a beach in El Nido
- Volunteering at your local food bank
- Walking across the stage at graduation
- Landing your dream job

Reflect on what values you were honoring in those situations. If we look at my example of sitting on the beach in El Nido, it coincidentally honors the values of freedom and growth. See what we're doing here? **What was the core principle or value in each experience that was being honored or upheld?**

Step 3

Go back through both of your lists from steps 1 and 2 and write down more details. Write down how you felt in those situations and why they were memorable. Keep asking yourself the question "Why was this important to me?" over and over again, digging deeper into your own reasoning and experience each time, until you can't answer it anymore. Here is an example:

> **An experience that made me feel alive:** landing my first client
>
> **Why was this important to me?** I took a risk starting my business, and this was an indication that I could actually make money through a career that I was passionate about.
> **Why is pursuing a career I'm passionate about important to me?** I care about helping people, and finding a career I'm excited about will allow me to make an impact on people's lives.
> **Why is helping people important to me?** I feel the most fulfilled and happy when I am able to help, support, or impact somebody's life.
> **Why is feeling fulfilled important to me? . . .** You get the idea.

Now I want you to look over everything you've written and pull out similar themes. Highlight the patterns that you notice.

- What were the common threads between your big meaningful experiences?
- Did the same values feel suppressed multiple times?
- What were the qualities or characteristics that stuck out to you?

Step 4

Now that you've reflected on some past situations, it's time to start brainstorming what your values are. There are no right or wrong answers, just write the words that come to mind. If you're struggling, you can use the values list I've provided below to help guide you. This is just a starting point and not an exhaustive list, so don't worry if you think of a word that's not included here.

List of Values

Achievement	Forgiveness	Loyalty
Ambition	Freedom	Open-mindedness
Authenticity	Fun	Optimism
Balance	Generosity	Patience
Collaboration	Gratitude	Perseverance
Community	Growth	Professionalism
Compassion	Hard work	Respect
Courage	Honesty	Responsibility
Creativity	Humility	Self-improvement
Diversity	Inclusivity	Spirituality
Empathy	Independence	Spontaneity
Empowerment	Innovation	Stability
Environmentalism	Integrity	Support
Equity	Justice	Teamwork
Excellence	Kindness	Understanding
Fairness	Leadership	Unity
Faith	Learning	Wealth

Once you have a list of 3–10 values, I recommend that you stop and take a break. Come back to step 5 after you've had some time away.

Step 5

Take your list of values from step 4 and organize them into categories. Many of the values that you have written down probably have some overlap, and categorizing them will help to eliminate doubles. The way you group values together will vary from person to person. Here's what that might look like:

Helping and service values:

- Community
- Generosity
- Leadership

Personal development values:

- Creativity
- Freedom
- Learning
- Growth

Look at your overall list of values and select the top 3 that feel most relevant right now. Try to avoid picking values that may represent the same thing (your category grouping should help with this). These should be the words that resonate the most with you; focus on the values that feel essential to your life and happiness.

Step 6

Now that you've selected your core personal values, the final step is to spend some time defining what those values mean to you. Don't just think about it—write down or record your definitions so that you can reference this exercise and remember exactly why you chose those specific words. One of my values is community, but for me this doesn't just mean a dictionary definition such as *"a unified group of people."* My definition means creating a sense of community wherever I go, building a strong community via my platforms where people can support one another, putting work into my local neighborhood, supporting social justice movements, spending quality time with loved ones, and so much more. **What do your chosen values mean to you?**

Remember that the values you just selected may be very different from ones you previously held, and they may change again in the future. Values can shift as you grow and evolve through life, and that's okay. I recommend revisiting your values every year and making sure they still hold true.

PASSING THE MIC

Michelle's Story: Reframing Shame and Embracing Your Values

Author, activist, speaker, CEO, and entrepreneur Michelle MiJung Kim (she/her) opens up about her own experience of trying to live in alignment with her values in a capitalist society, as a queer, Korean American immigrant woman. Michelle is the award-winning author of *The Wake Up*, is the CEO and founder of Awaken, and is passionate about creating meaningful and sustainable change. Here is her story:

I decided to pursue a career in management consulting right out of school, despite having been a really active youth organizer and activist throughout high school and college. I always thought I would go into full-time organizing or the nonprofit world, but I realized I needed money to immigrate my mom to the U.S. from South Korea. There was a lot of guilt and shame that came up for me having gone into corporate America for the purposes of earning money. I think that's a common struggle for marginalized people, especially people who hold social justice values, that prioritizing money can sometimes feel dirty. It can feel shameful. It can feel selfish.

I would describe my relationship with money today as a work in progress. I'm constantly checking in on it because now I have class privilege. I have to be really honest and ask myself, what is enough? What can I do to live in alignment with my values when it comes to money? What does that look like in a concrete way? Those are the questions that I've been asking myself constantly, and it's been challenging.

I think there's a lot of contradictions when it comes to trying to live out my values in a capitalist society. Is home ownership something that is in alignment with my values? Why or why not? I don't think that a lot of people ask those questions unless they've been thinking really deeply about social justice. Because for a lot of people it would be an obvious choice, but it was a very complex situation for me. I did end up buying a home, and I wrote in my book about how that process for me was really emotionally and logistically complicated.

I found that navigating these very different spaces gives me the understanding and the compassion to be able to hold a lot of gray areas, which I think is necessary for us to be able to do this work in a thoughtful and nuanced way. I wish that I could tell my younger self to not sulk in shame for having needed money to support my loved ones. I want people to not make themselves the source of shame but rather understand how the systems are set up in such a way that requires us to make difficult choices in order to survive.

SPENDING IN ALIGNMENT WITH YOUR VALUES

Michelle's interview emphasizes the important role that your values play in how you choose to live your life. Understanding your personal values provides clarity, especially when it comes to your finances. You can now use this information to evaluate your past financial decisions and your decisions moving forward. To start, I've got a question for you: **If I were to look at your spending for the past couple of months, would it be clear what your core values are?**

You might feel some shame creeping up as you read that sentence, and you're not alone in feeling that way. I want to take a moment to acknowledge the uncomfortable process of evaluating your spending habits, and all the negative emotions that can accompany that. Show yourself compassion in this moment; you couldn't have addressed an issue that you weren't aware of. Look at your spending and compare it with the values work that you just did. I recommend you pull up the spending tracker you completed back in Chapter 2 and review those purchases. If it's been a while since you tracked your purchases, you may want to complete that exercise again.

Do your financial choices and behaviors align with your values?

If your answer is *yes*, that means you're already spending in alignment with your values. Consider if there is any room for improvement as I cover values-based spending. If your answer is *no*, let me introduce you to intentional or values-based spending.

Values-based spending simply means using your money in alignment with your values. This means being intentional with what you're buying and where your money is going. You might find that the guilt you feel around your purchases has less to do with the money being spent and more to do with *how* the money is being spent. When you're able to shift your spending to support your core values, it feels like always putting on an outfit that

fits perfectly. Doing this will allow you to remove much of the guilt and shame that accompanies unintentional buying and instead move forward in alignment.

Earlier I shared with you that one of my values is community, but my spending didn't always reflect that. If you were to pull up my bank statements from a handful of years ago, you would see that I spent a lot of money on alcohol, food, Uber rides, and clothing. There's nothing wrong with that spending, but I wasn't using my money in a way that aligned with my core values. As a result, I often felt guilty and unfulfilled when reflecting on my purchases. When I'm practicing values-based spending, I prioritize purchases that uphold the value of community. Maybe that means going out for a nice dinner with a good friend, attending a local community event, donating to social causes I care about, or supporting small businesses.

Following values-based spending also allows you to make financial decisions with more confidence. If you're trying to decide whether you should keep renting or purchase a home, you can ask yourself which of those options would align more with your values. **Which decision supports what's important to you? What feels out of alignment?**

FINANCIAL SIDEBAR

We've talked a lot about spending in this book, and at this point you've hopefully set up your allowance card and maybe started dabbling in the 5-account system. The final step in that process is setting up automation, which makes it easier to make intentional, aligned purchases.

What is automation?
Automation is a way of keeping your money organized while still prioritizing your goals by setting up automated systems. Essentially your money can work for you behind the scenes, allowing you to be more hands off when you're having a tough mental health month, or

if you just don't want to think about your money as much. We are more likely to overspend when the flow of our money isn't organized.

Why is automation helpful?
- Lowers risk of late or missed payments
- Lessens your mental load so you don't worry and stress as much
- Can reduce impulsive spending

Note: Automation may not be the best option if you're living pay-check to paycheck or are in a tight financial position, as you may miss payments and get hit with overdraft fees. If you are living in this reality (60% of Americans are) and if you know this system isn't going to work for you, this is your permission slip to just skip this section and move on! You can always come back to this box in the future.

What should you automate?
1. **Your monthly bills and expenses:** Automate all your bill payments—everything from your internet payment to your rent—by logging on to your online account for each one and setting up the auto-pay feature. Even if the company itself doesn't have an auto-pay feature, you can often have your bank make the payment for you or mail something like a rent check on your behalf. I recommend using 1 account or credit card for all of your bill payments to keep things simple (like we covered in my 5-account system). If you're using a credit card for bill payments, then set up an automatic payment from a checking account to pay off that card each month.
2. **Your debt payments:** If you're currently working on paying off debt, automate your monthly debt repayment. For example, if it's credit card debt, set up an automatic payment from a checking account to your credit card. If your credit card is separate from where you do your daily banking, you can set up your credit card as a "payee." You can also automate payments to a line of credit and a personal loan, depending on your terms. If you're not

putting a consistent amount toward your debt each month, then you can just automate the minimum monthly payment and manually contribute anything additional.

3. **Your savings contributions (safety fund, mental health funds, etc.):** Set up automatic transfers through your bank to your savings account(s) each month, ideally as soon as you get paid, so you don't have a chance to spend that money elsewhere.

4. **Your investment contributions:** If you're currently investing money, set up automatic transfers to your investment accounts each month. If you're investing through your work for retirement, this can come automatically off your paycheck. PS: If your work offers employer matching plans, definitely take advantage of this, because it's like free money!

If you're implementing the 5-account system, you essentially want to automate the transfers from your hub account to all your other accounts.

Pro tip: Automate directly from your paycheck
Talk to your payroll department and see if you're able to submit direct deposit information for multiple accounts or see if your company's payroll service offers a paycheck splitter. This allows you to allocate money from your paycheck to go *directly* into different accounts. The ultimate automation.

Setting up automations will take work up front and can be overwhelming, so I suggest tackling this when you're in a good mental state. Once it's set up, however, there's minimal upkeep needed on your end!

VOTING WITH YOUR MONEY

The pandemic shifted how I viewed values-based spending. The collective trauma of the last few years forced me to look at my finances differently and showed me the power of voting with my money.

Voting with your money is the idea that you can support the issues you care about through the financial decisions you make. This is essentially values-based spending, but we are taking it a step further by thinking about how the way we use our money can impact the world. You can vote with your money through your spending by choosing to shop at a small business instead of a big-box store. You can vote with your money through investing by choosing socially responsible investments. You can vote with your money through donation by directly giving money to organizations and causes you care about.

Before I give any more examples, I want to take a moment to address the privilege and classism that surrounds the idea of voting with your money. It seems easy to tell people to stop buying fast fashion and to shop ethical clothing brands instead, but for many, fast fashion may be the only affordable option. You may want to buy organic groceries but struggle to do so while keeping up with the skyrocketing prices due to inflation.

Sometimes your financial situation may reduce the options that you have. The remainder of this chapter will introduce different ways to live in alignment with your values by using your money, even if your finances do not allow for much change. Some of it may be applicable to your life, and some of it won't be. Shifting your financial decisions to be more in alignment with your values is a process, and this process can occur over years. It's the accumulation of tiny decisions and changes over time that result in change for everyone.

Where You Invest Your Money

If you are currently investing already, this is a relatively easy shift to make. I wouldn't stress about moving your current investments; instead, focus on socially responsible investments that you can make moving forward. One type of sustainable investing is known as ESG investing, which assesses the environmental, social, and governance factors to determine the investment's impact and return. You can select these investments based on the issues that you care about. You may want to invest in companies that are woman run, or are sustainable and ethical, or have inclusive hiring practices. You get to decide what matters!

Another shift you can make is switching who you bank with if their policies don't align with your values. One example is banks investing in fossil fuels. Between 2016 and 2020, the four largest banks in the United States provided $976 *billion* in funding to fossil fuel companies. Financial institutions that dump millions of dollars of funding into destructive environmental initiatives play a role in climate change.

Socially responsible financial institutions do exist, and they have committed to not funding industries that cause harm to people or the environment. Typically, these institutions are very transparent with how they spend their money and will use their resources to support important economic, social, racial, and environmental causes. Each institution will vary on how they display their commitment, but just like socially responsible investing, you get to decide who to support. One way to tell the ethical banks from those that are greenwashing is to check what certifications they hold. Check out the resource section for a list of certifications and designations you can look for when choosing a socially responsible institution.

RESOURCE

Choosing a Socially Responsible Financial Institution,
page 315

Although it might feel as if who you bank with doesn't make a big difference, I assure you that it does. Not only are you choosing to manage your
money in alignment with your values but you're encouraging others to do
the same. If enough people start making the switch, these institutions will be
forced to start making changes.

Companies You Support

In addition to who you may invest in, also consider the companies that
you choose to support regularly. Is there one switch you can make? Perhaps
instead of grabbing your morning coffee at Starbucks, you decide to support
your local coffee shop, or instead of buying your clothes from a company
that isn't 2SLGBTQIA+ friendly, you shop at an equivalent that supports
the community. Now I'm not sitting here saying you need to make all these
switches or pretending that I have. If you know me, you know I love supporting local coffee shops, but I also love my Starbucks. Again, it's about making
small changes and choices when you can, but not beating yourself up when it
doesn't work. These examples might not even be important to you and your
values, and that's okay too. Refer back to your core values and reflect on what
matters to you.

What You Care About

How can you use the resources you have to support the causes you're
passionate about? You might be able to use the resource of money to support organizations or charities. If you want to make sure that's a priority, you
could add a donation to your monthly expenses or make a donation every
year on your birthday. Alternatively, the resource of time might be a better
option for you. Maybe you can donate your time to volunteering or protesting. Or perhaps you have some social capital—meaning you have a following on social media—and you can use that to share and boost important

content. There are a lot of things you can do that don't involve your finances at all, such as signing petitions, speaking up about injustice, educating yourself and others, and sharing resources.

The goal here is not to make you feel like you're not doing enough, or that you've been making wrong decisions, but rather to get you thinking about how to be more intentional. Choose what is important to you and make one small shift. Make more changes as you're able but give yourself grace if you fall short of the expectations you set for yourself. Even just the act of reflecting on your decisions is powerful.

MINDFUL MOMENT

My girlfriend cares a lot about sustainability and was almost completely zero waste for a period of time in her life. She had a pantry full of mason jars containing all her food, she made her own laundry detergent, cleaners, and deodorant, she only bought items secondhand, and much more. She felt really good about making the conscious decision to shop at zero waste stores and minimize the waste she created, but it came with a price to her mental health. My girlfriend also has ADHD and living zero waste can add a lot of extra steps to tasks that are usually simple. She found that she was putting so much extra effort into ensuring she was making sustainable choices that she had no energy to do anything else. I mean, when you're struggling to even do laundry, it's not fun to have to go out and collect soap nuts to create your own detergent. She's at a point now where she's found a good balance. We try to be zero waste where we can, and we still make our own cleaners, but we've started buying laundry detergent and shopping at regular grocery stores.

It's important to remember that your mental health outweighs your intentional spending. Sometimes the decisions that align with our values don't actually support us in the best way. Now she's able to complete daily tasks with ease and put more energy into her passions. Do the things you can and release the expectation to do more.

WRAPPING IT UP

After booking the trip that took me to the Philippines, Vietnam, Cambodia, Laos, and Australia, I did return home and finish my degree. I was in the process of discovering my own personal values and that moment on the beach in El Nido was the beginning. People often ask me if I regret my university degree as I don't really use it, and I'm still stuck with student debt, but my answer is always no. I believe that nobody is really clear on their personal values as children because we have too much outside influence. It's up to us to figure it out as adults. My moment of "what the hell am I going to do with my life?" sparked a year of self-discovery that allowed me to get clear on my core values.

Understanding your personal values gives you more clarity when making decisions about your life, especially when it comes to your finances. Evaluate the decisions you make through the lens of your values. If there isn't alignment, it's time to change course. Now that you have more awareness around how your spending is tied to your values, you can use that knowledge to make more informed and aligned purchasing decisions. When you're ready, you can take it a step further and begin voting with your money. Using your money to fight against social injustice is a powerful form of protest, and every small decision has an impact. Keep in mind that this is new information, and practice kindness when you fear you're not doing enough. Remember that your own mental health is most important, and the practice of living in alignment is a lifelong journey. You've made progress just by reading through this chapter. You're equipped with the tools, and all you have to do is start putting it into practice.

PUTTING iT iNTO PRACTiCE

1. Look at your top 3 values and write down all the financial behaviors and choices that align with those values. I mentioned one of my values is community, so some behaviors and choices that align with that for me are:

o   Donating money to social causes I care about
o   Spending money to share time with my loved ones (whether that's hopping on a plane to see my sister, date night with my girlfriend, or going bowling with my friends)
o   Investing in my business—which is growing this incredible community
o   Volunteering in my local neighborhood

2. Review your spending evaluation, and reflect on these questions:

o   What spending is currently supporting my values that I would like to maintain?
o   What spending is currently not supporting my values that I'd like to do less of?
o   What spending would support my values that I'd like to do more of?

3. Choose one way you'd like to vote with your money and either implement it right away or do so when it's possible for you.

CHAPTER 10

Love at First Swipe

A GUIDE TO BUILDING AN EQUITABLE RELATIONSHIP

If you've ever lived with a partner before, you know how much of a learning curve there can be when you first move in together. Suddenly you're in such close quarters to each other, wondering why you never noticed how they put the toilet paper on the roll completely wrong.

When my girlfriend and I moved in together, it was actually a more seamless transition than I was anticipating. There were still things we needed to figure out, but we quickly slipped into a rhythm and were operating as a solid team only a couple months in. The only problem was that we had overlooked one big aspect of this partnership—our finances. People assume that we must be excellent at managing our money together because I'm a financial expert. Let me assure you that we have had our fair share of financial challenges as a couple and are still finding our groove today.

I knew how important it was to talk about money before we moved in together, so we did. We had conversations about our current finances, our future goals, and how we wanted to split expenses based on our incomes. We talked about our budget for moving in together and what that would logistically look like. What we didn't talk about was what we would do when something went haywire. We were planning for the ideal situation, not reality.

My partner and I didn't just move in together, we moved to a new city where neither of us had ever lived before. We jumped straight from each living in small apartments to renting a house together. While I was able to keep working because my business operated online, my partner had to quit her serving job and find a new job when we moved. We had calculated the rent we could comfortably afford with my business income and her previous income, because we knew she could make a similar amount serving in our new city. I felt confident in our decisions and in my girlfriend's ability to quickly land a job.

What we both didn't foresee was the mental battle she was about to undergo. She had been through a lot in the year leading up to our move and had been operating in survival mode for a long time. After we moved, she was working through trauma from her previous job. As a result, she wasn't in the position to job hunt, let alone start working. I knew it was important for her to heal, so I paid for her to start seeing a therapist. I was happy to support her and to take on the financial burden for a while.

Well, a while turned into over 6 months. It became a point of tension in our relationship. I didn't want to push her to get a job before she was ready, but at the same time I was now in a tough financial spot. To cover all the bills, I had to stop contributing to my savings and investments. I felt pressure to make more money, and my business started to suffer. Every time we tried to talk about it, we both got emotional. I started avoiding the conversation because I thought it would make things worse. Resentment began to build up. While part of me felt good about helping her, the other part was stressed and upset that my goals and business were taking a hit.

Writing this now, I still feel a wave of shame for feeling frustrated, but it's important that I'm honest with all of you. I think the most challenging thing was not that I was paying for everything but that this happened unexpectedly, on top of us moving. If we had been able to have a conversation where my partner explained she needed some time off from working and I was mentally prepared to make this shift, it would have felt different. But this is real life, and there will always be unpredictable changes. That's why it's so important to have open and honest money conversations with your partner.

This will allow you to begin to understand and navigate your differences. We had started taking those steps, but before we could finish, we were thrust into the unknown, stuck navigating without a clear path forward.

Money plays a critical role in relationships. It not only defines what you can afford but also impacts your relationship dynamics, domestic labor, future goals, and your ability to raise a family. If you're not talking about money with your partner(s), you need to start now. Throughout this chapter I am going to share our journey from moving in together to where we are with our finances today. I will walk you through how to have these important and uncomfortable conversations so you can confidently overcome challenges together. You will also hear from some folks in interracial, intercultural, and 2SLGBTQIA+ relationships on how they have worked through their differences around money. I'll introduce them to you now, and you'll find their experiences and advice sprinkled throughout the following pages.

Maggie (she/her) and Yuvraj (he/him) have been together just over a year and are about to move in with each other. They received very different messaging around money growing up. Maggie is an artist who was taught to follow her passions while Yuvraj is an engineer who grew up being told to secure a stable job with a good salary. Together they are preparing to take a big financial step in their relationship.

Hannah (she/her) and Kristen (she/her) have been together for 1.5 years and are working toward living together. Kristen is a Black woman, comes from an immigrant family, and provides financial support for them. Hannah's family is white, her parents are divorced, and this is her first queer relationship. They've learned to openly communicate about money and are currently navigating Kristen being laid off.

Meenadchi (she/her) and Unika (they/them) have been dating for 5 months and are beginning to have serious conversations about the future. Unika was raised in the lower middle class and experienced trauma stemming from that socioeconomic positioning. Meenadchi grew up in the upper middle class and is self-employed. Together they've been cultivating a relationship with mutual care.

Rebecca (she/her) and Brendan (he/him) have been together for 9 years and moved in with each other about 10 months ago. Rebecca is half Indian, half African American; her parents had her when they were 20 and built their wealth from scratch. Brendan is white and benefits from generational wealth on both sides of his parents' families. They've learned to navigate these differences through open and honest conversation.

Janie (she/her), Maggie (she/her), and Cody (he/him) are involved in a polyamorous triad, own a home together, and are about to all be married. Maggie and Cody are currently married and have been together since 2016; they began dating Janie in 2017 and are now engaged to Janie. They've had to navigate a lot, from being raised in different religions, coming out to friends and family, and organizing finances both legally and logistically between 3 people. Of the 3, I interviewed Janie and will be sharing their story from her perspective.

THE IMPACT OF MONEY IN RELATIONSHIPS

Before we dive into the various dynamics around money that play out in relationships, I want to note that most of the research out there focuses on cisgendered, heterosexual (referred to as "cishet" throughout this chapter), traditional relationships. There's not a lot of discourse around the intersection of culture and finances, and there's hardly any research on 2SLGBTQIA+ and/or polyamorous relationships. Although academic literature has not caught up to modern-day relationships, a lot of the research will still be applicable. To keep things simple, I will often be referring to relationships involving two people and using terms such as "couple" or "partner," but feel free to adapt this information for whatever your relationship scenario is.

We've already explored some of the many ways that your identity impacts your money, but when you're in a relationship, there's another person's identity to consider as well. This merging of identities will impact your relationship whether you've been dating for a month or have been married for 10 years. It will spill over into something as simple as who pays for dinner and build up to big life decisions like whether or not you want children. The dynamics are also shifting constantly as the world moves around you. Moving in together, getting laid off from your job, getting a promotion, having children, and getting married are examples of shifts that could occur throughout your life together. You might be reading this right now and thinking, "My partner and I don't talk about money and our relationship is great!" You might even be tempted to skip past this chapter because you feel it doesn't apply to you.

Before you do that, let me remind you that one of the strongest predictors of divorce is money disagreements. Even if your relationship is rainbows and butterflies right now, or even if you've accepted the fact that you'll likely die alone with 30 cats, you need to hear this. One day you might be swept off your feet or decide to commit to a platonic partnership with your best friend, and I want you to be prepared to navigate finances in any kind of relationship with ease.

Navigating finances in a relationship is a lot like building a Lego house. The end goal is to have a beautiful home you equitably built together. You each start off with your own Lego pieces and decide that you want to pool them to build a cool new home. The ideal situation is one in which your Lego pieces will fit with each other perfectly and you'll work together brick by brick to create something beautiful. Assembling this Lego house means that you must be able to problem solve, communicate, and plan ahead as a couple. If you avoid talking about money, then you've already started laying down Legos before you've even decided what you want to build. This happens every time one of you feels resentment over paying for dinner, or teases the other for buying something "silly," or complains to your friends that your partner didn't spoil you for your birthday. By the time you decide this relationship is getting serious, and you might need to start having money conversations, a messy foundation already exists. The longer you go on without addressing the unstable foundation, the more rickety the house becomes.

One of the reasons money is so highly linked to divorce is because of how deeply money affects other aspects of the relationship. Here are some of the top money-related causes for divorce:

1. Differing or opposing attitudes toward money
2. Mismatched priorities (e.g., save for a house vs. save for a big trip)
3. Credit card debt
4. Financial "infidelity" (e.g., secret accounts, purchases, habits, or debt)
5. Overextended budgets
6. Unwillingness to compromise on spending
7. Big impulse buys
8. The stress of combined finances

It's shocking how many of these causes could be avoided with open communication. Not just about the finances themselves but about childhood experiences, past trauma, division of labor, career, and life goals.

I want each one of you reading this chapter to realize how important achieving equity is within your relationship, so that you don't end up with a Lego house that's falling apart. While *equality* means that you both are provided the same resources and opportunity, *equity* takes it one step further and allocates those resources based on your specific circumstances to achieve the same outcome for all. If we're talking about splitting expenses within a relationship, *equality* would mean you pay for everything 50/50 regardless of your income. *Equity* would mean you split expenses proportional to your income so it's fair for both of you. But equity isn't just about how you split expenses; it's about how you decide to build your entire life together. Navigating finances as a couple means facing systems of inequity in your relationship head-on. To do that, we must dismantle some deep societal conditioning around gender roles and the patriarchy. Buckle up!

THE BREADWINNER MODEL

The feminist movement has worked to achieve more equity for women. We've seen some progress (although this has mostly been for white women, with BIPOC and other marginalized identities getting left behind in these efforts), with more women earning college degrees, working in traditionally male-dominated spaces, and gaining more leadership and political positions. However, this movement has not made much headway when it comes to how women are treated at home. American mothers spend more time on childcare today than mothers did in the '60s even though they are more likely to also be working a job. Western media, politics, and social systems still idealize a traditional cishet family dynamic where the husband is the provider and the wife is the homemaker. A survey of US adults showed that 71% of respondents felt men must be able to support their family financially in order to be a good husband/partner but only 32% felt the same about women. The notion of a breadwinner is antiquated, yet widespread. The term comes from the time when most cishet households were single income and relied on the men making the money and the women managing the household. Even though trends have shifted toward many women earning as much as their partners, and more dual family income models, certain relationship expectations and norms have stayed the same. It's common for men to feel threatened when the woman takes on the role of the breadwinner, even if that's been previously discussed as a couple.

The hesitancy to acknowledge the woman in a cishet relationship as the breadwinner comes from both partners, with women being even less likely to label themselves as the breadwinner of the family. Oof, I told you there was some deep conditioning here. The icing on the cake is that the less men earn, the less likely they are to help out at home. Somehow the woman in this scenario is now both the sole income provider and household manager. Women who are the top earners in their relationship are more likely to get divorced due to the tension this fact causes. Make it make sense, please.

If you are reading this and are the breadwinner in your relationship, please know you are killing it. Your success deserves to be celebrated and not diminished because it threatens your partner's ego. You should be able to celebrate your own accomplishments and feel proud that you're the sole provider for your family.

Although this type of research is practically nonexistent around non-cishet couples, in my experience, it's not uncommon in 2SLGBTQIA+ relationships for partners to unknowingly "take on" similar roles as cishet couples. Regardless of who you're dating, you can still experience tension around income disparity. It may not even show up as anger toward your partner; rather, it may manifest as shame toward yourself because you feel inadequate. What's interesting is that the research shows that it's the mentality of being the breadwinner rather than the money itself that is the problem. If your income is causing stress or resentment in your relationship, that dynamic will never go away unless you work through it.

Please also know that if you're a stay-at-home parent or any kind of caregiver, you're killing it. Managing the household, taking on the domestic labor, and raising children is equally important labor, even if it's unpaid. Paid work is often valued over unpaid work, and that's another form of inequity. We'll be talking more about domestic labor later in this chapter.

To achieve true equity in your relationship, you first have to start with the gender gap that exists within your own home. To address this gap, you need to be aware of the gender roles within your partnership as those may actually be a stronger indicator of relationship satisfaction.

THE ROLES WE PLAY

I had dated men my whole life until I started dating my current partner. One aspect about dating women that I didn't anticipate was the sheer volume of ingrained gender roles I would need to dismantle. I consider myself a feminist and thought I was pretty good at challenging traditional gender norms until I met my girlfriend. Suddenly it became painfully obvious how many roles I had subconsciously integrated in my life. I would allow men to pay for dinner more often than I would foot the bill. (Although I really don't regret that—reparations for the patriarchy, am I right?) When walking on a sidewalk, I automatically took the "inside" lane so I wasn't closest to the road. Although I never lived with a man, I'm sure if I did, I would have a million more examples of "household duties" that I wouldn't question my role in.

I know many of my friends in cishet relationships who completely slip into these gender expectations. As if on autopilot, they take on the cooking and the cleaning. Simultaneously, the men in these relationships are also falling into traditional gender roles. I've witnessed men fail to clean up after themselves because they know their partner will do it for them. The same men might call taking care of their own children "babysitting." These ideals are pounded into us from such a young age that we don't even notice we're upholding them. Or even worse, we notice the inequity but convince ourselves that doing the expected labor makes us more valuable as a partner.

Dating my girlfriend meant everything I knew about gender norms went out the window. We couldn't just easily slip into the expectations that society had laid out for us. We had to rewrite the rules. As children, we had both grown up in households that modeled traditional gender roles. My mom stayed at home to raise us and take care of the house while my dad went to work. My partner had a similar upbringing, even though her mom also worked as a nurse. Growing up with brothers, she was assigned certain chores (like washing the dishes) that they didn't have to do. Research is consistent with her experience, indicating that girls do more chores and specifically kitchen-related tasks than boys. Together we questioned every gender role that had been taught to us and instead created our own roles in the relationship.

I want to help you do the same, no matter who you're with. If you're a woman, I want to help you dismantle the internalized misogyny and gender norms that might affect you. If you're a man, I want to show you how much you're probably perpetuating these roles even if you don't mean to. If you're trans, nonbinary, Two-Spirit, or gender fluid, you might be fighting with both those areas, and I want you to find that middle ground. If you can challenge the gender roles that exist in your relationship, that's another step toward equity.

Step 1: Recognize Ingrained Gender Roles

The discussion of gender roles is deeply nuanced and must be viewed through the lens of culture. Culture informs how children are socialized, what they are taught, and what roles they are expected to adopt as adults. In North America, there is very clearly still inequity between genders and even more so in the case of those with marginalized identities. We teach girls how to nurture and care for others, be kind and respectful, and not make a fuss. Boys, on the other hand, are raised to be outspoken, independent, and strong. When you take into consideration factors like race, class, and culture, this socialization process becomes even more nuanced. Women are constantly told that their path in life, the ultimate source of fulfillment for them, is to get married and have children. But in cishet relationships, men often get to maintain their independence while women take on the responsibilities of the household and the children. In fact, it's *because* women are taking on the domestic labor that many men are able to succeed in their career.

Domestic labor is one of the biggest examples of inequitable gender expectations that we still commonly see upheld. The distribution of domestic work remains unequal across genders in the United States. It's estimated that women could make up to an extra $40,000 a year for their unpaid household labor. Ironically, the calculation for that number uses the average hourly wage for Americans, which would actually be less for women, and even lower if you're disabled or a woman of color. That's not including or considering the additional income women could secure if they weren't the ones responsible for most of the domestic labor.

It's the societal norms of more "feminine" vs. "masculine" tasks that drive the unequal division of labor. Many typical day-to-day household responsibilities, as well as the mental load that comes along with them, tend to be categorized as "feminine" tasks while things like yard work fall under "masculine" tasks. We can even see this idea perpetuated in some lesbian and queer relationships, where the more "masculine" partner may be perceived as the "man" of the relationship by outside observers (and sometimes even by the couple themselves). The problem in any partnership, of course, is that if you're the one constantly taking on most of the domestic labor and mental load, that will ultimately lead to resentment in the relationship.

One statistic I find extremely illuminating is that 70% of the top 1% earners in the United States have stay-at-home partners. While their partner is at home managing the domestic labor, they have the autonomy and capacity to focus on their career. It's not uncommon in this scenario that the partner who is out working will also be the one to manage the finances in the relationship. My goal is to help you create equitable relationships, and domestic labor plays a major role in that conversation. When talking about money with your partner, both paid and unpaid labor should be discussed. Getting clear on the gender roles you both uphold and expect from the other will allow you to recognize what needs to change. For women especially, it might be challenging to even identify these, because of how intensely we've been conditioned to uphold the patriarchy.

Think about what gender expectations you might be bringing into your own relationship. Keep in mind that the gender of your partner(s) doesn't matter. You can still enforce or uphold these norms outside a cishet or monogamous relationship. A good place to start is to go back to the reflection you already did around your culture and family in Chapter 7. Consider how any systems or expectations might have transferred over into your romantic partnerships as you answer the following questions:

- What traditional (or nontraditional) gender roles did your parents/caregivers model for you?
- What traditional gender roles are being modeled to you in everyday life through your workplace, social media, and entertainment?
- What jobs/roles/responsibilities do you tend to take on in your relationships? Why do you think that is?
- What jobs/roles/responsibilities does/do your partner(s) tend to take on in your relationship? Why do you think that is?
- When it comes to your finances, what responsibilities do each of you take on? (e.g., managing accounts, planning for future goals, keeping track of who owes who)
- What do you expect your partner(s) to do for you in a relationship? Consider household cleaning, maintenance, cooking/meal planning, laundry, and taking care of animals or children as a starting point. (e.g., have dinner ready when you come home from work, do the trip planning, pay for dinner, put away dishes after you've cleaned them, etc.)

PASSING THE MIC

Relationship Stories: Identifying Expectations

Meenadchi and Unika

M: *"I was very clear right from the first date that they were not going to pay, and there was no expectation to uphold stereotypical 'masculine' roles."*

Rebecca and Brendan

R: *"We had none. Both sets of our parents are my relationship role models and nothing in the house was up to specifically Mom or Dad, they shared all tasks. It was really refreshing to find someone who had the same ideals around 'gender norms' or roles."*

Janie, Maggie, and Cody

J: *"The expectation was that we weren't going to have specific roles. We've figured things out over time by having lots of discussions."*

Step 2: Identify What Needs to Change

Use the answers to the gender role questions to identify any inequity that exists within your relationship. It's important to clarify that while you can start reflecting on your own, ultimately this work has to be done *with* your partner(s). You might be able to easily pinpoint the areas of inequity that exist for you, but without input from your partner(s) you might not realize what is burdensome for them. Plus, nothing is going to change if everyone in the relationship isn't willing to commit and take it seriously. Educator, equitable labor advocate, and author Laura Danger says a good starting point

238 | Keeping Finance Personal

for your first conversation around domestic labor is talking about how much that dynamic is costing everyone. She recommends getting honest about how you're feeling, specifically where it's taking a toll in your relationship. Here are some questions to consider with your partner(s):

- How is the domestic labor currently divided in your household? (Think beyond just the tasks themselves and also consider the mental load.) Who is thinking about, planning, and executing household tasks?
- What is the cost of your current domestic labor division and setup? (e.g., one person is constantly tired and stressed, resentment is building, one person is doing all the parenting)
- Do you have equal access to rest? (remember that household work is still labor and should not be treated as "rest" just because that partner isn't working a paid job)

If you can pinpoint where the gender gap exists at home, and how it costs you, then you can start to implement changes. Decide what you want to change moving forward and take responsibility together.

What needs to change to achieve a more equitable household? If you're overwhelmed with where to start, here is a process you can walk through.

Review the tasks that you typically take on and evaluate whether you're the best person to take on that responsibility. Do the same for your partner(s). Make sure to consider the unique identity and needs of everyone. For example, if one of you is disabled or has a chronic illness, that may impact that partner's ability to complete certain tasks. Spend some time considering what capacity you have and what household roles you can reasonably take on every week.

Evaluate the system that you're using to manage your household tasks. Perhaps a new structure would work better to ensure equitable division of household labor. For me personally, if I don't visually see the task I need to do, or a reminder of that task, I will forget about it. So, lists are a very important tool for our household. Discuss whether the system you're currently using is working for both of you and adjust if needed.

Discuss the quality standard you each expect for these responsibilities. This means clearly communicating how you envision a certain task to be done. For example, "tidying up" might mean putting away clutter and fluffing the pillows to one person and wiping down all surfaces and vacuuming to another. If you are not on the same page in terms of how a responsibility should be carried out, this leaves room for disappointment. Coming up with a minimum agreed-upon standard will help you feel confident trusting each other to get the job done right.

Step 3: Work Toward Dismantling Gender Roles

Dismantling these old-school societal norms will not be an easy task. You will have to work on this for the duration of your relationship. Now that you're clear on what needs to change, it's time to commit. Open, honest communication will be your best friend. Later in this chapter we are going to cover how to approach these conversations with your partner(s), so for now I'll just leave you with some quick tips:

- Be honest about what you can realistically give physically and mentally (because let's not forget about mental load) to household tasks each day/week/month
- Directly discuss and agree upon how to split up domestic labor based on personal capacity and priorities
- If you have tasks left over after assigning them based on your capacity, consider seeking additional support (friend, family member, cleaner, hired professional, etc.)
- Gently call out when one partner isn't completing their agreed-upon tasks and reassess your plan if need be
- Set up regular check-ins because life changes and things come up, and it's important to keep an open line of communication
- Create a "bad day protocol" that you can implement when one partner is struggling mentally or has reduced capacity

RESOURCE

Domestic Labor Resources, page 315

PASSING THE MIC

Relationship Stories: Working Toward Equity

Maggie and Yuvraj

M: *"We started using the Fair Play cards to spark discussions about dividing up household labor when we move in together."*

Hannah and Kristen

H: *"Because Kristen is more marginalized, I recognize that I have to give more in certain ways. To us, part of achieving equity means that Kristen doesn't need to educate me on race-related issues."*

Rebecca and Brendan

R: *"We assess situations as they come up, together. We never make assumptions on how the other person may feel or think. This way we can be flexible with each other about what's needed at home."*

Janie, Maggie, and Cody

J: *"We've had lots of conversations and continue to bring things up if one person feels they are doing more work than the others. We also approach things on a case-by-case basis, like if someone has a really busy week at work and communicates that, then we can pick up the slack."*

UNDERSTANDING AND NAVIGATING DIFFERENCES

One of my ex-boyfriends used to spend a lot of his money on weed and on takeout. There's nothing inherently wrong with that; it was his money and he could use it however he wanted. The issue was that this spending was starting to impact our relationship. He was spending outside his means and always ended up having to borrow money from people at the end of the month. As a result, we weren't able to do a lot of things together that we wanted to. As our relationship progressed, I began to think about our future. How would he afford half our bills if we moved in together? Would we ever be able to go on vacation? He had no desire to change his spending and wasn't willing to put much effort in to improve the situation for both of us. At this point, I knew we weren't a money match.

In contrast, when my girlfriend and I were navigating our financial struggles, we were both putting in the work to change our situation. She was regularly going to therapy and reprocessing her beliefs around work and money.

I was working on my own mindset around the situation and experimenting with different ways to approach the topic of money. I realized that I was trying to tackle too much in one conversation. We didn't need to solve all our problems in one night; in fact, attempting to do so was hurting both of us. Instead, we needed to have a little bit of fun and release the pressure. We shifted the conversations to focus on our exciting goals in the future, what engagement rings we wanted, and where we would love to travel. I reassured her that we were okay financially and that I could manage the bills for a while longer. She shared her breakthroughs in therapy and her plans for beginning to search for a job. We both held compassion for the other's experience and that allowed us to move through the challenges together. You cannot navigate finances as a team unless you truly understand each other's money story.

Understanding Yourself

To get on the same page with your finances, it's imperative that you understand your own money story first. Based on all the previous reflections we've done, you should have a pretty good idea of your underlying beliefs, habits, values, and goals. Refer back to your previous money story reflections to consider and share some of the important aspects with your partner, such as your childhood, cultural and familial values, past trauma, the impact of your identity, and other financial lived experiences.

Answer this question: **What does money mean to you?**

For some, money is a source of freedom. It allows for independence and the ability to make choices without restriction. For others, money provides safety and comfort. It allows for a sense of security because all basic needs are met. Defining what money means to you is important because this is the root of many of your motivations and goals.

 **QUEERD CO. COMMUNITY COMMENTS**

"Money has transformed me into an independent young lady that can do anything. I can raise money, I can spend money, I can grow it, I can keep it, I can channel it into ways that transform other people's lives. I'm no longer in survival mode. I'm in thriving mode, and now I want to share that wealth and service with everyone around me who will listen."

—Vanessa

"You cannot expect money to be the source of your happiness, but you also can't ignore that without the level that you need for your basic needs, it impacts your ability to find and access joy. I was able to understand that money doesn't equal happiness, but it does give you a certain level of comfort, and that comfort gives you privilege."

—Jenny

"I think one of the greatest examples is that I wouldn't have my toddler right now if I didn't have money, if I didn't experience the type of freedom that money provides you. I was very conscious, when I was debating whether or not I wanted to go through with my pregnancy, of whether or not I was financially stable enough to provide for this child. That was really important for me."

—Nina

List Out Your Personal Values

You've just completed the chapter on personal values, so this should be fresh in your mind.

Get Clear On Your Financial Goals

We will dive into goal-setting more a bit later (see Chapter 12), but for now, list your top 5 financial goals that you want to achieve in the next 10 or so years. This will give you a rough idea of your life direction, which you can discuss with your partner(s).

List Out Your Financial Non-Negotiables

Your non-negotiables are all the financial aspects you're not willing to compromise on. These could be priorities—like having X number of children or buying a home—that you're not willing to give up. Or they could be certain behaviors or habits that are deal-breakers for you. For instance, Lexa VanDamme, founder of the Avocado Toast Budget, says that she will likely never fully combine finances or live full-time with a partner. She set these boundaries based on her own experience, and they will serve as financial non-negotiables in future partnerships.

Understanding Each Other

You've put in the work to know your own money story; the next step is understanding each other's money stories. Finances are such an integral part of a relationship, and having a partner who is a money match is crucial. In a presentation on money and relationships, mindset coach and speaker Dr. Joi Madison pointed out that being a money match involves "compatibility, not carbon copy." Ideally, we want a partner who will complement our differences, not necessarily a partner who mirrors our money story. I would say that the biggest component of managing finances as a couple is having awareness and compassion for both of your money stories. Each of you brings your own trauma and lived experience to the table. If you're in an interracial or intercultural relationship, you're also navigating the different ways you move through the world. If you want to build a life together, you'll need to find a way to balance your different backgrounds, childhood experiences, values, goals, and worldviews. It can be done, but it's going to take some work. Here are a couple tips for understanding your partner's money story better:

Tip #1: Observe

Start observing the way that your partner approaches money without judgment. Pay attention to the language they use, and the habits they have. **How do they choose to spend and manage their money?**

Tip #2: Get Curious

Express interest in your partner's money story. In an open, nonjudgmental way, explicitly ask them about behaviors you observe and where they stem from. Ask them about their values, goals, and intentions with money. Share your own findings from the "understanding yourself" section of this chapter.

Tip #3: Acceptance

Recognize how your differences affect your relationship and also impact your finances. Notice if your dissimilarities complement or conflict with each other. If there's conflict between your differences, important decisions or compromises will need to be made.

PASSING THE MIC

Relationship Stories: Understanding Differences

Maggie and Yuvraj

M: *"The messaging we received growing up was very different. I was told to follow my passions and was encouraged to do that, but Yuvraj was told to get the good job and good salary. I also have celiac disease and so I have a very different relationship to food. This can cause conflict when we are planning a trip and decide to pay proportionally but my food cost is so much higher so the expectation of what we would be spending isn't accurate."*

Hannah and Kristen

K: *"We have racial and culture differences. Hannah is white, and I'm Black, from an immigrant family with expectations that I provide financial support to my family."*

Meenadchi and Unika

U: *"The differences I've noticed have been mostly in our upbringing, and the trauma I went through as a child and young adult. What is important to us when it comes to money is different."*

Rebecca and Brendan

R: *"I am half Indian, half African American. My parents had me when they were 20 and built their wealth without generational wealth to assist them. He is a white male, parents had him late in life, and he benefits from generational wealth from both sides of his parents' families. At the beginning of our relationship, it REALLY impacted our connection. He had to learn a lot about how the world outside of his privilege works. There was a long period of time—I want to say a year—where we were having very open and deep conversations with both of our families around our differences."*

I realized that my ex didn't want the same type of life that I was striving for and I had to either give up my dreams or walk away. Having differences isn't a bad thing, but how are you going to approach those differences? If neither of you is willing to find a middle ground, money will always be a point of tension in your relationship. It will likely hold one or both of you back and lead to resentment in the future. Be honest with each other about where you're at financially, where you want to be, and how you want to spend your money throughout life. This is not the time to hold back or to adjust your answers to please your partner(s). Understanding how you each envision the role of money in your life is just as important as knowing whether you want kids. If being a parent was the biggest dream in your life, would you marry someone who didn't ever want kids? Probably not. Decisions like what you want to save for, what type of lifestyle you want to live, and how you want to retire are just as major.

Choosing a partner you're going to build a life with involves so much more than love. If you're not willing to compromise when it comes to your finances, then it may not be the relationship for you. Listen, I don't want to break anyone up here, okay? I just want you to have an incredible, equitable, and rich life with your partner(s). Far too often we try to fit our lives into relationships instead of finding a relationship that just fits with our life.

MINDFUL MOMENT

While honest discussion is critical in a financially healthy relationship, it's also important to be on the lookout for any financial red flags from your partner. Financial abuse is defined as *"behavior that seeks to control a person's ability to acquire, use, or maintain economic resources, and threatens their self-sufficiency and financial autonomy."* It's an especially sneaky form of domestic abuse that creates a toxic power dynamic. A big red flag is when one partner takes charge of managing all the money. This might be the case for many of you right now, and I'm not suggesting your partner is abusing you, but it is something to be aware of. In my interview with Laura Danger, she said, *"If you don't have the choice to leave, then you might not be in that relationship willingly."* Whether either of you realize it or not, one partner having complete control over the finances gives them more power.

Examples of Financial Abuse:
- Running up large amounts of debt on joint accounts
- Controlling how all the money is spent
- Limiting (or removing) access to bank accounts
- Hiding assets
- Forbidding the victim to work
- Ruining a victim's credit score
- Not including victim in investment or banking decisions

I chatted with Lexa VanDamme, founder of the Avocado Toast Budget, about her experience with financial abuse. Her partner wouldn't allow her to quit her job to pursue content creation unless she had 6 months' worth of expenses saved up. Lexa told me, *"At the time, that seemed totally normal. Like, this is the person I'm in a relationship with. This is how things should go."* Then one day her partner came home and informed her they had quit their job without any notice. The financial abuse went further, and Lexa's partner persuaded her to put their expenses on her credit card. Lexa was in credit card debt herself but was under the impression her partner didn't have any money left. It came out later that her partner had $30,000 sitting in the bank that could have been used. Escape and recovery from these situations are challenging because the victim often cannot access the money they need to leave. Lexa recalls that a big reason she was able to leave that abusive relationship was because she had the financial means to.

"I had started saving for myself and just having that cushion and knowing that if I wanted to, I could have some more freedom, move, leave, or get access to resources that I needed was huge. And for me, building up that emergency fund, building up savings when possible, was so helpful in being able to help me with that freedom."

If you think you might be experiencing financial abuse, please seek out support and start saving up some money that your partner(s) doesn't have access to. I've included resources to help get you started in the resource section.

RESOURCE

Financial Abuse Resources, page 316

HOW TO TALK ABOUT MONEY

Why is it so damn *uncomfortable* to talk about money? Talking about money is often seen as "rude" or "probing." We are told it's not appropriate to ask people about their finances. Girls are told not to discuss topics like money, while boys get taught about finances, investing, and career advancement. It's no wonder women get paid less than men when their first money conversation is the salary negotiation for their entry-level job. The taboo around money was designed to maintain the status quo and leave folks with marginalized

MONEY TABOO CYCLE *

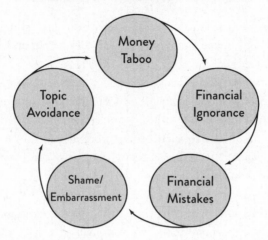

identities out of the conversation. Not talking about money upholds the capitalist system. We avoid talking about our finances, which leads to us not knowing how to ask for help, which results in financial mistakes that leave us feeling guilty and shameful, and the cycle continues.

In relationships, the shame you're carrying around money intensifies. Everything feels more serious because you love this other person and don't want to push them away. You might fear that disclosing your financial situation will make them see you as "flawed" or "unlovable." Many of my clients feel that their partner is "good with money" and that they are the weak link in the relationship. This belief is part of the money taboo, because instead of being able to talk about money and actually get clear on their situation, they are just speculating. Just because someone appears to be "good with money" doesn't mean that they don't have financial issues, or that they are superior to you, or that their system even makes sense for you as a couple.

If you're nervous to have money conversations with your partner, you're not alone. Nearly 40% of adults steer clear of talking about money with their significant other. By avoiding these topics, you risk ending up with that unstable Lego house foundation we talked about. Let's face it head-on, shall we?

---

* Adapted from: http://www.decisionfish.com/the-money-taboo-what-can-we-do
-about-it-talk/.

How to Have a Money Conversation

1. Release the pressure or expectation that you're going to cover everything in the first conversation. You won't, and you don't want to, either.
2. Give your partner a heads-up when you want to have a finance conversation so that you can both feel prepared and present.
3. Ease into the conversation with some lighthearted, general money questions to each other (prompts provided at the end of the chapter). You don't need to deep dive into your financial trauma right away!
4. If your partner isn't feeling comfortable yet, speak about your own situation first. Mention things you're struggling with, achievements you're proud of, and goals you have. Don't pressure them to share until they are ready.

Important Money Conversation Tips

- Talking about money isn't rude!!!
- Remember that both of you have a different money story, lived experience, and trauma.
- Someone's feelings around money are valid (even if they don't make sense to you!).
- Emotions may run high: take breaks when you need to.
- Avoid criticism and judgment.
- Just hold space for them! You don't need to have "answers" to people's struggles.
- Practice active listening.
- See a professional if you need help with facilitating these conversations.

My last piece of advice is: don't avoid the big, scary money topics! You can start small and dip your toes in, but make sure you still prioritize those heavier subjects. In the Putting It into Practice section, I provide a checklist of some key topics to cover together.

PASSING THE MIC

Relationship Stories: Talking About Money

Maggie and Yuvraj

M: "I had fears that I would be viewed as a gold digger or not pulling my weight or contributing enough because I'm an actor and he's an engineer. There was some awkwardness to it, but I was excited we were able to have those conversations. I was like wow, we can talk about this and it's fine."

Hannah and Kristen

H: "There was a lot of fear because I saw money be a huge conflict for my parents. It felt way too soon to talk about money because I thought that talking about money meant the relationship was really serious."

K: "I was nervous to share at the beginning, and I had seen relationships and marriages fail because of money. I don't want her to feel like she's responsible for my finances."

Rebecca and Brendan

R: "We had our first big money conversations when we were planning on moving in together and planning our futures together. We started to talk about what we made annually, how we see bills/household things being split, etc., and then the conversation evolved as we started talking about other expenses like vacations and getting married, getting a dog, etc. Brendan was way more used to having these conversations as his family dynamic with money was different. He knows everything now; he's helped me with my budget, and we have check-ins regularly as we have saving goals together!"

Janie, Maggie, and Cody

J: *"Our first money conversation was about a year into our relationship. Maggie and Cody bought a king-size bed so all of us could fit and put it on a payment plan and I asked to pay for part of it. I was always nervous to have those conversations initially, but it was less about money and more about communicating. I started going to therapy in 2017 because my communication skills weren't going to cut it anymore."*

STRATEGIES FOR MANAGING MONEY AS A TEAM

My girlfriend landed a job around 7 months after we moved. Our shift to more lighthearted conversation allowed us to feel excited about our finances. Now that we were adding a second income, our next hurdle was figuring out how we wanted to manage our money as a couple. How would we split expenses? What accounts did we want to use? Should we open joint accounts? What about savings and investments? There are a ton of different methods and strategies for merging your finances out there, so let's walk through some of the options.

As you've learned from the various interviews throughout this chapter, all relationship dynamics are unique, which requires a unique financial approach. You're likely going to have to compromise on some areas here because everyone has a different approach to money management. Remember that these tangible techniques are just one piece of a larger picture (or I should say, one piece of Lego within your Lego house). Don't forget about the gender roles, domestic labor, and money stories we discussed earlier. Take bits and pieces of my suggestions to build an ideal plan for your dynamic.

Split expenses based on income. This is perhaps my most controversial opinion when it comes to managing finances together. I believe that in order to achieve equity within your relationship, you shouldn't split expenses 50/50. Instead, it should be based on a percentage of your income (along with other relevant considerations, such as physical ability, capacity, domestic labor, etc.). Following a 50/50 split when you have different incomes means that one person will be at a disadvantage. Whoever is making less money will also then have less money to save or invest. For example, I make more money than my girlfriend. We calculated that I earn around 60% of our total household income. I pay 60% of our monthly expenses, she pays 40%. To do this, you can either divide each individual bill, or just divvy up your expenses so they equal out to an appropriate split.

Separate spending cards. I swear this advice saves relationships. Keep your spending cards separate; don't ever combine them. As long as you've discussed how much each of you are spending a month, and it's not interfering with your other joint goals, then you don't need to know anything else. That's just my personal opinion; however, some couples like setting guidelines such as purchases over a certain dollar amount should be jointly discussed. You may want a joint spending card in addition to your individual cards for ongoing purchases you make together.

Create joint savings for shared goals. I found it both easier and more encouraging to have joint savings accounts when working toward a common goal. This way you can track your overall progress more easily, and it's motivating when you see the other person contributing. Clarify expectations by discussing how much each of you is going to contribute each week or month. Make sure to consider other financial responsibilities you both have and how that would impact your savings goals.

Keep some savings separate. I'm a strong advocate for having completely separate safety funds (refer back to the financial sidebar in Chapter 3 for a refresher on these funds!) for a couple of reasons: (1) you might have emergency expenses that just apply to you and that wouldn't make sense for your partner to contribute to, and (2) it protects you. We just heard from Lexa about how her emergency fund made it possible to leave her unhealthy relationship. Lack of financial access keeps people trapped in abusive situations.

Like I said earlier, there are many different approaches to managing money as a couple. My parents have had completely combined finances since they married, and it works great for them. That can make any potential separation very messy, but hey, you do you. Currently, my partner and I keep our finances pretty separate, but we are both completely in the loop on what's happening. There's no one right way to combine finances, so take your time figuring out what's going to work best for you. Make sure to consider the needs of each other so that the plan is sustainable for both of you.

PASSING THE MIC

Relationship Stories: Figuring Out What Works

Maggie and Yuvraj

M & Y: *"If you can get those big conversations out of the way early, you don't have to stress about it so much. Ask yourself: Is this someone I want to date? Did they react in a way that feels in alignment to my values? Release expectations that there is a 'right' way and do what works best for you as a couple."*

Hannah and Kristen

H & K: *"We started doing a shared date fund, where we each set aside $100 for a date night and then we plan together what we want to do."*

Meenadchi and Unika

U: *"I tend to externally shut down when conversations are hard, and so we take breaks in our serious conversations."*

Rebecca and Brendan

R: *"Have ALL the open conversations, until it's no longer uncomfortable. Have deep conversations about what you want, in every aspect of your relationship, money included. Once it's out there, it's so much easier to navigate EVERYTHING, together! Talk it out."*

Janie, Maggie, and Cody

J: *"We have family meetings every Sunday and have lots of time to talk about finances. It's become a ritual of being in the same environment at the dining room table, everyone puts their phones away and gives their undivided attention. We make sure everyone has time to share their thoughts on a matter, and we don't move on until then."*

WRAPPING IT UP

My hope is that you're feeling way more confident about how to navigate your finances within your unique relationship dynamic. You've heard from folks in a variety of different relationships about the barriers they faced and the intersectional complexities that arose. You've also seen the potential repercussions of avoiding these conversations. All that's left to do is put what you've learned into practice. It's time to work on your Lego house. Stabilize your foundation, dismantle those gender roles, face your financial trauma, and start putting the pieces together. The more Lego pieces you add, the stronger the structure becomes. Brick by brick, you can build an amazing, equitable home together.

PUTTING IT INTO PRACTICE

Make sure you've answered the earlier reflection questions in this chapter first!!

1. Have a Money Date Night! Just because finances can be boring doesn't mean your money conversations have to be. Turn your nerve-wracking money talks into a fun date. Cook your favorite meal together or order takeout, make yummy drinks, put on good music, and light some candles. Use this time to have a serious money conversation, create a budget together, or set up some joint financial systems. Add on another fun activity you both love to make the experience more enjoyable.

As we've discussed, money conversations aren't one and done, so I suggest making your Money Dates a reoccurring thing. This could be once a week, month, or even quarter, depending on what's feasible for you. Whatever you decide, commit to it. You'll thank me later.

2. Use the following prompts as a starting point to talk about money:

   o How comfortable do you feel talking about money?
   o What did you learn about money as a child?
   o What did your parents think/say to you about money?
   o Did you get an allowance as a child? Where did that money go?
   o What financial choices are you ashamed or embarrassed about?
   o What is a money habit of mine that you admire?
   o What does "good with money" mean to you?
   o What does "financial freedom" mean to you?
   o Tell me about your current financial situation—what debts are you currently working on paying off? Are you saving for retirement? Do you have savings/investments?
   o What is your annual and monthly income?
   o How do you like to spend your money?
   o What would you like to learn more about when it comes to finances?
   o Do you want to support anyone else with your money? (partner(s), future children, parents, siblings, etc.)

o   How has the pandemic changed how you view your finances?
o   What is your biggest financial goal right now?
o   What are your future financial goals?
o   If you won the lottery, how would you spend that money?

3. Go through this checklist together to see what important topics you still have to cover.

o   Moving in together—When? Where? What will that look like?
o   Domestic labor—How will it be divided up? What's the standard of completion?
o   Marriage—Yes or no? And why?
o   Wedding—Yes or no? What's your vision? How much money do you want to spend?
o   Pre/postnuptials—Yes or no? What does that look like?
o   Children—Yes or no? And why?
o   If it's a yes to children—How are you planning to be parents? If you cannot conceive, are you prepared to pay for alternative options? How will you financially support them? Will you pay for their college?
o   Raising a child—Is there an expectation that one of you stays home with the child? How are you balancing work and parenting? Discuss household labor again!
o   Spending—What do we want to spend money on together? Separately?
o   Debt—Do you have any? Is there an expectation that you tackle debt together?
o   Big financial goals—What are they? How does your partner fit into those?
o   Owning a home—Yes or no? What does that look like?
o   Life insurance—Do we want it? What type makes sense for you?
o   Retirement—What will that look like? When will it begin? How much can we live off of?

CHAPTER 11

The Currency of Cool

THE KEY TO DITCHING SOCIETY'S DEFINITION OF SUCCESS

The year this book is published I will celebrate my 29th birthday. I'm right at the age when people look at you and think *you should have your life together by now.* I should be in my prime, making good money, working my dream job, getting married, buying a home, and having lots of children. It feels like I'm teetering on the edge of my twenties, when the world doesn't expect much from me yet, about to be thrust into my thirties when suddenly my success is measured and scrutinized. I think most of us have recognized, especially after learning about the generational divide, that the path to success laid out by older generations is not the way society operates anymore. Yet the narratives we are told still haven't caught up to that realization.

Society defines success as having a prestigious job, driving an expensive car, and owning a beautiful house. The goals that many people set for themselves are rooted in their desire to avoid shame and instead receive praise and respect from their peers. The societal expectations placed on young folks can feel debilitating and greatly impact decision making. If you follow that path and fall short, you've failed. If you dare to pursue your own path, live outside the box, and reject these definitions of success, you're ostracized. It can feel impossible to win when the system is working against you.

In this chapter I want to explore some of the overarching societal expectations of our times. There are many, but I'm going to stick to three broad expectations that we are told to pursue in order to be successful.

1. Work hard
2. Aim higher
3. Build wealth

For each one of these rules, I will be exploring the following:

The expectation: how society portrays this rule

The consequence: the side effects that come with pursuing this expectation

The reality: the very real barriers that make this rule unattainable for most

The transformation: how you can redefine this rule and work within your constraints

My goal is that you will leave this chapter feeling empowered to make your own decisions and design the life that you want while also accepting and understanding the barriers that are working against you. Ready?

EXPECTATION #1: WORK HARD

The Expectation

Hard work is a pillar of the American dream. Just work hard and you'll achieve whatever you want. With this mindset, we are told that it's normal to live for your job when you're first starting out. You need to grind and hustle now so that you can relax in retirement.

The Consequence

We design our lives in a way that leaves us perpetually chasing more. More money, more success, more power. As soon as we reach a milestone, we're on to the next one without stopping to catch our breath. Capitalism banks on this reality, which will only push you to work harder and devalue your previous accomplishments.

Hustle culture is the biggest capitalist trap. But we do it because we are told that hard work is something to be admired. Employees who can pick up any project and drop everything at a moment's notice are labeled as flexible and considered team players. The more you buy into hustle culture, the greater the pressure to perform, which opens you up to a lot of comparison. Resentment builds against all the people who are being rewarded despite them not working as hard as you.

We ultimately develop internalized capitalism, which is when we believe our self-worth is tied to our work. We are not worthy unless we are productive. If we are unable to work, we feel ashamed. If we rest too much, we feel ashamed. If we don't produce enough, we feel ashamed. It completely erodes our sense of self, making us an easy target for manipulation. Some examples of internalized capitalist narratives are:

- Feeling guilty for resting, even when sick or struggling
- Putting productivity above health
- Feeling shame over being "lazy"

Internalized capitalism is exploitative and creates a hierarchical ranking system of productiveness in society. Work is praised and rest is frowned upon. The more people adopt this narrative, the more big companies can exploit their workers while raking in the profits.

I know without a doubt that I have internalized capitalism, and I'd bet most of you do too. It's hard to escape it while living within a capitalist society. When I started my own business, I saw it as an opportunity to create the work environment I always wanted. I told myself I'd only work 5 hours a day, 5 days a week, and I'd be flexible with what days and times I actually worked. Ahh, what a lovely, naive lie I told myself. Instead, I worked all the time. I blew off friends to spend time working on a project. If I didn't finish my to-do list for the day, I would feel guilty all week. It never felt like I was doing enough, and if I'm honest, sometimes it still feels like that. I feel that right now as I'm writing this book, as though each day my best just isn't quite good enough.

The feeling of not being good enough and not doing enough will ruin your life. It will take everything you love away from you because it will make you believe that you're not worthy of any of it. That voice inside your head will convince you that nobody will want to be with you because of where you're at in your career, how much money you make, and what you've achieved. It will further isolate you from everyone and everything you know and love. You'll lose your hobbies and your passions as you toss them aside for work. You'll let your mental and physical health deteriorate just so you can impress your boss.

The Reality

Before we go further, I want to clarify that there is a difference between working hard at something and the extreme hustle culture that encourages overworking and burnout. It feels amazing to put your all into an endeavor and know that you did your best. There's nothing wrong with enjoying your work and doing it well, even in a society that struggles with internalized capitalism.

The reality is that it's not as simple as "just work hard." Being successful and building wealth is not dependent on how hard you work. There are people doing grueling, challenging jobs, and getting paid peanuts. Many people have to hustle to survive, but the glorification of hustle culture reduces the reality of those struggling to make ends meet. This mindset is inherently classist because hard work can only bring you success if you are already holding the key.

There are many reasons why someone cannot meet society's expectations of what constitutes "hard work." Mental health challenges and disability can impact your ability to find a suitable workplace environment, and even employment in general. You may have constraints on how many hours you can work due to an injury, disability, or your children. If you experience discrimination or harassment at your job, this could stop you from coming into work as often as you otherwise would. In the next section, we'll talk about wage gaps, another inequity that reveals the lie of the "work harder" mentality.

Constantly pushing ourselves to work harder and pursue money or career advancement over everything leads to burnout, plain and simple. Burnout is now recognized by the World Health Organization as a source of stress and poor well-being that demands mental health support. Common characteristics of burnout include cynicism, lethargy, and depression, as well as feeling alienated from yourself, a sense of purpose, and work. The more that you are exposed to chronic stressors, the more likely you are to experience burnout. In the context of hustle culture, we are told we don't deserve rest until we burn out, but even in less toxic work environments, rest is usually only encouraged when you're feeling tired, or your mental health is suffering. It's almost never suggested as a preventative measure.

If you are burying yourself in work as a coping mechanism, you could develop workaholism. Overworking could also be linked to your pursuit of wealth and an underlying scarcity mindset. Corporate culture practically breeds workaholism, giving young professionals seemingly justifiable reasons for obsessive working. We get stuck in these traps because of the deep desire to be appreciated and praised. The longing to be noticed by our boss, hear the verbal affirmation that we are doing a good job, or achieve some abstract recognition in our industry is insatiable. For some, there is also the pressure from family to reach a certain level of success. Workaholics will often defend their intense work ethic by saying that as soon as they reach a specific salary or promotion, they will slow down. But they barely even need to defend their unhealthy work-life balance, because society approves of it. The problem with hinging your access to rest on something as unmeasurable as success is that you'll never feel satisfied enough to stop.

Let's also not ignore the fact that perhaps we don't actually want to hustle our whole lives. Despite the deeply ingrained capitalist narratives, I desire a slow life. I want to work enough to support my needs and stop there. Hard work isn't a prerequisite for success and there isn't just one way to define success. The prioritization of rest in itself is anti-capitalist.

The Transformation

Fighting back against the narrative that we need to work hard to be successful is not going to be easy. What's challenging about internalized capitalism is that your socioeconomic status can make it difficult to distance yourself from this narrative. If you're living in poverty, or paycheck to paycheck, hearing me tell you to rest probably makes you want to put down this book. There is a lot of nuance involved when speaking about how to rest more, or fight internalized capitalism. It's true that there are very real, tangible systems of oppression and barriers working against people that make it hard to work less and rest more, and it's also true that it's important to do what you can to reimagine capitalism. Both can exist at the same time.

As I share some suggestions on how you can pave your own way in the world of hustle culture, please know that my intent is not to minimize your challenges. I'm not denying that there are valid reasons why you can't work less, or why you're pushing yourself so hard. I recognize that I hold a lot of privilege and will never understand some of your struggles. I know that it's damn near impossible to completely heal from internalized capitalism while still living within capitalism. Trust me, if I could burn all those systems to the ground tomorrow, I would. Unfortunately, I can't do that, but what I can offer you are some examples of small ways you can start to take back your power from the system that is working against you.

Set boundaries between yourself and work. This involves creating space and essentially defining your limits. Give yourself a hard start and end time and honor that. Delete the email app off your phone on weekends. Stop responding outside work hours. Start communicating the project load you have to your boss so that they understand when you're at capacity.

If that feels too scary . . . start small. Begin with something easier like simply taking a lunch break if you weren't doing so before. Work up to taking your full allotted time. Get out of the office, or out of the house during breaks. Take a 5-minute walk before and after your workday. Move your desk out of your bedroom. Or if that's not possible (I lived with my desk in my bedroom for years), try to create a visual and mental separation between your work-space and bed. My number one tip here is to create some sort of transition routine between the end of your work and whatever is coming next—whether you're going home to your family, out to meet friends, getting in a workout, or going home to sleep. Having a routine will tell your brain it's time to clock out and leave work stress behind. Other end-of-work transition ideas:

- Listen to a meditation or calming music
- Close your laptop, push in your chair, shut the office door, all with intention, mindfully recognizing you're closing the door on your workday
- Repeat a positive affirmation to yourself
- Wash your face or take a shower
- Take a walk

Advocate for yourself. This involves being able to recognize and artic-ulate your needs to others. If it's safe for you to do so, ask for necessary accommodations at work. These could include the type of work conditions or environment you need to thrive, understanding of how you best learn and understand, the way you approach tasks, and where you need support. If you're struggling in your current job, try to pinpoint the root of those chal-lenges and if there are any accommodations that might improve your situa-tion. Pay attention to your natural energy ebbs and flows and learn how to honor them. For example, if you menstruate, you could plan the type of work you do around your cycle and energy levels. The more you practice asking for what you need, the easier it'll become.

Celebrate your "done list." At the end of your workday, when you start thinking about everything you didn't accomplish and everything you have to do tomorrow, stop and take a second to celebrate what you *did* do. Look at everything you crossed off your list and then go beyond the list. Think about the intangible wins you had that day. It could be the delicious sandwich you had for lunch, the catch-up phone call with your long-distance friend, saying no to a project that you didn't have capacity for, or just getting through the day without crying. I highly recommend creating a habit around this, where you finish each workday with a mini celebration of your "done list" and a more realistic understanding of what you accomplished.

Learn how internalized capitalism impacts you. Understanding where it comes from and how it shows up in your daily life can be a validating practice. Recognize that internalized capitalism is widespread in our culture. When you find yourself feeling guilty for resting, or like you haven't done enough, ask yourself where that comes from. Get curious about who initiated the narrative in the first place, you or capitalism?

Give yourself permission to rest. You don't need to earn rest. Resting does not mean you're lazy or self-indulgent. Rest is necessary. It's a human right. You are worthy of rest. Does wealth give you more access to rest? Yes. But that doesn't mean we can't incorporate intentional rest into our lives now. There are actually 7 different types of rest: physical, mental, emotional, spiritual, sensory, social, and creative. Here are some ways you can practice each of them:

1. **Physical:** full night of sleep, napping, stretching, massage
2. **Mental:** being present, taking work breaks, medication
3. **Emotional:** talking to a loved one or therapist, advocating for your needs
4. **Spiritual:** meditation, community involvement, gratitude practice
5. **Sensory:** turning off overhead lighting, sitting in a quiet space, unplugging from technology
6. **Social:** spending time alone, hanging out with people who you can be yourself around, avoiding a packed social calendar
7. **Creative:** being out in nature, doing a hobby for fun, going to an art exhibit

When you're experiencing burnout, you probably need to engage in all 7 types of rest, but that in itself is exhausting. Start with the area that you're lacking the most rest in first. Carve out 10 minutes of your day to simply rest. 10 minutes a day that you reclaim for yourself.

MINDFUL MOMENT

Anti-capitalist money coach Ada Vargas (they/them) shares their advice as a nonbinary, queer, first-generation immigrant on how to prioritize rest and navigate guilt while trying to survive in a capitalist society.

One of the things that changed my financial journey is having a vision of not just keeping our heads above water. This is a tricky thing because we do live in an environment that is trying to keep us just barely there or below the water. We live in an environment that requires money in order for us to have rest.

I think that people who come from marginalized and systemically oppressed communities deserve to live in those environments of rest and abundance, and all of us do. But there can also be feelings of guilt that come with access to those things. If you start to accumulate money, there's a lot that gets triggered. You're, like, now I'm different than my tribe, and are they going to disown me? But in a way, you can really flip the script and have the rest that your ancestors before you never had.

I want people to realize that investing is accessible to them and that they don't have to have hundreds or thousands of dollars to start building wealth. Like, you don't even have to have a Social Security number to invest. It's not your responsibility to fix the system by abstaining from it in a world where there isn't another way that you're going to get to have a funded retirement with the rest you deserve. Enough has been taken from you over the length of history that you don't have to carry the burden of morality on your shoulders. Use that money to do the things that capitalism hates. Like resting, or providing mutual aid for other people in your community, or having options to leave a toxic workplace, the choice to retire early, and to do the kinds of things that maybe don't seem at all possible. Just have that vision of your future self in order to not be stuck in that just barely above water moment forever.

EXPECTATION #2: AIM HIGHER

The Expectation

You should always be aiming higher. Get a degree or professional designation, land a good, high-paying job, and climb the corporate ladder in order to be successful and make a lot of money. If you work your way up in a company, you'll be rich. Once you've maxed out career income, monetize every other aspect of your life. Use that money to buy nice things, go on a fancy vacation, or build your dream home and show off your success.

The Consequence

Building off the idea that you must "work hard" for success comes the expectation of climbing the corporate ladder. Pair the toxicity of hustle culture with company loyalty and you've got the perfect recipe for easily manipulated employees. Corporate America created an army of loyal workers who bought into the facade of stability. We were all sold on it. You want to land a solid, steady 9-to-5 job that you can rely on. Don't stop there, though, keep climbing higher, work your way up to management, that's where the real money is.

If you went to college (which you were likely encouraged to do as it's painted as a straight shot to a successful life), you were essentially trained how to be cutthroat in the pursuit of wealth. College creates a breeding ground for competition, consistently pitting your success against that of your classmates. That environment is replicated in the workplace. Many companies don't care about the well-being of their employees, they just want to keep everyone always striving for more. Within this culture, all the boss has to do is dangle the carrot and their entire team is putting in overtime for a chance to bite it.

Sometimes, it's not even about climbing the corporate ladder and getting a promotion but the prestige that comes with it. Being able to tell your peers or your family your professional title and bask in the adoration that follows.

Because as long as you have that validation that you checked the right box, you can ignore what it's costing you. In fact, you can curate a public perception of yourself entirely detached from reality with material goods. You can bury the fact that you're struggling or unfulfilled with expensive clothes and a fancy new car. But this holds only until you perceive someone else to be doing better than you. Suddenly what you have isn't enough; you need to strive for more.

You may not resonate with the need to purchase material goods like cars or handbags, but there are sneakier ways this comparison shows up. It comes down to a deep dissatisfaction with being where you are, having what you have, and existing as you are. You scroll on social media and you see these people your age who seem to be doing it all. Maybe they are a student, running their own business, staying in shape, and still finding time to hang out with their friends. You wonder why you can't do more as a student. You feel less than for not working in addition to studying for your courses.

I've never cared about what car I drove, and I'm not sure if or when I'll want to buy a home, but like everyone I do chase "more" in smaller ways. The biggest area this shows up for me is in my business. I want my business to be the best it can be, so I invest a lot of money into it. Quite honestly, some of these investments have been driven by comparison. I see other businesses and I feel like I need to be doing more. There's always the next level waiting for me after each accomplishment.

Our society has created an obsession with money, to the point that we will monetize every aspect of our lives. Those art projects you do for fun could be posted on Etsy instead. The passions that used to bring you joy and happiness turn into stress and productivity in adulthood. By now this desire to aim higher has become an unquenchable thirst.

The Reality

When you spend your life perpetually chasing more, you're left with a warped perception of your own success. You view promotions or career changes through the lens of monetary success and prestige, always considering what the "right" move would be and suppressing your concerns or desires. Keeping your head down and climbing higher with the expectation that lots of money is waiting for you further up the ladder.

The truth is "paying your dues" does not necessarily give you access to success and wealth. We are all looking at the same corporate ladder, or more generally, the ladder to success and wealth. Those with more privilege and power are first in line and get to start climbing while everyone else waits their turn. Then when those with marginalized identities finally get their turn to climb, they realize the rungs of the ladder have been coated in oil. Not only did they get a late start, but now they are going to have a much harder time climbing and will likely go slower. Wage gaps are a clear demonstration of this struggle.

Most of us are aware of the gender wage gap. Women make less than men. There is variability in the numbers depending on what factors you take into consideration, but women earn approximately $0.82 for every $1 that men make. There are many possible reasons behind this gap. Fields dominated by women tend to pay less in general, women are often the primary caregivers, meaning they may need to work less to take care of their children. Women are also less likely to advocate for themselves when it comes to getting a raise or promotion. There are also patriarchal and misogynistic biases in the workplace, which limit the hiring and progression of women's careers. The wage gap remains across all industries, all occupations, and levels of education.

The gender wage gap is far more significant for most women of color. For every $1.00 that white men make, here's how much women get paid when you account for race:

Asian women—$0.90
White women—$0.79
Black women—$0.62
Indigenous women—$0.57
Hispanic women—$0.54

While white women obtaining bachelor's degrees does contribute to a slight closing of the gender gap, we do not see the same with women of color. It's not just women of color who suffer, though: Black and Hispanic men earn $0.87 and $0.91, respectively, to every white man's dollar. The origins of the racial wage gap stem from colonialism and slavery. In 1963 Martin Luther King Jr. observed that America had given Black communities *"a bad check, a check which has come back marked 'insufficient funds.'"* Today it could be described as "occupational segregation," with the history of disparity and Jim Crow laws keeping women of color in domestic (usually lower-paying) positions. Factors such as visa and class status, discriminatory hiring practices, and red lining would also explain some of the racial wage gap.

The wage gap that exists within the 2SLGBTQIA+ community is hard to pin down due to the many crossroads of identity present in this case. What we do know is that 2SLGBTQIA+ folks are more likely to live in poverty than cishet folks, and that's even more likely for those who are transgender. Men in the community have the smallest gap, at $0.96 earned for every $1.00 a "non-2SLGBTQIA+ worker" earns. The gap for women is at $0.87, then drops to $0.70 for nonbinary, genderqueer, genderfluid, Two-Spirit, and trans men, and then to $0.60 for trans women. The gap originates largely in underemployment and unemployment, as well as discrimination.

The wage gap also exists for people with disabilities, who generally earn $0.74 for every dollar nondisabled people make. Many disabled folks, especially in America, are essentially forced to not work or risk losing their benefits. It's a really messed-up system. The primary disability benefits available in the United States, SSDI and SSI, have strict limits on how much you're allowed to work before losing some of your government support. This varies depending on the situation, but most disabled folks can't work more than a part-time job without being disqualified from those benefits. If they do decide to work more and forgo their benefits, they will also lose access to their health insurance and often be left earning less than if they were working part-time, or not at all. Closing the disability wage gap could help remove the need to choose between having a job and being able to cover healthcare costs. Clearly, the reality facing people as they strive to fulfill the "aim higher" mentality is much more complex than we've been led to believe.

I want to emphasize the importance of talking about disability rights. This is a conversation we should all be a part of, because anyone can become disabled at any point in their life. These conversations need to be led by disabled folks, and to that end, I had the pleasure of speaking to Laura Andert (she/her) and Allison Lang (she/her) about their experiences navigating the restrictions placed on disabled folks when it comes to building wealth.

PASSING THE MIC

Laura and Allison's Stories: Navigating Disability and Money

Laura Andert (she/her) is a disability consultant and benefits coach who helps individuals navigate their Social Security cash assistance and other federal, state, and local benefits. She was born with cerebral palsy and has been on disability benefits since her early twenties. Here is her story:

> For people receiving disability benefits every year, there's a certain level called the SGA level, substantial gainful activity, which is a specific amount of income you can't go over. With the jobs I've taken, I've had to really communicate with my supervisors that I can't go over this amount. This affects my ability to accept a raise.
>
> I've had a nervous, anxiety-related relationship with money all my life so far because any money I make can't go over a certain

amount. And if I want something that is expensive and nice, I worry about how much I'm spending. I'm just like, well, if I buy these, I won't do this next month, or I won't do this next week.

Allison Lang (she/her) is a disability advocate, content creator, model, and athlete for Team Canada's sitting volleyball team. She was born missing the lower half of her left leg. Here is her story:

I've been disabled my whole life. You qualify for the RDSP (Registered Disability Savings Plan) at the age of eighteen, and I didn't get permission for it until I was twenty-eight. So, I missed out on ten years of contribution room because of a medical practitioner saying that I wasn't disabled enough to qualify for government grants and contributions. That's thousands of dollars that I could have in my retirement disability savings plan, and I could have invested that money and seen immense growth over time.

Nondisabled people are always making decisions around disabled people's benefits, funding, and medical stuff, and it is about time for that to change. They need to not only really focus and home in on the support that they're providing for disabled people but bring disabled people to the table, have the discussions with us to see what we need. There are a lot of things that are lost in translation because people don't have the life experience that we do. Next year [the government] could say, "Oh, we have to contribute more taxpayer money in this area and cut disabled funding." We're always on the chopping block, which is not a way for us to live.

It's so bad that I have to prove to people that I can make money. It's, like, why do I have to prove anything? I'm human, just like you. It's been a tough discussion with my partner because if we do ever live together or get married, I would lose a lot of the government benefit system. And so that is a fear of mine moving forward, which also makes me wonder how am I going to afford a mortgage in the future? How am I going to afford having kids?

One of the most effective ways to combat inequalities in the workplace, such as the wage gap, is to openly talk about money more. If we can normalize discussing topics like salary and negotiation, this gives back power to everyone, but especially to marginalized groups. Start asking people at your job or in your personal life how much money they make. If that question feels too blunt, try the classic higher or lower tactic. Do you make more or less than $40,000 a year? Talk to your friends about if and how they negotiated their salary. The more transparent people are about money, the less exploitation can occur behind the scenes.

Let's put the wage gap aside for a second and discuss the idea that higher income is more important than every other aspect of the job. We get so focused on the status and recognition of our careers that we don't pay attention to our overall enjoyment and fulfillment doing that work. Society tells us that a prestigious job is an immense achievement, but we don't hear the same narrative for creative or humanitarian careers. We are sold two options: work a job you hate for lots of money or pursue your passion and accept less. I'm here to tell you that not only are there far more options than this but there's also no right choice.

I don't think there is anything wrong with working a job that you don't inherently love doing, if it gives you the lifestyle that you want. On the flip side, I think it can be incredible to follow your passion and do work that you're obsessed with, if it gives you the lifestyle you want. That's what it comes down to. Just be honest with yourself about what you want your life to look like, and what sacrifices you're willing to make to get there.

The Transformation

When we place so much value on wealth and success, we often forget that all we can see is the *appearance* of wealth and success. I've received over 500 applications for my coaching services and I've learned that owning a home and a nice car (or two) doesn't dictate financial success. I've had clients who have the house and the car and take multiple vacations a year but are secretly drowning in debt and living paycheck to paycheck. Instead of asking yourself why you don't own a home, or why you are $50,000 in debt, consider these important questions instead:

- What is your definition of success? What does success look and feel like to you?
- How much money do you need to sustain your ideal lifestyle? What kind of career can give that to you?

Set boundaries to limit comparison. If there are people you follow online who you're constantly comparing yourself to, I recommend unfollowing or muting them. While this isn't a permanent solution, it can be helpful as you're working through redefining success.

Whether you're applying for jobs, looking to advance within your current career, or running your own business, spend some time thinking about how that would fit into and support your life.

- What are the most important aspects of your job? Aka the non-negotiables that **need** to be included (e.g., salary, benefits, WFH options, working for yourself, flexible schedule, time off, etc.)
- What would you like to gain from your career? (e.g., recognition, wealth, security, comfort, socialization, stimulation, challenge, etc.)
- What do you believe about the value that you bring to the workforce/the world?

If you notice little voices of doubt coming up, telling you that you're not good enough or that you'll be worth more when you achieve XYZ, take a pause. Try to pinpoint where this belief stems from. Write it down and make it a priority to work through those limiting beliefs.

We're accustomed to working and living life on autopilot. I'm going to challenge you to *just exist* for a hot minute. Stop trying to grow in every area of your life every single day. Reconnect with why you're chasing more. Why do you feel like what you have isn't enough? Is it that you truly don't have enough, or that society told you that you didn't? Bring intentionality back into your daily life.

EXPECTATION #3: BUILD WEALTH

The Expectation

If you want to build wealth, then you need to follow a formula. Pay off all your debt as soon as humanly possible because debt is bad. Don't have any fun and put all your money toward savings and retirement. Buy a home, it's the ultimate investment. There you go! *Easy peasy*, anyone can do it. There's some variability to the wealth formula, but for the most part, it goes something like this:

- Pay off all your debt
- Start investing as soon as possible
- Focus on maxing out your retirement account
- Invest $500/month
- Buy a home ASAP
- Always aim to increase your net worth
- Let compound interest do its thing
- Retire early

The Consequence

The classic guidelines for how to build wealth are the Brandy Melville of finance. It's marketed as one-size-fits-all, but when you take a closer look, you realize it's inaccessible to most people. We attempt to follow this formula because all of us want some level of wealth (what that means will vary for everyone) and we think this is what will get us there. All you have to do is stick to a tight budget, max out your investment accounts, become debt-free, and buy up property. Bonus points if you achieve retirement early. If you fail to stick to these guidelines, it's your fault.

Another expectation when it comes to building wealth is that you should aim to exponentially increase your net worth. All the investment advice out there is hinged on getting richer and richer. This ties back into hustle culture and internalized capitalism as well, because hard work will *allegedly* give you more money to invest. We are told to aim for millions of dollars for retirement and to keep our net worth rising. We stop questioning and automatically chase this path to wealth that has been marketed as accessible to everyone. The promise of the American dream has achieved a cultlike following because we all desperately want to believe in the possibility of a better life.

We're told to meet rigid expectations like owning a home or reaching specific investment milestones depending on our age. The inability to reach certain age-based metrics for investments leads to a shame spiral. If you hear that you should have X amount of money invested by age 25, and you're 27 and haven't started investing, this is going to incite panic. That deep feeling of failure keeps us in analysis paralysis, unable to make sound decisions.

When I first started talking about money online, I had $5,000 invested. That was a lot for me, but compared to the other financial creators out there, I felt like a fraud. At the time, I had paid off a chunk of high interest debt, but not all of it. I had saved up a small safety fund and finally was feeling in control of my money. I really had no awareness of where other people my age were financially. To see these finance creators talking so openly about their money and to realize they were "ahead" of me was almost enough to make me quit when I had barely started. It took a lot of work to overcome those feelings of inadequacy. I almost let societal expectations hold me back from creating a multi-6-figure business that would lead me to securing this book deal and being able to share my story with all of you. *Thank god I didn't.*

The label of being inadequate leads to immense shame. The long-term impact is that many people will stop trying to save for retirement or reach financial milestones or goals because they don't see the point anymore. If you can't complete the formula for success, why bother starting? This compounds into more shame and guilt, and you end up feeling very isolated.

FINANCIAL SIDEBAR

If you just read that last section and thought *welp* I should be investing, or I'm already so behind, I want to tell you that today is the perfect day to start. Whether you've been investing for years or haven't started yet, it's not too late. Here's a simple breakdown of how to get started:

Step 1: Open up an investment account (e.g., traditional IRA, Roth IRA, TFSA, RRSP)
One of the easiest ways to do this is through an online brokerage such as Questrade or Wealthsimple (essentially these are online investing platforms). You can also open investment accounts through your bank, if that feels more comfortable. Pay attention to the brokerage fees involved. If your employer offers a company-matched 401(k) plan, I highly recommend taking advantage of that first!

Step 2: Fund your investment account
Once you've opened an account, next you need to actually put money in there. Some investing platforms have minimum requirements to start investing, so you might need to save up a bit if that's the case. Other platforms allow you to start investing with any amount. As soon as there is money in your investment account, you're ready for step 3.

Step 3: Purchase your investments
A lot of people will stop at step 2 thinking that they've invested their money, but that's not the case. Right now, the money sitting in your account is not invested; it's in holding, just waiting to be invested. The final step here is that you actually use that money to buy different assets, such as stocks, mutual funds, index funds, ETFs, and bonds. You'll also want to keep an eye out for different fees here as

well. If you're not sure which assets to choose, check out the resource section at the back of the book for some guidance.

Quick reminder that you do not have to know everything about investing and do not have to spend years studying the stock market: you just need to know enough to get started. And many of you already know enough. So just start. Even if you only have $10 to invest, *just start.*

The Reality

The path to wealth has not been, and will not ever be, one-size-fits-all. It doesn't make sense to propose the same wealth-building advice to the single mom living in rural Georgia as you would to the 20-year-old college student living in downtown Los Angeles. Even if we ignore the geographical differences, there are major lifestyle differences. It's highly unlikely that they both have the exact same financial goals that would warrant the same advice.

I'm not saying that this formula for wealth is *wrong* per se, but rather that it's not *right* for everyone. More importantly, beyond the advice we implement when it comes to investing and creating wealth, there are factors out of our control that will create barriers for some and opportunity for others. The impacts of capitalism, white supremacy, and colonialism have ensured that one size won't fit all, as we learned in Chapter 5.

We previously explored the wage gap, and now I want to touch on the *wealth* gap. At the time of signing the Emancipation Proclamation in 1863, only 0.5% of the wealth in America belonged to the Black community. Take a guess at how much that number has changed in the last 150 years? If you answered hardly at all, you'd be correct. Over 150 years later, the Black community still only owns around 4% of total household wealth even though Black Americans account for 13.4% of the population. If you're floored by that fact, you're not alone; the racial wealth gap is 6x greater than most Americans think it is.

A lifetime of being underpaid means you'll be less likely to build savings, handle economic downturn, and ultimately reach financial stability. Black and Indigenous women lose out on almost $1 million to the wealth gap, and Hispanic women lose a staggering $1,163,920. The growing racial wealth gap is something we should all be concerned about. It can lead to increased mental health challenges, a greater likelihood of crime and violence, community instability, and it also undermines democracy.

The guidelines we are told to follow make no sense when everyone is playing by a different set of rules. It's important to consider what barriers you're up against and what place you're starting from. Your path to wealth will look a lot different depending on if you're born into generational wealth or poverty. And your path *should* look different because we don't all want or need the same outcome.

The constant drive for higher net worth is exemplified in the way we talk about home ownership. It's interesting to me that we prioritize the goal of owning a home over other financial goals like retirement. Whenever I bring this point up, I'm met with responses like "At least I'll have a home to live in when I'm 80, unlike you," as if you're cut off from renting at a certain age. Sure, you may own a home at 80, but do you have money to survive? Yes, you could sell that home and cash out on your "investment," but that likely isn't a full retirement fund. There's also the possibility that your home doesn't end up being a good investment once you account for all the money you put into it. This will largely depend on where and when you buy. In reality, the conversation around homeownership is much more complex than we realize.

The push for the traditional upward trajectory of wealth until you die is often rooted in scarcity. The author of *Die with Zero*, Bill Perkins, breaks down the issues with hoarding our wealth for retirement. It's become completely normal to talk about all the countries we want to travel to and the hobbies we will pick up once we are retired. We cushion the blow of not being able to afford these experiences now by convincing ourselves we can do them later. Bill Perkins argues that this way of thinking isn't helpful, as many of the experiences you want to have now may not be an option later on when your health isn't as good. He suggests that instead you aim for your net worth to follow a bell curve, meaning that you spend more of your money throughout your life instead of waiting until retirement. Money can bring you freedom and happiness and you deserve to experience some of that now rather than grinding for 40 years first. Bill Perkins states, *"The sad truth is that too many people delay gratification for too long, or indefinitely. They put off what they want to do until it's too late, saving money for experiences they will never enjoy."*

I acknowledge that this advice comes with a layer of privilege. Some of you may not have the option to forgo savings for opportunities. But for those of you who are meeting your basic needs, working toward your goals, and putting some money away for retirement, this is important to consider. That doesn't mean you should spend all your disposable income on experiences instead of saving for retirement, but rather that there can be a balance. It doesn't have to be all or nothing.

> ### *Money is a tool and a resource I can use to create a better quality of life for myself.*

The Transformation

By now I hope that I've already proven that the formula for wealth simply will not work the same for everyone. When it comes to the advice you hear around building wealth, I want to encourage you to question absolutely everything. You know your life and your ambitions better than anyone. On that note, you cannot meaningfully build wealth for yourself without first considering what wealth actually means to you.

- What is your definition of wealth?
- How much money do you actually need in retirement?*

*Not the percentage or amount everyone says you need—the amount you would actually need to live comfortably and have the lifestyle you want, adjusted for inflation. Check out the resource section to find some useful calculators.

RESOURCE

Retirement Calculators, page 316

When making decisions about your retirement, the accounts you want to use, and where you want to invest your money, education is key. Once you have some basic knowledge on the topic, you can begin to adapt it to your needs, values, and life.

If it scares you to even think about retirement, if you are struggling with a scarcity mindset, or you don't believe you'll live to be that old, this next one's for you. I'm challenging you to experiment with planning for the future. Start small by preparing for something coming up in the next couple of months and move out the time frame as you get more comfortable. **What would it feel like to plan financially for next month or next year?**

REIMAGINING SUCCESS

My goal in this chapter is not to say that you don't need to work hard, aim higher throughout your life, or build wealth. What I want you to do is question *why* you're doing everything. Why are you saving $500 a month for retirement? Because someone told you to? Where is that money going and why? Does that monthly amount make sense in the context of your life?

If you are chasing after success and accomplishment without clearly defining and understanding what those mean to you personally, you will end up disappointed. You will look back and realize that the trajectory of your life was dictated by your need for acceptance and validation.

In an interview with trauma-informed clarity coach and mentor Dr. Joi Madison, I asked this question, *"What advice would you give to someone who maybe knows this isn't the life they want but is unsure of how to reimagine this 'American dream' they've been taught?"*

I loved her response so much I need to share it with all of you. Dr. Joi shared that she went through this experience herself and that questioning the expected path inevitably results in a process of untangling. You will need to untangle yourself from the expectations, the internalized beliefs and conditions, and the aspects of your identity that were tied up to the American dream.

Ask yourself: How do I want my life to feel?

Dr. Joi goes on to suggest homing in on an internal gauge, something inside you that can help you determine if you're following the right path. For most people, their reference is outside themselves. It's the job title, salary, money in the bank, awards, or material goods. The problem with chasing an external reference is that it can move and change without notice. For instance, inflation could spike and suddenly your dream home, which you spent years saving for, is out of reach. You'll never be in control of these things and that can prevent you from feeling grounded in the decisions you make. For Dr. Joi, her internal gauge was how she wanted to feel each day when she woke up in the experience of her life. Instead of being motivated by what she wanted her life to *look* like, it was more about how she wanted to *feel* inside that life.

WRAPPING IT UP

This whole chapter comes down to understanding what makes you happy in life, discovering what kind of life you want to live, and aligning your decisions with that vision. You can start to show up each day as the person who is embodying that life and really question if your current decisions will set you up for what you want in the future. Decide what expectations or rules work for you, which ones no longer fit, and the new guidelines you want to set for yourself. That's when you'll truly be able to reimagine what success and wealth look like and live a life of fulfillment.

CLEAN OUT YOUR EXPECTATIONS

UNWANTED EXPECTATIONS

EXPECTATIONS THAT NO LONGER FIT

DONATE!

CLOTHING SWAP

CLOTHES R-US!

NEW EXPECTATIONS

PUTTING IT INTO PRACTICE

1. Reflect on what your ultimate dream life would look like using Ramit Sethi's Rich Life exercise. For this exercise you're essentially going to imagine what an ordinary week would look like inside your dream life. Imagining your future can be challenging, so do your best to get yourself into a creative headspace before starting. Go through these questions to help imagine your dream life:

o   What would your morning routine look like? What time do you wake up? What do you do first?

284 | Keeping Finance Personal

○ Where do you live? What does your home look like?
○ What kind of work do you do? Where do you work? What's your day like? If you have an office, what does it look like? Who do you interact with?
○ What do you do after work? What does your evening look like?
○ What do you do for fun? What kind of hobbies do you have?
○ What's your next vacation? Where are you going? What type of vacation? What would you do differently than you do right now?

2. Using the questions below, and your current money story as a guide, reimagine what success and wealth look like to you.

○ What current beliefs do you hold around wealth and success?
○ In what ways does internalized capitalism show up for you?
○ How can you prioritize rest moving forward?
○ What is your definition of success? What does success look and feel like to you?
○ How much money do you need to sustain your ideal lifestyle? What kind of career can give that to you?
○ What is your definition of wealth?
○ Based on your personal values, how do you want to spend your wealth?
○ How much money do you actually need/want in retirement?
○ How do you want your life to feel?

CHAPTER 12

Begin Again (Your Version)

HOW TO LIVE OUT YOUR NEW MONEY STORY

My grandma passed away at the age of 94 from complications related to her dementia. I want to tell you part of her story, both to honor her and to inspire you. Near the end, she was no longer mentally with us. She couldn't recognize her son, my dad, or even remember that she had children. The last handful of times I visited her she couldn't recall my name or who I was. I would talk to her about random things, like how I liked the color of her nail polish or how her day had been. It was incredibly painful and sad to experience someone you love forget your existence. Ironically, although her mental capacity was rapidly deteriorating, her physical body was not. Up until the last couple months before her death, she was still mobile and able to move around on her own using a walker.

While residing at an assisted-living facility for the last 5 years of her life, she sustained numerous falls. Usually when an 80- or 90-year-old individual takes a spill, you'd expect there to be a broken hip. But despite her falls, she never fractured anything. One day, my grandma even made a big escape from the facility she lived in. She somehow managed to reach the window high up at the top of the wall in her room by standing on her bed, and then essentially do a chin-up and pull herself out onto the ground outside.

So how did my little grandma pull the ultimate Houdini act and maintain such incredible physical health into her 90s? My family attributes this to the consistent walking habit my grandparents had when they were younger. When both my grandparents were still alive, they would go outside for a walk almost every day. They would walk less in the winters ('cause hello, we live in Canada), but even then, they would often go for indoor mall walks. As my sister and I were growing up, our grandparents would encourage us to go walking with them. After my grandpa passed away, my grandma kept walking without him. Even as her dementia worsened, she still knew the route to walk to the bank, about 3 blocks away from her house. She didn't need to do any banking, but she would walk there and back to get her steps in.

Although we can't say for sure that this walking habit was the reason for her amazing physical health, it's safe to say it had an impact. Something that seems so small and mundane as a daily walk gave her an incredible gift of physical health and likely more years to live. The return on investment of this consistent habit was immeasurable.

Sometimes small actions can create an immense ripple effect in your life. You may not realize how much of an impact that habit is having until you reflect back on it when you're 90. The decisions you make and actions you take today will affect your future self. Each small habit that you gain and choice that you make adds up to a changed life. My grandma's story is a reminder to focus on your foundation because that will set up your life in a profound way.

The journey you're on with your money is lifelong, and you won't change your situation overnight. It's the culmination of the little things that lead to a solid foundation you can build your life on.

WHAT'S NEXT?

I did not set out to write a finance book that will teach you how to be rich. I knew that you needed something different. You were frustrated with traditional financial advice because it never seemed to work quite right for you. I set out to show you how to leave your expectations about money management behind and instead forge a new path forward, one that celebrates and honors the complexity of your identity and experience. I challenged you to look at yourself and your money in a new way.

I've read a lot of self-help, business, personal development, and finance books. Only a handful of these have been truly life-changing for me. They stood out because they either (a) changed my mindset or way of thinking in a radical way or (b) provided actionable steps on how to implement the material they taught. Too often I'm left overloaded with information and overwhelmed with where to start. While I did likely inundate you with new ideas, questions to ponder, and complex concepts, I'm not going to leave you wondering where to go from here. At this point you have a greater understanding of your identity, your values, the role of family, and broader cultural and societal systems, what kind of life you desire, and perhaps some changes you want to make, but how do you begin to live out your new money story?

Consider this chapter the road map for how to integrate everything you've learned and accomplish what you set out to do. You've already begun to rewrite your story as you've read this book, through every piece of homework you completed and action step you implemented. You're doing the work, and I'm so proud of you. Redefining your relationship with money will have a ripple effect on your life, because as you know now, money is woven into the very fabric of your existence. No matter where you are in life, no matter what your background or circumstances, my hope is that this book can serve as a tool for you. One that you can continue to revisit as you need and dig into chapters more deeply as they become relevant in your life. There is not just one edition of your money story; it will continue to be edited and written throughout the coming years. Whenever you feel a little lost or disconnected or recognize harmful patterns emerging, this book will be here to offer solace and provide a new way of looking at your money.

The editing has begun, but you'll need to take it a step further to create remarkable change in your life. To help you do so, I've created a framework for intentionally embracing and living out your new money story. This is the process that gets you from where you are to where you want to be.

1. LET GO

Your first step is deciding what you're ready to leave behind. Step away from the old narratives, limiting beliefs, and shame or guilt that is no longer serving you. It's time to forgive or release the hold that people and systems in your life have on you. To do this, you need to be honest with yourself about what aspects of your money story you want to edit. At the beginning of this book, you wrote out the money story you held at the time. Read over that version and pinpoint the aspects that feel misaligned or stick out as needing to be adjusted. It's normal for you to feel uncomfortable, frustrated, sad, or even angry while doing this. Continuing to cling to a story that doesn't serve you will hold you back from seeing the changes you desire in your finances. You can be grateful for the version of yourself that led you to this point while also recognizing it's time for a change.

There may be feelings of resentment toward yourself, your family, or even society because of the role they played in your current situation. Part of letting go is forgiving yourself and others for the mistakes or missteps that were made with your money, particularly ones you might feel guilt or shame around now. Reflect on the following questions and write down everything that comes to mind:

What resentment are you carrying toward yourself, society, or others when it comes to your finances? Where are you placing blame?

Make the decision that you will no longer allow this pain or resentment to have a hold on you (with the exception of trauma—we need to call in professional reinforcement for that!). For every answer that you wrote down, hold onto it in your head as you repeat the following statements out loud:

I choose to no longer dwell on this situation.
I choose to let go of the hold this has over me.
I choose to no longer wait for an apology.
I choose to not let this affect my daily life anymore.
I choose to release this in the new edition of my money story.

If you'd like to take this practice one step further, I suggest writing the things you're holding onto on a piece of paper and then (safely) burning that paper as you repeat the statements out loud.

Choosing to let go of these things does not magically erase the feelings and emotions we have. Some of those deep-rooted wounds and trauma take professional guidance and years to move past. The powerful part of this practice is the intentionality. It's about you recognizing what parts of your story you're ready and willing to leave behind. Those parts of us take courage to face; I am proud of you for finding the courage.

2. FIND SUPPORT

The very first chapter in this book talked about the importance of having safe spaces where you can learn and ask questions without judgment. In other chapters, we explored the need for safe spaces in every aspect of our life. It's imperative that you work on finding comfortable, supportive environments and communities to lean on. Do not underestimate the importance of a strong support system. When it comes to your finances, make it your mission to find people and companies that you trust. This includes a bank, credit union, or financial institution you feel comfortable giving your money to, a financial professional, advisor, coach, or educator you can learn from, and friends or family members you can openly discuss money with.

What you consume is an important but often overlooked part of your support system. You may not think of media as your support system, but for many people, their little corner of the internet may be the only place they experience true connection. The people you follow, podcasts you listen to, and books you read will feed you ideas and information. These sources may uplift you and push you in the direction you want to go, they might hold you in place, stunting your growth, or they may pull you backward. Curate an Instagram feed and a reading list that is going to encourage you to keep growing. Choosing who you follow is almost as important as choosing your friends.

Speaking of choosing your friends, it's challenging to be surrounded by friends who don't understand your situation or can't relate to your lived experience. No matter how kind or compassionate they are, it's impossible for them to really know the impact of things they haven't lived through. As a white person, I will never be able to fathom the lived experience of BIPOC folks. My heterosexual friends will never understand what it's like to be queer, or the fear that comes with holding my partner's hand in public. Those without kids cannot know the exhaustion that comes with raising a child. It's imperative that you find at least one person in your life who can relate to you and make you feel less alone.

If you notice that there is some unresolved trauma, or that you're not managing your mental health as well as you could be, put time into creating a healthcare community for yourself. This may take years and, depending on where you live, can be expensive, but it will be worth it. Having a team of healthcare professionals who know and understand your struggles and are there to help you in a crisis will allow you to bounce back that much quicker.

If you feel like you have a good support system currently, think about potential areas of improvement. Are there boundaries that need to be set with family members? Do you and your partner need to have more discussions about creating an equitable household? Is your best friend willing to chat about their money goals with you and listen as you share what's stressing you out? Share what you've learned in this book with your community so you can move forward together. Here's what I've found to be a solid foundation for a support system:

3 people you can talk openly about money with

3 people who challenge you to improve and better your life *(not in a climb the corporate ladder kind of way, more like a "rest is sexy" kind of way)*

3 people or sources that are safe spaces for you to learn more about money/ask questions

2 people who will help you in a mental health crisis *(ideally at least 1 healthcare professional)*

1 bank, credit union, or financial institution you trust

Before you panic, I'm not suggesting a total of 12 people in your support system. Some of you might have that, but if you're like me, you have a very small circle. Many of these roles can be played by the same person (though make sure they're not *all* the same person. That's not fair to you or them). Your partner may be someone you talk to about money, who challenges you to keep growing and helps you in a crisis. This is also not a hard-and-fast formula but a guideline I've found to be helpful.

I struggle a lot with making friends, and especially when it comes to trusting and leaning on them for support. This is due to my ADHD, which can make socializing and connecting with new people hard, as well as my own past trauma around friendships. I'm working on a lot of these issues with my therapist, and I can't wait till the day I have an amazing support system. I'm going to have that, and so will you, if you don't already. Let's commit to putting the work in together, okay?

3. TAKE ACTION

In the previous chapter, I had you redefine what success and wealth mean to you and envision the life you want to live. Now it's time to plan out the action steps that will get you there. To do this, you'll need to reverse engineer your life vision, so that you can get a clear idea of what to do this week, month, and year.

Step 1: Figure out what you need to achieve to give you the life you want. Reference your new vision of success from the previous chapter.

- What decisions and actions align with your definition of success?
- What does your reimagined life look like?
- What are 1 to 3 long-term financial goals that would bring you closer to your dream life?

Step 2: Adjust and hone your goals by running them through the SMART goal acronym. Be sure to be specific in wording your goals. A goal such as "I want to be financially stable" is great, but it isn't specific! Instead, the goal should be something like "I want to be earning $80,000 a year so that I can cover all my bills and live my life without constant worry."

SPECIFIC: What exactly do you want to achieve? What are the details of this goal? Be specific!

MEASURABLE: How will you be measuring success or progress with this goal? How will you know that you have accomplished your goal?

ATTAINABLE: What are the limitations and constraints of this goal? Is this something you can realistically dedicate time and energy to achieving right now?

RELEVANT: Why is this goal important to you?

TIME-BASED: When would you like to have accomplished this goal? (You don't necessarily need an exact date, but at least have a rough estimate of the timeline.)

I suggest working backward from your goal and doing a little math to see what a realistic timeline might be. Let's say you want to buy a home in 5 years and need a down payment of $50,000. That would mean you'd need to save $10,000 a year. That's also assuming you're not saving for other goals and don't currently have high interest debt that needs to be paid off. While facing these numbers can feel discouraging, it's ultimately empowering because it forces you to stop saying "someday" and actually be pragmatic about your timeline. Without looking at the math, you'd be hoping that you'll have a house in 5 years, but those years will pass and you likely still won't own a home. Using reverse engineering, you find out it's going to take you 10 years to buy a home, but at least your chances of owning that home in 10 years is exponentially higher.

If you cannot answer the "SMART" questions, your goal probably needs to be changed. It may be too broad, or unmeasurable, or just might not be as important to you as you initially thought.

Step 3: Complete the goal pyramid

This is a tool that I created to help break down the enormity of a goal. One of the biggest challenges when it comes to goal setting is mapping out the path to achieve it. Setting the goal is the easy part: it gives you the dopamine hit. Follow-through is the hard part, and that's where the goal pyramid comes in.

THE GOAL PYRAMID

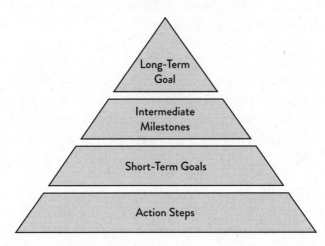

Long-Term
Goal

Intermediate
Milestones

Short-Term Goals

Action Steps

Draw a giant triangle on a piece of paper and then draw four horizontal lines through your triangle so that you have four different "levels." Choose one of your goals to start with. As you work your way down the pyramid, you'll be breaking that goal into smaller, more manageable pieces.

Level 1 = the big goal you want to achieve

The top of the pyramid is where you put one of the long-term SMART goals you just identified.

Level 2 = intermediate milestones

In this section you want to list all the big milestones that you'll need to accomplish in order to complete your long-term goal. If you imagine your goal as a book, the milestones would be the major chapters inside. You likely won't have more than 10 milestones, and usually I find most goals are associated with approximately 5 milestones.

Level 3 = short-term goals

Next look at your milestones and break them down into smaller, short-term goals that you could realistically achieve within 6 months to 1 year. Your big goal is likely several years away, and the milestones have covered what needs to happen on a large scale between now and then. In order to not get bogged down with all the things you need to do, start by focusing only on this year. Forget about the top of the pyramid and just focus on the milestones level above. **What needs to happen this year that will help you get closer to achieving those milestones?**

Level 4 = action steps

Finally, think about all the small daily, weekly, and monthly action steps or habits that you need to complete to achieve the short-term goals you just identified. Again, you're just focusing on the one level above and thinking about all the tiny bite-size tasks that will help you accomplish your short-term goals.

Step 4: Flesh out your action steps

The very last step when it comes to reverse engineering your vision is to break down your action steps once more. You want to get to a point where you can look at your list of action steps and know exactly how to approach each one. You don't want to have any steps or tasks listed that your brain would look at and be overwhelmed or confused by.

For example, the action step "create a visual tracker for monthly savings goals" could be broken down even further into: search for savings tracker templates on Canva, customize it with the colors I like and numbers I need, print out the tracker, and hang it up in my office. Especially if you're neurodivergent, the task of creating a visual tracking system may feel like a lot, which could hold you back from accomplishing it. Keep breaking it down until the tasks are so small it feels silly to write them out.

Once you've done that, go through and assign deadlines to these action steps. Schedule them on your calendar and to-do lists. Incorporate the motivation and reward systems we covered in Chapter 4 and celebrate every single completed action step (which I touch on more in the last part of this framework).

Goal pyramid example: Buying my dream home

Level 1 = the big goal you want to achieve

Buying my dream home. Diving into the "S" of the SMART goal acronym, my specifics would be that I want to purchase my dream, single-family home in the city. I want it to be a home with 3 bedrooms, big windows, wood floors, and a fully updated kitchen. I want the monthly mortgage to be no higher than $2500 per month.

Level 2 = intermediate milestones

- Save up $50,000 for the down payment, legal fees, and closing costs
- Save up a personal safety fund and home safety fund of $20,000 each
- Build my credit score up to 750
- Get approved for a mortgage

Level 3 = short-term goals (remember that you're referencing the milestones now, thinking about what's realistic to start working on this year!)

Let's assume in this example I have $500 per month ($6,000 per year) available to go toward savings and debt repayment.

- Put $2,000 into my safety fund
- Pay off $1,500 of credit card debt
- Find a mortgage broker to start discussing next steps
- Save up $2,500 this year for a down payment

Level 4 = action steps

- Automate my monthly savings contributions
- Stick to my allowance each month
- Create a visual tracker for monthly savings goals
- Ask friends and family for mortgage broker recommendations
- Pick up 3 extra shifts a month
- Negotiate phone and internet bill
- Have monthly money date nights to check in
- Do daily affirmations and meditation

The breakdown of the goal pyramid is another example of how all your small actions add up and create the foundation for your big goals. You're mapping out the route to the life you want to live. Revisit this pyramid at least once a year, and ideally more often, to update your short-term goals and action steps. This is a great tool to include as part of your check-in practice, which I'll tell you about next.

4. CHECK-IN

Just like you visit the doctor to check your health and the dentist to check your teeth, you want to be regularly checking on your financial well-being. Staying connected and up-to-date with your finances allows you to course correct if you're drifting off track, reflect on your progress, and review your current situation. A check-in practice allows you to not leave behind what you've learned from this book and instead show up consistently to put in the work. Your check-in practice could be . . .

- **A version of the money date I introduced in Chapters 4 and 10.** You decide on an itinerary of what you want to cover, in what way, and pair the heavy stuff with something fun to lighten it up.
- **A journaling session.** Your ideal check-in might look like getting cozy under a bunch of blankets and writing out how you've been feeling. If this is a helpful way for you to process, it can be very powerful.
- **A list of reflection questions.** I've provided some questions at the end of this chapter that could help guide you with a check-in practice. You may want to think about these questions, talk through them out loud, write or type them out. This is a more structured approach than journaling.

Of course, there are many more ways that you could structure this check-in; just make sure that it makes sense for you and will be simple to repeat. During your check-in practice you want to go through what I like to call your finance M+Ms. These include: money, mindset, mental health, and miscellaneous. Reflect on these four Ms, and your bases will be covered.

Money: Look over your numbers, systems, and tangible financial aspects. You can look at your progress toward your money goals, review your spending, and transfer money to necessary accounts.

Mindset: Check in with your money story and where your mindset is at. This is where you'll want to reflect on how you felt around spending recently, or areas that you noticed negative thought patterns coming up. You could review your rewritten money story and see if you need to adjust your decisions or behavior.

Mental health: This will look different depending on if or how you struggle with your mental health. This is an opportunity to assess where you're at mentally, book necessary health appointments, notice if your mental health is impacting your finances, and assess where different systems may need to be set up. Take note of any larger societal issues or injustices that may be affecting your mental wellness.

Miscellaneous: This is a catch-all to cover everything else. In this book we've gone over many different aspects of your identity and life that may play a role in your finances. Every one of you is going to have a different

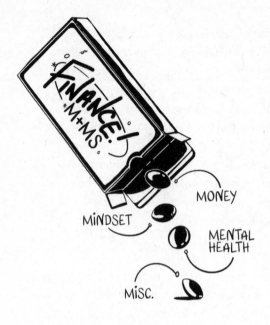

experience, so I wanted to leave this category broad. The miscellaneous check-in practice covers those other areas that you might be actively working on, such as identity struggles, personal or collective trauma, habit changes, family systems, personal values, relationship dynamics, and societal expectations. You would want to check up on how you're implementing the Putting It into Practice homework, where you're at, and what you want to continue to focus on.

Ideally your check-in practice should improve your self-awareness and help you realign your money story. It can be whatever it needs to be in order to be sustainable and easily added to your life. Customize it based on your needs and the areas you tend to struggle with the most.

I'll leave it up to you how often you check in. It could be daily, weekly, biweekly or monthly. Don't try to start with some big, 2-hour-long weekly reflection if that's not realistic for you. It's less important how *often* you do it than how *consistently* you do it. Stay accountable to this practice by scheduling it into your calendar, adding reminders to your phone, and maybe even recruiting someone to be your accountability buddy. Treat this just as seriously as you would a health appointment.

5. CELEBRATE

The final step in this framework is to celebrate! But not just one celebration: I'm challenging you to implement a celebration system or routine, something you can engage in repeatedly every time you reach a goal or have any sort of win with your money. I'm talking about celebrating any time, for any win, big or small.

Some example wins to celebrate:

- Every time a paycheck hits your bank account
- When you sign a new client
- Successfully upholding a boundary
- Contributing to your savings
- Getting a promotion

I suggest you come up with two different types of celebration, one for your smaller wins, which happen more frequently, and one for rarer, bigger wins. This can look however you want it to, and it doesn't have to involve money at all. I'll start you off with some ideas.

Small win celebration ideas:

- Have a dance party
- Repeat a celebratory affirmation
- Put a little extra sugar in your coffee or drink the fancy tea
- Sit with the good feelings
- Jump up and down
- Write it down in your journal
- Share with a friend or loved one
- Thank the universe/God/karma/Taylor Swift

Big win celebration ideas:

- Bake cookies for yourself
- Take a bath with your best bath bombs
- Transfer $5 into your savings
- Order your favorite takeout
- Go on a date night with your partner
- Take yourself on a date
- Buy yourself something small on your wish list

Whatever you choose as your big win celebration routine, make sure it feels fancy and special to you. That doesn't mean it has to be expensive or luxurious, just that it's not something you do or get to enjoy on a daily basis. You're rewriting your relationship with your finances, which involves getting comfortable with positive feelings and emotions around money. You deserve the happiest, healthiest, and most fulfilling relationship with money, and that starts today. Be proud of yourself for everything you've accomplished so far, and everything that's to come. You're actively doing it: *you're changing your story.*

PASSING THE MIC

Advice to Help You Begin Again

I'm passing the mic back to some of the incredible voices you've heard from throughout this book to share their final tips for embracing your new money story.

Michelle MiJung Kim, award-winning author of
The Wake Up
  Something that has helped shift my relationship with money is going to therapy and asking the tough questions. I've been in therapy for 5 years. It's such an integral part of my work. I also have an incredible group of friends and support system who are able to see the complexity of who I am and can help me practice accountability. I think that just learning from other marginalized people who are grappling with similar questions around money, around investing, and around building wealth—all of those things have been instrumental for me to navigate my relationship with money and also how I show up in this world now with this privilege that I didn't grow up with.

Candace Linklater, founder of Relentless Indigenous Woman

An Indigenous practice that could help with healing your relationship with money is the idea that everything has a spirit. Money has a spirit, so consider the place of that spirit in your life. Is that spirit controlling you? Do you allow it to consume you? Money could be used as a very manipulative tactic, but it could also be used for a very empowering one as well. So how are you using the spirit of money for yourself, community, and the global everything, every living being? When you're coming into financial success, think about how you could bring your community with you.

Don't forget to cultivate joy. Don't let money be the sole focus of your every day and the reason for burnout and mental health challenges. Question the systems, challenge the systems and the narratives that are surrounded in our exploitation, but remember the human parts, remember nature, remember joy, remember connection. And rest. You deserve to rest.

Dr. Joi Madison, international coach and speaker

When it comes to rewriting your money story, it really just requires giving yourself permission to evolve and not being stuck in rigid ideas of who you should be. Cultivate a practice that allows you to constantly check in with yourself. Get curious about what it means to commit to showing up every day as the truest version of your understanding of who you are. What does that mean about your relationship with money? What does that mean about how you show up to your work? What does that mean about the choices you make, about the life that you create with yourself, for yourself, with others?

Nina Huynh, mom, YouTuber, and entrepreneur

I now have an abundance mindset where I definitely used to have scarcity. And I think it's very fair to have a scarcity mindset when money is really tight. But then as you start making money, you see there is so much money to be made.

The reason why I love taking risks so much is because I've taken so many and I've seen where it's gotten me. I think back and reflect and if I was of a scarcity mindset, thinking, "I can't afford to take that risk and I need to just stockpile my money and do what's safe," I would never be where I'm at today. I would never become the kind of entrepreneur that I want to be.

I feel like now I definitely have the mindset of no matter what, I'm going to be okay, and money will ever flow. Sometimes there will be more, sometimes there will be less, but there is so much out there.

WRAPPING IT UP

In this book I promised to help you ditch the "shoulds" and the shame and rewrite your money story. Every piece of homework, reflection question, resource, or suggested action step was thoughtfully curated with that promise in mind. I've upheld my end of the bargain by writing this book and taking you through this journey. Now it's up to you to follow through with the work.

PUTTING IT INTO PRACTICE

1. I recommend starting a check-in practice right away, so that you can continue the work of this book now that you've reached the end. Here is a list of reflection questions that could help guide you. Pick 1 to 3 to go through now:

o What's been going well with your finances? What hasn't been going so well?
o What areas do you want to prioritize moving forward?
o What do you need to change or do differently?
o How can you stay accountable to these changes?

o How has your mindset been around money? What positive
   thoughts/beliefs did you notice coming up? What negative
   thoughts/beliefs did you notice coming up?
o What's something you're really freaking proud of?
o What progress have you made toward your goals? Are you still
   on track to reach those goals or do you need to adjust?
o Have you been spending in alignment with your identity and
   values? If not, what needs to change?

2. At the beginning of this book, I had you reflect on your current money
story. You've already begun the work of challenging harmful money beliefs
and interrupting disruptive patterns and now it's time to decide how you'd
like to move forward. Here are some questions to assist in the processing of
embracing your new story:

o What still needs to change within your money story? What
   does that look like?
o How will you see this new money story represented in your
   finances? (e.g., will you spend money differently, donate
   more, let go of the guilt around your debt, have no more late
   payments, commit to more money conversations, invest in your
   education, etc.)
o What habits or actions do you need to implement to embrace
   your rewritten story?
o How does your new story make you feel about yourself, your
   money, and your life?

3. Start implementing the framework you just learned to help you embrace
your new money story. You've rewritten your story—now it's time to live it!

Epilogue

Hi, friend! You did it. Take a second to reflect on the changes that have occurred since you started this book. Appreciate how you've grown, not just within your finances but in terms of your mindset and relationship with money. This is the moment where we part ways and you get to decide what comes next. I encourage you to continue investing in yourself and honoring the rest you deserve. Remember that you are capable of rewriting your money story at any time. Think back to the shelf of knickknacks that represents your money story, as discussed in the Introduction. Each object has been carefully examined and dusted off, and now it's up to you to choose which items to retain or release, which hold the most significance, and how to curate your shelf moving forward. You have the power to change the beliefs and habits that are holding you back. You are the one who gets to decide what success and wealth look like and what kind of path will get you there.

As I said in the very beginning, this book is not a step-by-step manual on how to get rich. You can google a lot of tangible financial advice, but you can't google how your values, identity, mental health, habits, and trauma all affect your finances. These are invaluable answers you've gained in this book that will help you change your relationship with money. The beautiful thing is that you can continue to build on the foundation of what you've learned by diving into more complicated financial topics. Now you'll be able to view that advice through a new lens, one that is more informed, intersectional, and personal. So put down this book and go out and live your rewritten story!

Acknowledgments

Writing this book has been far more challenging, frustrating, and rewarding than I ever could have imagined. If you have ADHD, you know that staying invested in an endeavor for over 2 years is nothing short of a miracle. But I did it. I wrote a whole damn book, a feat that wouldn't have been possible without the team of people behind me. The support I've received before, leading up to, and during the process of writing this book is what kept me going.

First, to the Queerd Co. community and anyone who has engaged with my work, you are the reason this book even exists. Every follow, like, comment, share, listen, email, and DM led us to this moment. Together we created a safe space to talk about money. This isn't my book, it's our book. Thank you for the continuous support, encouragement, friendship, and most of all, for sharing your stories and allowing me to include them in this book.

To my wonderful parents, I would not have finished this book without your support. Thank you for believing in me from the beginning, cheering me on every single step of the way, brainstorming ideas, answering my endless FaceTime calls, editing with me on Zoom, celebrating my wins, and talking me through my moments of doubt. A lifetime of your love and encouragement made this all possible. An extra special shout-out to my mom, the first writer of our family, who showed me the ropes of the writing world, spent countless hours (and even a weekend away) with me writing, editing, and being my sounding board. Thank you for never letting me give up.

To my partner and best friend in the world, Erica, I am so grateful for your emotional support, encouragement, and unwavering love. I appreciate your willingness to take on more at home and make sure I was fed when I was writing 10 hours a day. Thank you for always wiping my tears, reminding me to take care of myself, having dance parties in the kitchen, and giving me kisses when I crawl into bed at 2 a.m. I love you.

To my incredible agent, Kirsten Neuhaus, you were the one who made me believe that people actually wanted to read my book. Thank you for championing my idea, helping refine my abstract thoughts into a stellar proposal, and finding a publisher who aligns so well with my vision. To Aaron Karo, who changed the entire course of my career by sending one random email, asking if I've ever considered writing a book. Thank you for seeing something in me, and introducing me to Peter and Kirsten at Ultra Literary Agency.

To my two amazing editors, Alison and Gwen, you took my ramblings and shaped them into a masterpiece. Alison, your support and check-ins along the way kept me accountable, and you made this overwhelming process a lot more manageable. Gwen, thank you for welcoming my manuscript with open arms and bringing this project home. To the entire team at Hachette Go, and especially—Cisca Schreefel, Monica Oluwek, Irina du Quenoy, Kindall Gant, Ashley Kiedrowski, Michael Barrs, Michelle Aielli, Bart Dawson, YY Liak, and Maya Chessen—your dedication to this book and willingness to listen to my input every step of the way meant the world to me. I'm so proud of what we've created together.

To everyone who dedicated their time and energy to interview for this book, I am forever grateful. You helped create a safe space with your stories.

To the online community of other personal finance creators, your variety of unique experiences, and willingness to be vulnerable about your own financial challenges constantly pushes me to improve my craft. A special shout-out to Alyssa Davies, for showing me what's possible and supporting me along this journey.

To my illustrator, Steffanie, who went above and beyond to make this book aesthetic and accessible. I appreciate your dedication and helpful feedback when it came to the interior design and cover. This book is my baby, but you've become the cool aunt, creating interior illustrations that exceeded my expectations and becoming my friend in the process.

To my DEI consultant and friend, Jalali, I appreciate you helping me approach topics through an intersectional and compassionate lens, and minimize any unintentional harm my words could cause. Beyond the book, thank you for coming in and educating the Queerd Co. team on how we can incorporate diversity, equity, and inclusion values into everything we do.

Thank you to Meggie, my research assistant, for spending endless hours compiling research in order to back up my theories. You're a superstar, truly. To the Queerd Co. team during the time I was writing this book, Emma, Lizzie, and Danae, thank you for keeping things organized, and taking work off my plate so that I could focus more on writing.

To my sister, Rachel, thank you for being such a role model when it comes to working hard and pursuing your dreams. I'm so blessed to have you.

To my long-time friends, Shandelle and Annika, I am so grateful for your friendship and enthusiasm over any project I take on. Shandelle, you've believed in my dreams from day 1 and that means more than you'll ever know. Annika, your texts, voice memos, and accountability check-ins kept me going and literally are the reason I met my manuscript deadline. I love you both so much.

To Charlotte, the friend who "gets" it, you've made the isolating life of being an entrepreneur a lot less lonely. I'm forever thankful to have someone in my corner to share business ideas with, complain about trolls on the internet, and remind me that my message is worth sharing. Our Voxer messages give me life.

To Madi, Zoe, Lewis, Pat, Mykelti, and Bustos, thank you for continuing to invite me to things and check in on me even when I ghosted you during the final months before my manuscript delivery. Your friendship is so important to me. To Mallory, for walking me through numerous meltdowns and encouraging me to advocate for myself. To every other friend who has been a part of this journey, thank you for everything.

Finally, to you, for reading this book and listening to our stories. Thank you. I am so grateful for your support. I encourage you to go out there and continue the conversation around money.

Resources

I created this resource section to provide you with additional tools to continue doing the important work you have begun. For every plant illustration you saw throughout the book, there is a corresponding resource here to guide you.

Beyond the chapter-specific resources, I have compiled an overarching list of recommended books, podcasts, social media creators, and other material to check out. Here is where you will also be able to support and connect with all the wonderful folks who you heard from in this book. This list, along with the digital version of the resource library, can be found at **www.queerdco.com/book-resources**.

Chapter 1

Working with a Financial Advisor

To avoid working with a financial advisor who's putting their profits over what's best for you, you want to make sure they are a fiduciary. This is just a fancy word that means they are legally required to act and make decisions that are in your best interest and are not allowed to profit from your investments. When going into a meeting with a financial advisor, I suggest coming in with a list of the topics you want to cover. Here are some examples to start with:

- How to manage your money better (creating a budget, organizing your finances)
- Setting up your financial foundation (e.g., what your safety fund should look like, how much you should be saving, what systems to put in place)
- Creating a debt repayment plan
- How to build your credit score

- Navigating any upcoming big life changes (e.g., starting a family, big promotion)
- How to achieve your short- and long-term financial goals
- Retirement planning

Finding Safe Spaces

I've compiled a curated list of the Queerd Co. community's favorite online resources and safe spaces for a variety of demographics, available at **www.queerdco.com/book-resources**. I kept this list digital, so that it can be periodically updated.

Chapter 2

Financial Audit and Spending Tracker Template

A fillable PDF and GoogleSheets version of the Financial Audit and Spending Tracker can be found at **www.queerdco.com/book-resources**.

Chapter 3

Choosing an HYSA

Here are some websites that you can use to compare HYSAs:

- **NerdWallet:** www.nerdwallet.com (US) www.nerdwallet.ca (CAN)
- **Investopedia:** www.investopedia.com (US)
- **MoneySense:** www.moneysense.ca (CAN)
- **Canadian HYSA rate comparison chart:** www.highinterestsavings.ca/chart/ (CAN)

Don't spend too much time stressing over this! Pick one that's at a financial institution you like and trust and make sure it's FDIC, CDIC, or NCUA insured.

> **FDIC:** Use the BankFind tool to check if your institution is FDIC insured. https://banks.data.fdic.gov/bankfind-suite/bankfind.
> **CDIC:** See if your financial institution is a CDIC member. https://www.cdic.ca/your-coverage/list-of-member-institutions/.
> **NCUA:** Find out if your credit union is insured by NCUA by looking for the NCUA insurance sign on your credit union's webpage. Check out https://mapping.ncua.gov/.

Free Mental Health Resources

Find my list of resources with a mental health and money lens, as well as online mental health resources, at **www.queerdco.com/book-resources**.

Canada:
- **Wellness Together:** call 1-866-585-0445 or text WELLNESS to 741741
- **Talk Suicide Canada:** call 1-833-456-4566 for 24/7 support
- **Hope for Wellness** (for First Nations, Inuit, and Métis peoples): call 855-242-3310 (toll-free) for 24/7 support

US:
- **Suicide & Crisis Lifeline:** call or text 988
- **National Alliance on Mental Illness:** call 1-800-950-6264 or text "HelpLine" to 62640
- **The Trevor Project (for 2SLGBTQIA+ folks):** call 1-866-488-7386 or text START to 678-678 for 24/7 support

Chapter 4

Choosing an Allowance Card

You can find my suggestions for allowance cards, along with all the other financial tools I recommend, at **www.queerdco.com/money-tools**.

Chapter 5

Accessing Your Window of Tolerance

- Say today's date out loud (if your trauma is linked to a specific event that you're now safe from)
- Meditation: check out the Calm or Headspace app!
- Moving your body (running, walking, yoga, stretching, weight lifting)
- Any type of breathing or breathwork
- Somatic shaking or stomping
- Using a weighted blanket or heating pad
- Smelling essential oils

Using Money as Medicine

You can find an updated list of organizations to consider donating to at **www.queerdco.com/book-resources**.

Chapter 6

Dopa-Menu Template

A fillable PDF and GoogleSheets version of the Dopa-Menu template can be found at **www.queerdco.com/book-resources**.

Chapter 7

Boundary-Setting Resource

Nedra Glover Tawwab, *Set Boundaries, Find Peace: A Guide to Reclaiming Yourself* (New York: Penguin, 2021).

Chapter 8

Mortgage Calculators

- **RateHub:** https://www.ratehub.ca/mortgage-payment-calculator (CAN)
- **Government of Canada:** https://itools-ioutils.fcac-acfc.gc.ca/MC-CH/MCCalc-CHCalc-eng.aspx
- **US bank:** https://www.usbank.com/home-loans/mortgage/mortgage-calculators
- **Bankrate:** https://www.bankrate.com/real-estate/new-house-calculator/

Recommendations for Will Services

- **Willful:** https://www.willful.co/ (CAN)
- **Trust & Will:** https://trustandwill.com/ (US)

Investing Educational Resources

- **Wealthsimple:** https://www.wealthsimple.com/en-ca/learn/category/investing
- **Nerdwallet:** https://www.nerdwallet.com/h/category/investing

You can find a more comprehensive, updated list of investing resources at **www.queerdco.com/book-resources** and some of my favorite investing tools at **www.queerdco.com/money-tools**.

Chapter 9

Choosing a Socially Responsible Financial Institution

One thing you want to be aware of when it comes to picking a socially responsible institution is the certifications they hold. These certifications are proof that they are serious about minimizing any harmful impact. Here are some certifications to keep a lookout for:

- Certified B Corporation*
- Global Alliance for Banking on Values*
- Fossil Free Certified
- 1% for the Planet
- Green America Certified
- Community Development Financial Institution
- Community Development Credit Union
- Minority Depository Institution
- Women-Owned Bank

*These certifications have some of the highest standards and represent a strong commitment to upholding socially responsible values.

Chapter 10

Domestic Labor Resources

- Mia Birdsong, *How We Show Up: Reclaiming Family, Friendship, and Community* (New York: Hachette Books, 2020).
- K. C. Davis, *How to Keep House While Drowning: A Gentle Approach to Cleaning and Organizing* (New York: Simon Element, 2022).
- Angela Garbes, *Essential Labor: Mothering as Social Change* (New York: Harper Wave, 2022).
- Eve Rodsky, *Fair Play: A Game-Changing Solution for When You Have Too Much to Do (and More Life to Live)* (New York: G.P. Putnam's Sons, 2021).

Financial Abuse Resources

Domestic violence hotline (US):
Call: 1-800-799-7233
Text: "START" to 88788
Website: https://www.thehotline.org/
Where to go for help by province (CAN):
https://cba.ca/where-to-go-for-help

The Allstate Foundation offers an educational course called the "Moving Ahead Curriculum" to help domestic violence survivors rebuild their finances and create security. Access it here: https://allstatefoundation.org/what-we-do /end-domestic-violence/resources/.

Chapter 11

Investing Educational Resources

- **Wealthsimple:** https://www.wealthsimple.com/en-ca/learn /category/investing
- **Nerdwallet:** https://www.nerdwallet.com/h/category/investing

You can find a more comprehensive, updated list of investing resources at **www.queerdco.com/book-resources** and some of my favorite investing tools at **www.queerdco.com/money-tools**.

Retirement Calculators

- **Retirement income calculator (CAN):** https://www.canada.ca /en/services/benefits/publicpensions/cpp/retirement-income -calculator
- **Retirement savings calculator:** https://www.wealthsimple.com /en-ca/tool/retirement-calculator
- **Retirement calculator:** https://www.financialmentor.com /calculator/best-retirement-calculator

Notes

Chapter 1

13   **only a quarter of millennials:** Global Financial Literacy Excellence Center, *Millennials and Financial Literacy: The Struggle with Personal Finance*, report, September 2016, https://gflec.org/wp-content/uploads/2016/09/pwc-millenials-and -financial-literacy-3.pdf?x93521.

13   **over half of Americans:** "Gauging the State of Financial Capability in the U.S.," Finra Foundation, accessed June 12, 2023, https://finrafoundation.org/knowledge -we-gain-share/nfcs.

13   **according to the 2021 TIAA Institute:** Paul J. Yakoboski, Annamaria Lusardi, and Andrea Hasler, "Financial Literacy and Well-Being in a Five Generation America: The 2021 TIAA Institute-GFLEC Personal Finance Index," SSRN, TIAA Institute Research Paper Series no. 2022-01, October 2022.

13   **over 60% of adults struggle:** Leona Klapper, Annamaria Lusardi, and Peter van Oudheusden, *Financial Literacy Around the World: Insight from the Standard and Poor's Ratings Services Global Financial Literacy Survey*, report, Global Financial Literacy Excellence Center, November 2011, https://gflec.org/wp-content/uploads /2015/11/3313-Finlit_Report_FINAL-5.11.16.pdf?x37611.

13   **"A safe space":** "Equipping Adolescent Girls with Health, Life Skills and Financial Literacy Through Safe Spaces—Learning Brief," Communication Initiative Network, October 3, 2017, www.comminit.com/content/equipping-adolescent-girls-health -life-skills-and-financial-literacy-through-safe-spaces.

19   **women face different systemic:** Financial Consumer Agency of Canada, "Make Change That Counts: National Financial Literacy Strategy 2021–2026," July 14, 2021, www.canada.ca/en/financial-consumer-agency/programs/financial-literacy /financial-literacy-strategy-2021-2026.html.

19   **women make up only 23%:** Julia Boorstin, "Survey: It's Still Tough to Be a Woman on Wall Street—but Men Don't Always Notice," CNBC, June 26, 2018, www.cnbc .com/2018/06/25/surveyon-wall-street-workplace-biases-persist---but-men-dont -see-t.html.

19   **lower for women of color:** Stacey Chin, Alexis Krivkovich, and Marie-Claude Nadaeau, "Closing the Gap: Leadership Perspectives on Promoting Women in Financial Services," McKinsey & Company, 2018, www.mckinsey.com/industries /financial-services/our-insights/closing-the-gap-leadership-perspectives-on -promoting-women-in-financial-services.

19   **According to a study from Wealthsimple:** Jean Chatzky, "Why Women Invest 40
      Percent Less Than Men (and How We Can Change It)," NBC News, September 25,
      2018, www.nbcnews.com/better/business/why-women-invest-40-percent-less-men
      -how-we-can-ncna912956.

19   **over half of women:** "Majority of Millennial Women Have Money to Invest, but
      Fear Holds Them Back," press release, SoFi, April 5, 2018, www.sofi.com/press
      /majority-millennial-women-money-invest-fear-holds-back/.

19   **A 2021 survey from CNBC:** Michelle Fox, "As Interest in Investing Grows,
      People of Color Still Lag Behind, CNBC Survey Finds," CNBC, August 23, 2021,
      www.cnbc.com/2021/08/23/as-interest-in-investing-grows-people-of-color-still-lag
      -behind-cnbc-survey-finds.html.

19   **are even greater for BIPOC folks:** Terri Friedline, Seyoung Oh, Thomas Klemm,
      and Jase Kugiya, "Exclusion and Marginalization in Financial Services: Frontline
      Employees as Street-Level Bureaucrats," working paper, Poverty Solutions at the
      University of Michigan Working Paper Series, January 29, 2020, https://poverty
      .umich.edu/files/2020/01/Friedline-Oh-Klemm-Kugiya-2020-Exclusion-and
      -Marginalization-in-Financial-Services-1.pdf.

22   **In clinical settings:** Michael S. Roth, "Don't Dismiss 'Safe Spaces,'" *New York Times*,
      August 29, 2019, www.nytimes.com/2019/08/29/opinion/safe-spaces-campus.html#
      :~:text=As%20the%20idea%20of%20safe.

Chapter 2

31   **"a person's self-identification":** "All About Race and Ethnicity in the Census—
      MCDC," Missouri Census Data Center, accessed April 27, 2023, https://mcdc
      .missouri.edu/help/race-ethnicity.html#:~:text=Race%20is%20a%20person.

32   **table of social identities:** "Social Identity Wheel," College of Literature, Science and
      the Arts, University of Michigan, accessed June 12, 2023, https://sites.lsa.umich
      .edu/inclusive-teaching/wp-content/uploads/sites/732/2020/07/Social-Identity
      -WheelDefinitions.pdf.

33   **What part(s) of your identity:** LSA Inclusive Teaching Initiative. The Spectrum
      Activity, Questions of Identity. University of Michigan, 2021. https://sites.lsa.umich
      .edu/inclusive-teaching/wp-content/uploads/sites/853/2021/12/The-Spectrum
      -Activity.pdf.

34   **understand how our identities impact:** Kimberlé Crenshaw, "Demarginalizing
      the Intersection of Race and Sex: A Black Feminist Critique of Antidiscrimination
      Doctrine, Feminist Theory and Antiracist Politics," *University of Chicago Legal Forum*
      1, no. 8 (1989): 139–167.

34   **emphasized the need for an intersectional approach:** Crenshaw, "Demarginalizing
      the Intersection of Race and Sex," 141–143.

35   **Wheel of Power and Privilege:** "Wheel of Privilege and Power—Canada.Ca."
      Government of Canada. Accessed August 22, 2023. https://www.canada.ca/content
      /dam/ircc documents/pdf/english/corporate/anti-racism/wheel-privilege-power.pdf.

36   **introduced the concept:** "Identity Economics," Decision Lab, accessed April 19,
      2022, https://thedecisionlab.com/reference-guide/economics/identity-economics.

37   **Subaru was struggling with sales:** Alex Mayyasi and Priceonomics, "How Subarus
      Came to Be Seen as Cars for Lesbians," *Atlantic*, June 22, 2016, www.theatlantic

.com/business/archive/2016/06/how-subarus-came-to-be-seen-as-cars-for
-lesbians/488042/.

41   **sense of self through the products:** H. Dittmar, "The Costs of Consumer Culture and the 'Cage Within': The Impact of the Material 'Good Life' and 'Body Perfect' Ideals on Individuals' Identity and Well-Being," *Psychological Inquiry* 18, no. 1 (2007): 23–24.

46   **gap between who you are:** Dittmar, "Costs of Consumer Culture and the 'Cage Within,'" 25–27.

46   **root causes of materialism:** Grant E. Donnelly, Masha Ksendzova, Ryan T. Howell, Kathleen D. Vohs, and Roy F. Baumeister, "Buying to Blunt Negative Feelings: Materialistic Escape from the Self," *Review of General Psychology* 20, no. 3 (2016): 300–304.

46   **further align or assimilate:** Donnelly et al., "Buying to Blunt Negative Feelings," 300–304.

47   **Material goods you own:** Dittmar, "Costs of Consumer Culture and the 'Cage Within,'" 23.

Chapter 3

55   **are more likely to struggle:** Naijie Guan, Alessandra Guariglia, Patrick Moore, Fangzhou Xu, and Hareth Al-Janabi, "Financial Stress and Depression in Adults: A Systematic Review," *PLOS ONE* 17, no. 2 (2022): 14.

58   **choices become closed off:** Christopher Bergland, "How Does Anxiety Short Circuit the Decision-Making Process?" *Psychology Today* (blog), March 17, 2016, www.psychologytoday.com/us/blog/the-athletes-way/201603/how-does-anxiety -short-circuit-the-decision-making-process.

64   **52% of people:** Maureen Connolly, "The United States of Stress 2019," Everyday Health, May 7, 2019, www.everydayhealth.com/wellness/united-states-of-stress/.

65   **Some common ways:** "The Link Between Money and Mental Health," Mind, April 2022, https://www.mind.org.uk/information-support/tips-for-everyday-living/ money-and-mental-health/the-link-between-money-and-mental-health/.

65   **Folks who are low income:** Christopher G. Hudson, "Socioeconomic Status and Mental Illness: Tests of the Social Causation and Selection Hypotheses," *American Journal of Orthopsychiatry* 75, no. 1 (2005): 3–18.

65   **depressive symptoms as a result:** "4 Tips to Cope with Debt Depression," *PsychCentral* (blog), July 21, 2021, https://psychcentral.com/blog/stressed-about -money-tips-to-cope-with-debt-depression.

66   **53% of people:** "United States of Stress 2019—Effects of Stress on Americans— Special Report," Everyday Health, accessed April 27, 2023, www.everydayhealth.com /wellness/united-states-of-stress/#financial-instability-is-making-us-stressed-and-sick.

67   **highest rates of mental health issues:** Katherine M. Harris, Mark J. Edlund, and Sharon Larson, "Racial and Ethnic Differences in the Mental Health Problems and Use of Mental Health Care," *Medical Care* 43, no. 8 (2005): 22–23.

67   **3x more likely:** "LGBTQ+ Community," Anxiety and Depression Association of America, 2021, https://adaa.org/find-help/by-demographics/lgbtq.

67   **2–4x more likely:** Lisa F. Platt, Julia K. Wolf, and Christopher P. Scheitle, "Patterns of Mental Health Care Utilization Among Sexual Orientation Minority Groups," *Journal of Homosexuality* 65, no. 2 (2018): 135–153.

67   **more affordable options:** "What to Do When You Can't Afford Therapy,"
      PsychCentral (blog), May 7, 2021, https://psychcentral.com/blog/what-to-do-when
      -you-cant-afford-therapy.

70   **only half of Americans:** Mark Moran, "Mental Health Stigma Persists in the
      Workplace, Poll Shows," *Psychiatric News*, June 18, 2019, https://psychnews
      .psychiatryonline.org/doi/10.1176/appi.pn.2019.6b21.

70   **If you are an *employer*:** Izabela Z. Schultz, Terry Krupa, and E. Sally Rogers, "Best
      Practices in Accommodating and Retaining Persons with Mental Health Disabilities
      at Work: Answered and Unanswered Questions," in ed. Izabela Z. Schultz and E.
      Sally Rogers, *Work Accommodation and Retention in Mental Health* (New York:
      Springer, 2011), 448–452.

71   **If you are an *employee*:** Schultz, Krupa, and Rogers, "Best Practices in
      Accommodating and Retaining Persons with Mental Health Disabilities at Work,"
      453–456.

74   **more low-cost:** Charlotte Darr, "The Wealth Building Bootcamp" (presentation,
      Save Live Thrive, Zoom, 2022).

Chapter 4

79   **"developmental disorder characterized":** Dorien F. Bangma, Janneke Koerts,
      Anselm B. M. Fuermaier, Christian Mette, Marco Zimmermann, Anna K. Toussaint,
      Lara Tucha, and Oliver Tucha, "Financial Decision-Making in Adults with ADHD,"
      Neuropsychology 33, no. 8 (2019): 1065.

79   **With ADHD you can present:** Penny Williams, "What Are the 3 Types of
      ADHD?," *ADDitude*, February 9, 2017, www.additudemag.com/3-types-of-adhd/.

81   **65% of folks with ADHD:** Rupert Jones, "'Shopping Is a Nightmare': How ADHD
      Affects People's Spending Habits," *Guardian*, June 25, 2022, www.theguardian.com
      /money/2022/jun/25/shopping-adhd-spending-habits#:~:text=Those%20with
      %20ADHD%20are%20twice.

81   **earning less and paying more:** Janneke Koert, Dorien F. Bangma, Anselm B. M.
      Fuermaier, Christian Mette, Lara Tucha, and Oliver Tucha, "Financial Judgment
      Determination in Adults with ADHD," *Journal of Neural Transmission* 128, no. 7
      (2021): 969–970.

82   **brain and cognition differs:** Cleveland Clinic, "Neurodivergent: What It Is,
      Symptoms and Types," June 2, 2022, https://my.clevelandclinic.org/health
      /symptoms/23154-neurodivergent.

84   **ADHD impairs your executive function:** Bangma et al., "Financial Decision-
      Making in Adults with ADHD," 1065–1066.

86   **"a motivation deficit disorder":** Russell A. Barkley, *Attention-Deficit Hyperactivity
      Disorder: A Handbook for Diagnosis and Treatment*, 4th ed. (New York: Guilford
      Press, 2018).

89   **adults with ADHD struggle:** Bangma et al., "Financial Decision-Making in Adults
      with ADHD," 1066.

89   **more prone to impulsively spend:** Dorien F. Bangma, Lara Tucha, Anselm B. M.
      Fuermaier, Oliver Tucha, and Janneke Koerts, "Financial Decision-Making in a
      Community Sample of Adults with and Without Current Symptoms of ADHD,"
      PLOS ONE 15, no. 10 (2020): 2.

89   **Financial Competence Assessment Inventory:** Koerts et al., "Financial Judgment Determination in Adults with ADHD."

89   **low savings, high debt:** Theodore P. Beauchaine, Itzhak Ben-David, and Marieke Bos, "ADHD, Financial Distress, and Suicide in Adulthood: A Population Study," *Science Advances* 6, no. 40 (2020): 1–2.

89   **use impulse spending:** Linda Roggli, "Neurotypical Budgeting Tips Don't Work for ADHD Brains. These Do," *ADDitude*, October 26, 2020, www.additudemag.com /budgeting-tips-for-adhd-brains/.

89   **difficulty paying bills:** Chi Liao, "ADHD Symptoms and Financial Distress," *Review of Finance* 25, no. 4 (2021): 1131.

90   **"ADHD symptoms essentially increase":** Liao, "ADHD Symptoms and Financial Distress," 1133.

96   **lack of communication:** Amy Marturana Winderl, "Defining Impulsiveness with ADHD," *Health Central*, August 30, 2022, www.healthcentral.com/article/adhd -symptoms-impulsiveness.

96   **more likely to engage in impulsive behaviors:** Beauchaine, Ben-David, and Bos, "ADHD, Financial Distress, and Suicide in Adulthood."

96   **low levels of dopamine:** Mareen Dennis, "12 Ways to Resist Impulse Buying: ADHD Shopping Secrets," *ADDitude*, February 18, 2021, www.additudemag.com /impulse-buying-money-problems-adhd-adults/.

99   **reducing the burden:** Rick Webster, "The ADHD Tax Is Draining—Financially and Emotionally," *ADDitude,* October 17, 2022, www.additudemag.com/adhd-tax -financial-wellness-money-problems/.

Chapter 5

108   **"Trauma is not":** "Trauma, Resilience and Addiction: Hoffman Interviews Dr. Gabor Maté," Hoffman Institute, accessed July 12, 2023, www.hoffmaninstitute.co.uk /trauma-resilience-and-addiction-hoffman-interviews-dr-gabor-mate/.

108   **mimic symptoms of:** Anya Meyerowitz, "What Is Financial Trauma and How Can You Escape It?," Refinery29, accessed December 1, 2022, www.refinery29.com /en-gb/financial-money-trauma.

108   **examples of financial trauma:** Chantel Chapman, "The Trauma of Money Framework" (presentation, Trauma of Money, Vancouver, BC, September 20, 2022).

109   **financial behaviors that:** Morgan Noll, "4 Signs of Financial Trauma and What You Should Know About It," Real Simple, accessed April 27, 2023, www.realsimple .com/work-life/money/signs-of-financial-trauma.

111   **motivate your amygdala:** J. Douglas Bremner, "Traumatic Stress: Effects on the Brain," *Dialogues in Clinical Neuroscience* 8, no. 4 (2006): 445–461.

111   **Window of Tolerance:** Daniel J. Siegel, *The Developing Mind: Toward a Neurobiology of Interpersonal Experience* (New York: Guilford Press, 2012).

112   **characterized by anxiety, panic, anger:** Siegel, *Developing Mind.*

112   **narrow your window:** "How to Help Your Clients Understand Their Window of Tolerance," National Institute for the Clinical Application of Behavioral Medicine blog, November 2, 2017, www.nicabm.com/trauma-how-to-help-your-clients -understand-their-window-of-tolerance/.

113   **"false window of tolerance":** "Working with Emotional Distress—with Janina Fisher, PhD," National Institute for the Clinical Application of Behavioral Medicine blog, August 13, 2021, www.nicabm.com/working-with-emotional-distress/.

115   **Guilt shows up:** Joseph Burgo, "The Difference Between Guilt and Shame," *Psychology Today*, May 30, 2013, https://www.psychologytoday.com/ca/blog /shame/201305/the-difference-between-guilt-and-shame.

115   **Guilt = I did something bad:** Chantel Chapman, "The Trauma of Money Framework" (presentation, Trauma of Money, Vancouver, BC, September 20, 2022).

121   **After slavery was abolished:** Mehrsa Baradaran, *The Color of Money: Black Banks and the Racial Wealth Gap* (Cambridge, MA: Belknap Press of Harvard University Press, 2019), 1–50.

121   **quarter of US households:** Dominique Stewart, "The Cost of Being Unbanked and Underbanked," Anti-Racism Daily, March 21, 2022, https://the-ard.com /2022/03/21/the-cost-of-being-unbanked-and-underbanked%EF%BF%BC/.

121   **difficult to pay bills:** Emily Guy Birken, "The Costs of Being Unbanked or Underbanked," Forbes Advisor, July 28, 2020, www.forbes.com/advisor/banking /costs-of-being-unbanked-or-underbanked/.

121   **12% of white Americans:** "The Fed—Report on the Economic Well-Being of U.S. Households in 2020—May 2021—Banking and Credit," Board of Governors of the Federal Reserve System, May 2021, www.federalreserve.gov/publications/2021 -economic-well-being-of-us-households-in-2020-banking-and-credit.htm.

121   **Freedman's Savings Bank:** Baradaran, *Color of Money*, 1–50.

122   **The capitalist system in America:** Matthew Desmond, "American Capitalism Is Brutal. You Can Trace That to the Plantation," *New York Times*, August 14, 2019, www.nytimes.com/interactive/2019/08/14/magazine/slavery-capitalism.html.

122   **3.2 million enslaved people:** Baradaran, *Color of Money*, 10.

122   **creation of new financial tools:** Baradaran, *Color of Money*, 10–11.

123   **"If today America promotes":** Desmond, "American Capitalism Is Brutal."

126   **Indigenous Worldview:** Edgar Villanueva, Money as Medicine, 2020.

128   **impede your cognitive:** Sendhil Mullainathan and Eldar Shafir, *Scarcity: Why Having Too Little Means So Much* (New York: Picador, 2014).

128   **Living in scarcity:** Mullainathan and Shafir, *Scarcity*.

129   **"scarcity, of any kind":** Anuj K. Shah, Sendhil Mullainathan, and Eldar Shafir, "Some Consequences of Having Too Little," *Science* 338, no. 6107 (2012): 683.

129   **bandwidth tax:** Sendhil Mullainathan and Eldar Shafir, "Freeing Up Intelligence," *Scientific American Mind* 25, no. 1 (2013): 58–63.

129   **weeklong vacation:** Chantel Chapman, "The Psychology of Scarcity" (presentation, Trauma of Money, Vancouver, BC, November 15, 2022).

130   **Unbudgeting:** Bridget Casey, "The Unbudget: Giving up Limits, Getting Back Your Life," *Money after Graduation* (blog), October 14, 2021, www.moneyaftergraduation .com/unbudget/.

Chapter 6

135   **Dopamine is a neurotransmitter:** "Dopamine: What It Is, Function & Symptoms," Cleveland Clinic, March 23, 2022, https://my.clevelandclinic.org/health/articles /22581-dopamine#:~:text=Dopamine%20is%20a%20neurotransmitter%20made ,%2C%20mood%2C%20attention%20and%20more.

135   **adequate levels of dopamine:** "Dopamine: What It Is, Function and Symptoms," Cleveland Clinic, March 23, 2022, https://my.clevelandclinic.org/health/articles/22581-dopamine.

136   **pleasure and pain battle as a scale:** Anna Lembke, *Dopamine Nation: Resetting Your Brain in the Age of Cheap Pleasures* (New York: Dutton, 2020).

136   **This set of behaviors:** Shadiya Mohamed Saleh Baqutayan, "Stress and Coping Mechanisms: A Historical Overview," *Mediterranean Journal of Social Sciences* 6, no. 2 S1 (2015): 479–488.

137   **"survival resource" and "creative resource":** Pat Ogden and Janina Fisher, *Sensorimotor Psychotherapy: Interventions for Trauma and Attachment* (New York: W. W. Norton, 2015), 255–285.

137   **Survival resources:** Ogden and Fisher, *Sensorimotor Psychotherapy*, 255–285.

138   **Creative resources:** Ogden and Fisher, *Sensorimotor Psychotherapy*, 255–285.

139   **more dopamine released:** Lembke, *Dopamine Nation*, 1–2.

140   **smartphones:** Lembke, *Dopamine Nation*, 1.

140   **Pursuit of our potential:** Stephen Joseph, "What Is Eudaimonic Happiness?" *Psychology Today Canada* (blog), January 2, 2019, www.psychologytoday.com/ca/blog/what-doesnt-kill-us/201901/what-is-eudaimonic-happiness.

141   **symptoms of harmful cellphone use:** José De-Sola Gutiérrez, Fernando Rodríguez de Fonseca, and Gabriel Rubio, "Cell-Phone Addiction: A Review," *Frontiers in Psychiatry* 7, no. 175 (2016): 2–3.

143   **retail therapy:** Scott I. Rick, Beatriz Pereira, and Katherine A. Burson, "The Benefits of Retail Therapy: Making Purchase Decisions Reduces Residual Sadness," *Journal of Consumer Psychology* 24, no. 3 (2014): 373–380.

143   **feelings such as:** Wendy Wisner, "6 Tips for Stopping Emotional Spending," Verywell Mind, accessed June 12, 2023, www.verywellmind.com/how-to-stop-emotional-spending-retail-therapy-5218151.

143   **compulsive buying:** Astrid Müller et al., "Buying-Shopping Disorder—Is There Enough Evidence to Support Its Inclusion in ICD-11?" *CNS Spectrums* 24, no. 4 (2019): 374–379.

143   **risk factors include:** Joel L. Young, "Compulsive Spending: What You Need to Know," December 9, 2016, *Psychology Today*, www.psychologytoday.com/us/blog/when-your-adult-child-breaks-your-heart/201612/compulsive-spending-what-you-need-know.

143   **stuck in a loop:** Donald W. Black, "Compulsive Buying Disorder: A Review of the Evidence," *CNS Spectrums* 12, no. 2 (2007): 124–132.

146   **a cost-benefit analysis:** Adam Hayes, "What Is Cost-Benefit Analysis, How Is It Used, What Are Its Pros and Cons?," Investopedia, accessed June 12, 2023, www.investopedia.com/terms/c/cost-benefitanalysis.asp.

149   **operate on autopilot:** Charles Duhigg, "Habits: How They Form and How to Break Them," NPR, March 5, 2012, www.npr.org/2012/03/05/147192599/habits-how-they-form-and-how-to-break-them.

150   **your cravings strengthen:** "Breaking Bad Habits: Why It's So Hard to Change," *NIH News in Health*, January 2012, https://newsinhealth.nih.gov/2012/01/breaking-bad-habits#:~:text=Enjoyable%20behaviors%20can%20prompt%20your.

151   **In his book *Atomic Habits*:** James Clear, *Atomic Habits: Tiny Changes, Remarkable Results* (New York: Penguin Publishing Group, 2018).

154   **The framework:** Lembke, *Dopamine Nation*, 71–88.
155   **which types of creative resources:** Ogden and Fisher, *Sensorimotor Psychotherapy*, 255–285.
157   **the Dopa-menu:** How to ADHD, "How to Give Your Brain the Stimulation It Needs," YouTube video, accessed June 12, 2023, www.youtube.com/watch?v=-6WCkTwW6xg.

Chapter 7

161   **by age 3:** Beth Kobliner, "Money Habits Are Set by Age 7. Teach Your Kids the Value of a Dollar Now," PBS NewsHour, April 5, 2018, www.pbs.org/newshour/economy/making-sense/money-habits-are-set-by-age-7-teach-your-kids-the-value-of-a-dollar-now.
162   **financial socialization:** Clinton G. Gudmunson, Sara K. Ray, and Jing Jian Xiao, "Financial Socialization," in *Handbook of Consumer Finance Research*, ed. J. Xiao (Cham, Switzerland: Springer, 2016), 61–72.
171   **Kuri Kalyanam:** Clare Frizell, "5 Interesting Ways Different Cultures Deal W/ Cash," *Happy Nomad* (blog), March 14, 2018, https://blog.bambatravel.com/5-ways-different-cultures-deal-cash/.
173   **losing money in interest:** Kamal M. Amjad Mian, Frank E. Vogel, and Samuel L. Hayes III, "Islamic Law and Finance; Religion, Risk, and Return," *Journal of Law and Religion* 15, no. 1/2 (2000): 475–479.

Chapter 8

187   **the average woman:** Kristen Bialik and Richard Fry, "How Millennials Compare with Prior Generations," Pew Research Center, Social and Demographic Trends Project, February 14, 2019, www.pewresearch.org/social-trends/2019/02/14/millennial-life-how-young-adulthood-today-compares-with-prior-generations-2/.
187   **Historically, women could not:** Jamela Adam, "When Could Women Open a Bank Account?," Forbes Advisor, accessed April 27, 2023, www.forbes.com/advisor/banking/when-could-women-open-a-bank-account/#:~:text=Technically%2C%20women%20won%20the%20right.
187   **choosing to not have children:** Bialik and Fry, "How Millennials Compare with Prior Generations."
188   **Millennials are less likely:** Bialik and Fry, "How Millennials Compare with Prior Generations."
188   **The cost of education:** Cameron Huddleston, "Boomers vs. Millennials: The Financial Gap," GOBankingRates, April 24, 2017, www.gobankingrates.com/saving-money/savings-advice/financial-gap-boomers-millennials/.
189   **millennial college graduates:** Huddleston, "Boomers vs. Millennials."
189   **pandemic housing bubble:** Lance Lambert, "The Pandemic Housing Market Correction, as Told by 3 Home Price Charts," Yahoo Finance, February 28, 2023, https://finance.yahoo.com/news/pandemic-housing-correction-both-mild-144622809.html?guccounter=1&guce_referrer=aHR0cHM6Ly93d3cuZ29vZ2xlLmNvbS8&guce_referrer_sig=AQAAAMZ3zDJzyn4rj84anGCe1m25XW-Y2Ailj2qCDo2YguIZwWtXmzSN7SC6tnyRTuCuuAQg5QX7V21WiETtxF_wnLJZr.

189   **cost of living:** BER staff, "Baby Boomers and the Future of Homeownership in the United States," *Berkeley Economic Review*, April 22, 2019, https://econreview .berkeley.edu/baby-boomers-and-the-future-of-homeownership-in-the-united -states/.

189   **Over half (51%) of boomers:** BER staff, "Baby Boomers and the Future of Homeownership."

190   **housing prices have increased:** Huddleston, "Boomers vs. Millennials."

191   **collective trauma is decontextualizing:** Miriam Taylor, "Collective Trauma and the Relational Field," *Humanistic Psychologist* 48, no. 4 (2020): 382–388.

192   **"Terrorism, by its very intent":** John A. Updegraff, Roxane Cohen Silver, and E. Alison Holman, "Searching for and Finding Meaning in Collective Trauma: Results from a National Longitudinal Study of the 9/11 Terrorist Attacks," *Journal of Personality and Social Psychology* 95, no. 3 (2008): 709–722.

192   **the economy as a whole:** History.com editors, "September 11 Attacks," History .com, August 25, 2018, www.history.com/topics/21st-century/9-11-attacks.

192   **The cost of cleaning up debris:** History.com editors, "September 11 Attacks."

194   **subprime mortgages:** Sam Thielman, "Black Americans Unfairly Targeted by Banks Before Housing Crisis, Says ACLU," *Guardian*, June 23, 2015, www .theguardian.com/business/2015/jun/23/black-americans-housing-crisis-sub -prime-loan.

195   **Millions of jobs were lost:** Manoj Singh, "The 2007–2008 Financial Crisis in Review," Investopedia, accessed April 27, 2023, www.investopedia.com/articles /economics/09/financial-crisis-review.asp#citation-26.

195   **10 million Americas were displaced:** Investopedia team, "How the 2008 Housing Crash Affected the American Dream," Investopedia, accessed June 12, 2023, www.investopedia.com/ask/answers/062515/how-was-american-dream-impacted -housing-market-collapse-2008.asp#:~:text=The%20Crash.

197   **the Great Resignation:** Kim Parker and Juliana Menasce Horowitz, "Majority of Workers Who Quit a Job in 2021 Cite Low Pay, No Opportunities for Advancement, Feeling Disrespected," Pew Research Center, April 25, 2023, https://www.pewresearch.org/short-reads/2022/03/09/majority-of-workers-who -quit-a-job-in-2021-cite-low-pay-no-opportunities-for-advancement-feeling -disrespected/.

Chapter 9

218   **(60% of Americans are):** "60% of Americans Now Living Paycheck to Paycheck, down from 64% a Month Ago." Corporate Profile, February 28, 2023. https://ir .lendingclub.com/news/news-details/2023/60-of-Americans-Now-Living-Paycheck -to-Paycheck-Down-from-64-a-Month-Ago/default.aspx.

221   **ESG investing:** Alana Benson, "What Is ESG Investing and How Does It Compare?," NerdWallet, March 14, 2022, www.nerdwallet.com/article/investing /esg-investing.

221   **Between 2016 and 2020:** Spencer Tierney, "Ethical Banking: What Are Socially Responsible Banks?," NerdWallet, accessed June 12, 2023, www.nerdwallet.com /article/banking/socially-responsible-banks.

221   **check what certifications:** Tierney, "Ethical Banking."

Chapter 10

230 **strongest predictors of divorce:** Jeffrey Dew, Sonya Britt, and Sandra Huston, "Examining the Relationship Between Financial Issues and Divorce," *Family Relations* 61, no. 4 (2012): 615–628.

230 **highly linked to divorce:** Lauren M. Papp, E. Mark Cummings, and Marcie C. Goeke-Morey, "For Richer, for Poorer: Money as a Topic of Marital Conflict in the Home," *Family Relations* 58, no. 1 (2009): 91–103.

230 **top money-related causes for divorce:** Sharon Feiereisen, "The 12 Biggest Money-Related Reasons People Get Divorced," *Business Insider*, July 7, 2019, www.businessinsider.com/divorce-money-issues-financial-relationship-couple-2019-7.

232 **more women earning college degrees:** Aliya Hamid Rao, "Women Breadwinners Still Do Most of the Family's Chores," *Atlantic*, May 12, 2019, www.theatlantic.com/family/archive/2019/05/breadwinning-wives-gender-inequality/589237/.

232 **American mothers spend:** Rao, "Women Breadwinners."

232 **Western media, politics:** Tara Siegel Bernard, "When She Earns More: As Roles Shift, Old Ideas on Who Pays the Bills Persist," *New York Times*, July 6, 2018, www.nytimes.com/2018/07/06/your-money/marriage-men-women-finances.html.

232 **A survey of US adults:** Kim Parker and Renee Stepler, "Americans See Men as the Financial Providers, Even as Women's Contributions Grow," Pew Research Center, September 20, 2017, www.pewresearch.org/short-reads/2017/09/20/americans-see-men-as-the-financial-providers-even-as-womens-contributions-grow/.

232 **The notion of a breadwinner:** Julia Kagan, "Breadwinner: What It Means, Word Origin, and Examples," Investopedia, December 11, 2022, www.investopedia.com/terms/b/breadwinner.asp.

232 **trends have shifted:** Bernard, "When She Earns More."

234 **girls do more chores:** Deborah L. Best and Angelica R. Puzio, "Gender and Culture," in *The Handbook of Culture and Psychology*, ed. David Matsumoto and Hyisung C. Hwang (Oxford: Oxford University Press, 2019), 235–291.

234 **The discussion of gender roles:** Best and Puzio, "Gender and Culture."

235 **The distribution of domestic work:** Abigail Johnson Hess, "Here's How Much More Women Could Earn if Household Chores Were Compensated," CNBC, April 10, 2018, www.cnbc.com/2018/04/10/heres-what-women-could-earn-if-household-chores-were-compensated.html.

235 **70% of the top 1%:** Lila MacLellan, "70% of Top Male Earners in the US Have a Spouse Who Stays Home," Yahoo Finance, April 30, 2019, https://finance.yahoo.com/news/70-top-male-earners-us-162154561.html.

247 **Financial abuse is defined:** "About Financial Abuse," National Network to End Domestic Violence, accessed June 13, 2023, https://nnedv.org/content/about-financial-abuse.

247 **Examples of Financial Abuse:** Emily H. Brachter, "8 Signs of Financial Abuse in Marriage," *US News & World Report*, September 7, 2022, https://money.usnews.com/money/personal-finance/family-finance/articles/signs-of-financial-abuse-in-marriage.

249 **Money Taboo Cycle:** Brett F. Whysel, "The Money Taboo: What Can We Do About It? Talk!," Decision Fish: Decide For Yourself, February 18, 2020, http://www.decisionfish.com/the-money-taboo-what-can-we-do-about-it-talk/.

249   **Nearly 40% of adults:** "The Currency," *Empower* (blog), accessed April 27, 2023, www.personalcapital.com/blog/whitepapers/2022-love-money-report/.

Chapter 11

260   **internalized capitalism:** Alia E. Dastagir, "If You Keep Putting Work Before Health and Happiness, You May Be Suffering from Internalized Capitalism," *USA Today*, June 17, 2021, www.usatoday.com/story/life/health-wellness/2021/06/17 /internalized-capitalism-harms-mental-health-productivity/7723416002/.

260   **examples of internalized capitalist narratives:** Christine Organ, "I Suffer from Internalized Capitalism—and You Probably Do Too," Scary Mommy, October 2, 2020, www.scarymommy.com/internalized-capitalism.

261   **many people have to hustle:** Matthew Thompson, "How Hustle Culture Is Slowly Killing Us," *Mighty Pursuit* (blog), July 30, 2022, https://mightypursuit.com/blog /how-hustle-culture-is-slowly-killing-us/.

262   **characteristics of burnout:** Melinda Wenner Moyer, "Your Body Knows You're Burned Out," *New York Times*, February 15, 2022, www.nytimes.com/2022/02/15 /well/live/burnout-work-stress.html.

262   **exposed to chronic stressors:** Ashley Abramson, "Burnout and Stress Are Everywhere," American Psychological Association, January 1, 2022, www.apa.org /monitor/2022/01/special-burnout-stress.

265   **7 different types of rest:** Heather White, "7 Types of Rest: The Key to Becoming the Prepared Adult," *MontessoriLife* (blog), December 21, 2022, https: //amshq.org/Blog/2022-12-21-7-Types-of-Rest.

269   **women earn:** Carolina Aragão, "Gender Pay Gap in U.S. Hasn't Changed Much in Two Decades," Pew Research Center, March 1, 2023, www.pewresearch.org/short -reads/2023/03/01/gender-pay-gap-facts/.

269   **Fields dominated by women** *Highlights of Women's Earnings in 2020: BLS Reports*, Bureau of Labor Statistics, 2021, www.bls.gov/opub/reports/womens-earnings/2020 /pdf/home.pdf.

269   **Women are also less likely:** Erin Coghlan and Sara Hinkley, "State Policy Strategies for Narrowing the Gender Wage Gap," Berkeley University, Institute for Research on Labor and Employment, April 10, 2018, https://irle.berkeley.edu/publications/irle -policy-brief/state-policy-strategies-for-narrowing-the-gender-wage-gap/.

269   **The wage gap remains:** Elise Gould, Jessica Schieder, and Kathleen Geier, "What Is the Gender Pay Gap and Is It Real?" Economic Policy Institute, October 20, 2016, www.epi.org/publication/what-is-the-gender-pay-gap-and-is-it-real/.

269   **far more significant:** "Race and the Pay Gap," AAUW, accessed December 19, 2022, www.aauw.org/resources/research/race-and-the-pay-gap/.

270   **women obtaining bachelor's:** "Race and the Pay Gap."

270   **Black and Hispanic men:** Stephen Miller, "Black Workers Still Earn Less Than Their White Counterparts," SHRM, June 11, 2020, www.shrm.org /resourcesandtools/hr-topics/compensation/pages/racial-wage-gaps-persistence -poses-challenge.aspx.

270   **"a bad check":** Martin Luther King Jr., "'I Have a Dream' Speech, in Its Entirety," NPR, broadcast January 16, 2023, www.npr.org/2010/01/18/122701268/i-have-a -dream-speech-in-its-entirety.

270   **"occupational segregation":** "Systemic Racism and the Gender Pay Gap: A Supplement to the Simple Truth," AAUW, July 2021, www.aauw.org/app/uploads /2021/07/SimpleTruth_4.0-1.pdf.

270   **more likely to live in poverty:** M. V. Lee Badget, Soon Kyu Choi, and Bianca D. M. Wilson, *LGBT Poverty in the United States: A Study of Differences Between Sexual Orientation and Gender Identity Groups*, report, UCLA School of Law, Williams Institute, October 2019, http://williamsinstitute.law.ucla.edu/wp-content/uploads /National-LGBT-Poverty-Oct-2019.pdf.

270   **Men in the community:** "The Wage Gap Among LGBTQ+ Workers in the United States," Human Rights Campaign, accessed December 19, 2022, www.hrc.org /resources/the-wage-gap-among-lgbtq-workers-in-the-united-states.

270   **The gap originates:** Cirrus Jahangiri, "LGBTQ+ Equal Pay Awareness Day Highlights Economic Disparity for LGBTQ+ People," Legal Aid at Work, June 15, 2022, https://legalaidatwork.org/blog/lgbtq-equal-pay-awareness-day/.

270   **people with disabilities:** "Economic Justice Is Disability Justice," Century Foundation, April 21, 2022, https://tcf.org/content/report/economic-justice -disability-justice/.

278   **the Black community:** Emily Moss, Kriston McIntosh, Wendy Edelberg, and Kristen Broady, "The Black-White Wealth Gap Left Black Households More Vulnerable," *Brookings* (blog), December 8, 2020, www.brookings.edu/blog /up-front/2020/12/08/the-black-white-wealth-gap-left-black-households-more -vulnerable/.

278   **the racial wealth gap:** "Wealth and Asset Ownership Data Tables," US Census Bureau, accessed December 19, 2022, www.census.gov/topics/income-poverty /wealth/data/tables.html.

278   **lifetime of being underpaid:** Robin Bleiweis, Jocelyn Frye, and Rose Khattar, "Women of Color and the Wage Gap," Center for American Progress, November 17, 2021, www.americanprogress.org/article/women-of-color-and-the-wage-gap/.

278   **Black and Indigenous women:** Jasmine Tucker, "The Wage Gap Has Robbed Women of Their Ability to Weather COVID-19," National Women's Law Center, March 16, 2021, https://nwlc.org/resource/the-wage-gap-has-robbed-women-of -their-ability-to-weather-covid-19/.

279   **increased mental health challenges:** Vanessa Williamson, "Closing the Racial Wealth Gap Requires Heavy, Progressive Taxation of Wealth," Brookings Institution, December 9, 2020, www.brookings.edu/research/closing-the-racial-wealth-gap -requires-heavy-progressive-taxation-of-wealth/.

279   **"The sad truth":** Bill Perkins, *Die with Zero: Getting All You Can from Your Money and Your Life* (Boston: Houghton Mifflin Harcourt, 2021), 3.

283   **Ramit Sethi's Rich Life:** Ramit Sethi, *I Will Teach You to Be Rich: No Guilt, No Excuses—Just a 6-Week Program That Works* (New York: Workman, 2019).

Resources

315   **Here are some certifications:** Spencer Tierney, "Ethical Banking: What Are Socially Responsible Banks?," NerdWallet, updated March 4, 2022, www.nerdwallet.com /article/banking/socially-responsible-banks.

Index